The
Conquest
of
Inner
Space

LEARNING THE LANGUAGE OF PRAYER

Sunder Krishnan

The
Conquest
of
Inner
Space

LEARNING THE LANGUAGE OF PRAYER

Scarlet Cord
press

ISBN 0-9732038-0-3
Printed and bound in Canada
10 9 8 7 6 5 4 3 2 1

Editor: Kathryn Dean
Designer: Warren MacDonald

For information and book orders, please contact:
Scarlet Cord Press
26 Winslow Street, Toronto, Ontario, Canada M8Y 3C1
www.scarletcordpress.com

Contents

Foreword

Any prayer is good enough to get us going in the life of prayer. One does well not to be too careful about the etiquette or protocol of prayer. God doesn't grade the grammar of our prayers.

But that doesn't mean that anything goes. We all have a sound instinct to prayer, but instinct is not a reliable guide to a developing and maturing life of prayer. Prayer that relies on emotion and instinct and circumstance for its impetus and syntax, while not exactly inauthentic, is hopelessly stuck in immaturity. There is nothing reprehensible about being immature; but it is irresponsible to remain so. Falling to our knees or lifting our hands to heaven and saying "God" is always a good thing to do, but our souls require instruction and guidance if these spontaneous beginnings are to stay on track and avoid the many detours and dead ends of false teaching and ignorance introduced by our own sin. Praying has as many heresies at its disposal as thinking.

We have a prayerbook bound into our Bibles, put there to train us in our prayers. That prayerbook is the Psalms. And we do well to be alert to it, apprenticing ourselves to these prayers, putting ourselves in a school that trains our souls in God. It is a school in which our prayers are stretched and deepened into the largeness of God.

Sunder Krishnan is a faithful guide and master teacher for Christians who come together to pray. The unique element in this book is the attention he gives to the missionary dimension of prayer. He demonstrates that the Psalms insistently guide us into forms of prayer that are often neglected in our fragmented and ego-isolated culture, taking us out of ourselves, moving us from our home base, into the neighborhood, and finally into "all the world." A generation of Christians that supposes that a daily hour or so with television or newspaper is the way to "keep up with" the world needs to know that many of us are convinced that prayer in Jesus' name is the only effective way to get in touch with and deal responsibly – *Christianly* – with a world that is as large as God's creation and salvation.

Praying, because it is so intensely personal, is always in danger of becoming exclusively private – me-centered. Sunder Krishnan shows us how the psalmists, while never letting themselves be distracted from personally dealing with God, were, at the same time, constantly preoccupied with the others in the world who were not yet in on the revelation: the nations and peoples, the ends of the earth, the outsiders to God. Entering into and cultivating such prayer works two ways: it keeps our world mission activities informed by prayer and it keeps our prayers stretched into world mission. Prayer that begins in the closet, as it so often (and properly) does, ends up in concert and companionship with the angels in the cosmos.

Eugene H. Peterson
Emeritus Professor of Spiritual Theology
Regent College, British Columbia

Introduction

The familiar voice of the air traffic controller crackled through the cockpit headphones: "Flight 407 cleared to descend to 10,000 feet." "Check. Descending to 10,000 feet," replied the first officer as he twiddled a dial. A similar conversational exchange was repeated periodically as the plane gradually made its way down to the appointed runway. When he was only a few hundred feet off the ground, the captain switched off the autopilot and took over manual control. With a steady hand, borne of years of experience, he landed the big jumbo jet so gently that the passengers did not even feel a bump. (Scattered applause in the economy section.) The captain exited from the cockpit and while leaving the plane, accidentally stubbed his toe. A string of expletives streamed from his lips.

Question! What allowed that pilot to gain such mastery over a massive and complicated piece of technical equipment and yet did not help him control his own speech in an unguarded moment? We could multiply many such examples to illustrate a truth that is all too familiar: human beings have done an amazing job of understanding and controlling the world outside of themselves, but conquering inner space, the world inside, remains as formidable a challenge as ever.

The problem, however, is not only a modern one. It has been with humanity since time immemorial. Let's travel back three thousand years to a scene where a young shepherd boy is lying on a Middle Eastern hillside. His sheep are probably bedded down for the night. Looking up into the crystal-clear, starlit night, he's amazed by the order that he sees in Creation. He expresses his feelings in poetry: *"The heavens declare the glory of God; the skies proclaim the work of his hands. Day after day they pour forth speech; night after night they display knowledge"* (Psalm 19:1–2). But then he looks inward, and this is what he writes: *"Who can discern his errors? Forgive my hidden faults. Keep your servant also from willful sins; may they not rule over me. Then I will be blameless, innocent of the great transgression"* (vv. 12–13). Even as he marvels at the order of the world outside of him, he's aware of the disorder inside, and he wants to set it right.

What is the secret to the ordering of his inner space? The psalmist tells us in the intervening verses: *"The law of the LORD is perfect, restoring the soul. The statutes of the LORD are trustworthy, making wise the simple. The commandments of the LORD are radiant, giving light to the eyes. The ordinances of the LORD are sure and altogether righteous. By them is your servant warned; in keeping them there is great reward"* (vv. 7–8; 10–11). The same order that the psalmist finds in Creation, he finds to an even more marvellous degree in the law of God. It is God's law alone that can create order from the chaos of inner space. And how will this come about? The psalmist's concluding words tell us: *"May the words of my mouth and the meditation of my heart be pleasing in your sight, O LORD, my rock and my redeemer"* (v. 14). The psalmist's worship and prayer, fuelled by his meditation on the law of God, arises as an acceptable offering to God and in the process brings order to his inner space.

What was true and necessary for a young shepherd boy three thousand years ago remains desperately necessary for us today. Most of us are frantically trying to carve out little islands of peace in a chaotic and frazzled society – largely by attempting to control our external circumstances, a project that is doomed either to total failure or to infinitesimal successes separated by long periods of time. God's Word prescribes an entirely different route to peace – peace in the middle of a chaotic world – through the conquest of inner space through precisely the same route that Psalm 19 described so beautifully for us. A mind given to regular meditation on God's Word lets that Word become fuel for acceptable worship and prayer, and this connects us to the only one who is in absolute and sovereign control over the circumstances of our lives.

How can this peace, rooted in God's sovereignty, penetrate our disordered souls? One way is through corporate worship. American pastor and author Calvin Miller observes that even though we may not be aware of it, this is why many people really come to church. They do not come, he says, to find answers to questions. They come to be put in touch with another world that they know exists but from which they are disconnected – the invisible world in which God reigns sovereignly through His lifegiving, ordering, and hence peace-bestowing Word.[1]

Certainly, this calls for a worship service, each of whose elements are carefully and prayerfully structured with this need in mind. I have, however, struggled throughout my ministry with the flip side of this issue. Is it possible for someone who has not met God all week long to suddenly get familiar with Him on Sunday? It's somewhat like being thrown into a room full of strangers and being told to hold a meaningful conversation with one or more of them. It's possible; but only by sheer accident would a significant interchange result. What's far more likely is a strained or superficial conversation (or both). Of course, God is sovereign, and certainly His Spirit can meet us at our driest and thirstiest. How often the psalmists look back to great "sanctuary moments" when they participated in corporate worship that gladdened their hearts and magnified God's greatness and power. But are we intended to count only on that? How much richer our corporate worship would be if we regularly came to it from a week of communion with God. That is why much of my ministry in the local church (which I have served for twenty-one years) has focused on helping people encounter God in personal, private communion both during and outside of formal worship. As I have attempted this through preaching, leading smaller corporate prayer meetings, spiritual direction in small groups, and "one-on-one" encounters, the key issues that needed to be addressed slowly crystallized.

A Problem with Words

When Jesus taught His disciples how to pray, He introduced the specifics with two general warnings: against the Pharisaic sin of hypocrisy and the Gentile sin of babbling. The more familiar King James Version's admonition against "vain repetitions" is a somewhat misleading way of describing babbling because it appears to warn against repetition, which is essential to perseverance in prayer. *Babbling*, on the other hand – aimless wandering and verbal diarrhea – is the real problem, not repetition. A classic example is our recurring use of a certain phrase whenever we pray for God to be with a specific individual.

We say, "Lord, be with them in a very real way." If we only paused to think for a moment, we would realize that we almost never speak that way to a human being whose presence is important to us. Imagine leaving your precious infant for the first time with a babysitter with these parting words: "Now, Sandra, make sure that you are with the baby in a very real way." That message conveys nothing specific to Sandra about your expectations of her or your concern for the well-being of your child. You would more likely tell her something like this: "Make sure to check her every thirty minutes, make sure the intercom's turned on at 9 p.m., and don't forget the bottle if she wakes up. Make sure to heat it for three minutes on low in the microwave before you give it to her, and if you have any problems, you can always call us at _____ ." If God is a person and we are talking to Him about matters that concern us, why don't we speak to Him normally, the way we would to any other person (I mean, as far as language is concerned). Why do we resort to "be with them in a very special way"? John Stott calls it "praying with our mouths disengaged from our minds."

The other side of babbling is *silence*. Because we do not want to babble, we say nothing. Now, there is a silence that concentrates and improves our speech, a silence that is essential to prayer. The silence I am referring to, however, sets the mind wandering so we are no longer drawing near to God with our hearts. To put it in the proverbial nutshell, the first practical problem that I wrestled with was this: *How do we find the balance between silence that invites our mind to wander and babbling that is an affront to God?*

Now, some people have resorted to prayer lists and denominational prayer *manuals* to solve this problem. We need to be thankful for these many mighty prayer warriors that God has raised up, who have daily, monthly, yearly, and even through decades ploughed through prayer manuals, battling on their knees for Christian workers and missionaries, tilting the balance of power in the warfare that is going on in the heavenly realms. This book is not for people like this, who pray very effectively with those tools. It is equally true, though, that for many people, lists and manuals become boring in very short order. They "hang in" there because of guilt and free-floating anxiety and because discipline is good for the soul. But as for delight, that seems an elusive, almost unachievable dream when it comes to prayer. That's the second problem I grappled with: *How do we bring delight into the discipline of prayer?*

The answers to both problems, in my own experience, consisted of the same elements. We need to *listen* to God in His Word before we say anything and then *speak* out of a mind well furnished with the plans and purposes of God, aided by an *imagination* fuelled by the powerful metaphors and images that abound in Scripture. As I tried to share these answers in the various settings I mentioned earlier, I began to see a third problem.

Pastor, How Do I Do It?

Simply suggesting this approach to praying the Psalms seems to be enough for some people. They don't need anything else to "kick-start" or sustain them in their subsequent journey. Several such testimonies can be found at the end of Eugene H. Peterson's book *Answering God*. One of these "pray-ers," however, suggests that "something more" may be necessary for others and gives us a clue as to what that might be. He writes: "I found that a *background of study*, such as from class, is especially helpful, as it 'takes off the blanket,' making the Psalms become alive, meaningful and relational in my prayer. *A balance of these two modes is essential for the authentication of each:* prayer to 'become'; study to illuminate the story."[2] That has certainly been my experience as a pastor. Even when I have directed people to "ready-made" scriptural prayers like the Psalms, even when I have pointed out that the Holy Spirit directed the composition and collection of these Psalms with the express purpose of creating a worship and prayer manual that one could use with confidence, even when I have given them excellent books on the Psalms, explaining this specific function, they most often come back to me with this question: "Great book, pastor. But now how do I do it? How do I pray through a Psalm?" Something more is needed.

Something More

This book is a humble attempt at providing that "something more," drawing upon the "treasury of David," the Psalms. Why the Psalms? you might ask. What makes them particularly suited to this enterprise of learning to listen to God and exercising our imagination so we can find that balance between silence and babbling and bring delight into the discipline of prayer?

- The simplest answer is that *God has ordained it to be so*, by causing the Psalms to be written and collated for that specific purpose. They are Israel's worship manual. We would be unwise to look elsewhere, at least at the beginning of our pilgrimage in prayer.

- They are also unique in that they represent *human beings' attempts to speak to God*, whereas the rest of Scripture, by and large, is a record of God speaking to humans. And in speaking to God they reflect the full gamut of human emotions. The psalmists "laugh, sing, weep, rail, they cry out in pain, fright, derision, joy and the sheer delight in life."[3] Because of that, as author Leonard Griffith puts it, everyone can "find themselves somewhere in the Old Testament Psalter."[4] And because they are inspired by the Holy Spirit and are therefore "not merely human folk songs reflecting the common experience of men, the Psalms also relate the wisdom and release that ensue when a hurt or a joy is laid at the feet of God."[5] This is important in an era when human feelings have gained an unwarranted autonomy and dangerous ascendance in fashioning responses to life, even Christian responses in prayer.

- A third critical function of praying the Psalms is described by Robert Johnston. In his brief commentary, he states, "In an era when life has been wrongly divided into the sacred and secular, it is hard for us to realize *the importance of worship in Israel's life*. Worship was widespread and related to the whole of life's experiences. Thus when you planted a field you had a religious ceremony. When you harvested your crop you did likewise. When you were sick, you came to God for help along with God's people. When you sinned, you sought forgiveness and restitution in worship. When your king was enthroned you first of all worshipped God."[6] Praying the Psalms will serve to integrate life – something we desperately need, because our lives bear the marks of the fragmentation and compartmentalization that characterize our society at large.

- The final reason is one I have not come across in any of the books on the Psalms that I have read. There are seventy-eight references to the "nations" and another twenty-eight to the "peoples" in the Psalter. Both these words refer to the natives of nations other than Israel. A complete survey of all these references is beyond the scope and intent of this introduction, but this recurring reference to the "nations" in the Psalms would never let Israel's worship degenerate into mere private enjoyment of God's blessings: every time they gathered to worship God, they would be reminded that *they had been chosen and blessed of God so that, through them, all nations of the earth would come to know and worship Israel's God.*

Psalm 47 is perhaps the quintessential representative in this regard: "*Clap your hands, all you* **nations***; shout to God with cries of joy. How awesome is the* LORD *Most High, the great King over all the earth! He subdued* **nations** *under us, peoples under our feet. He chose our inheritance for us, the pride of Jacob, whom he loved. God has ascended amid shouts of joy, the* LORD *amid the sounding of trumpets. Sing praises to God, sing praises; sing praises to our King, sing praises. For God is the King of all the earth; sing to him a psalm of praise. God reigns over the* **nations***; God is seated on his holy throne. The nobles of the* **nations** *assemble as the people of the God of Abraham, for the kings of the earth belong to God; he is greatly exalted.*" The last verse paints a vivid picture of the day when the nobles of the nations will "assemble" as the people of the God of Abraham (the Hebrew root for "assemble" is apparently closest in meaning to the New Testament concept of the "Church").

The "nations" are also featured in Psalm 2 (which, along with Psalm 1, serves as an introduction to the whole Psalter). Psalm 2 portrays the Father saying to Jesus, the Son, "*Ask of me and I will make the nations your inheritance, the ends of the earth your possession.*" From the very beginning, Israel's training in prayer included intercessory prayer for the nations, so that they would one day be gathered to the people of God. It is an emphasis we desperately need to recover. At last count, thousands of nations (or people groups) have yet to hear about Jesus Christ. We, no less than Israel, cannot be allowed to forget, in our private acts of contemplation and prayer, no matter how enjoyable, that God's purposes embrace all the nations. As American pastor and author John Piper argues so convincingly, one of the main reasons prayer has malfunctioned is that we Christians have turned what was intended as a wartime "walkie-talkie" that enables us to stay in touch with "command headquarters" into a domestic "intercom" that makes life more comfortable in the den.[7] Praying the Psalms will at least serve as a regular reminder of, and partial corrective to, religious myopia.

Where Are We Headed?

Part 1 contains two long chapters devoted to the two critical disciplines of *listening to God* and *exercising the imagination*. They are long because they are critical. If I fail to convince you here, the rest of the book is merely academic. In Part 2, I have included expositions of several Psalms. Since I first began preaching the Psalms in 1985 (about seventeen years ago), I have had the wonderful privilege of studying and expounding nearly thirty-five of them and praying through several others. Not surprisingly, therefore, it was a challenge to determine which ones to include in this book and which ones to leave for another day.

What criteria did I use for this selection? I finally settled on these: *uniqueness*, the *practical relevance* of the human emotions and predicaments addressed, and above all, their *effectiveness as tools* in training us to pray. While each chapter is intended as a "stand-alone" exposition, all are presented in a logical sequence. Psalm 84 begins our journey by describing the blessedness of those who have *"set their hearts on pilgrimage."* This pilgrimage to Zion (the temple in Jerusalem) sets the scene for Psalm 48, which extols a Mount Zion that is *"beautiful in its loftiness."* When the pilgrims reach Mount Zion, they worship with the gathered people of God, as we do every Sunday in church (our spiritual Mount Zion). That is why the next Psalm is Psalm 92, the only one titled *"A Song. For the Sabbath Day."*

We are not on this pilgrimage alone, and we will eventually "pass the baton" to the generation coming after us. Psalm 127 describes this task exquisitely as launching our children as arrows so they can do battle at the city gates, the place where decisions are made. At those "city gates," we and our children are called to mix religion and politics effectively, as described in Psalm 72. That Psalm, in turn, ends with an affirmation of the universal spread of God's glory, thus setting the stage for our first medley of Psalms (2, 110, and 118), teaching us to advance the Kingdom of God on our knees against virulent opposition.

The pilgrimage begun in Psalm 84 ends with the worldwide acknowledgement of God's glory. But as with the Hebrew pilgrim's journey to the physical Zion, we encounter obstacles along the way to the spiritual Zion. In the next four chapters, we look into some of these challenges. Psalm 51 teaches us how to confess our sins, a second medley (Psalms 22, 129, and 139) guides us in handling sins committed against us, and Psalm 37 offers answers to tyrannical questions raised by the intellect, which cannot harmonize life's harsh realities with "pat" theological assertions. Finally, Psalm 90 helps us tame time with a touch of eternity.

At the end of each expository section, interspersed throughout the book, I have included a Prayer Guide – the "something more" that some pray-ers will want to use, in addition to being encouraged to pray the Psalms. Without these guides, I would have felt no justification for adding this book to the many commentaries on the Psalms that are already available. A few words on how they could be used might be helpful. (I am indebted to my daughter, Sheila, for agreeing to be a spiritual "guinea pig." She was the first one to "field-test" a few of these guides by actually using them in her own prayer closet. Her feedback helped me tie up several loose ends and make the guides more "user friendly.")

So here are the "user instructions":

- *Read the Psalm*. The NIV version of the Psalm has been included at the beginning of each chapter and at appropriate points in the exposition, for ready accessibility.

- *Read the expositions of the Psalm* (in the main text of the chapter), skipping the Prayer Guides for the moment. This will give you the proverbial "bird's-eye view" of the issues the psalmist is grappling with, the emotions engendered by these issues, and how he responds to God.

- *Read through the expositions again*; only this time, stop whenever you come to a Prayer Guide – which is also the point where the word "Selah" appears in the full Psalm at the beginning of the chapter. Scholars tell us that the precise meaning of this word is uncertain, but its most likely function in the Psalms is to say to us, "Stop and reflect on what you have read." At any rate, that's the function I intend it to serve in my expositions. It says to you, "Stop here and go through the Prayer Guide." At each "Selah," or Prayer Guide, then, take some time to respond to God, using the suggestions in the guide to shape your prayers. When you feel you have finished responding, move on to the next Psalm exposition and continue until the next Prayer Guide. Then respond to that part of the Psalm, using the questions and suggestions in that guide.

The number and position of the Prayer Guides are my

attempt to provide a reasonable balance between a "choppy" exposition (where Prayer Guides would appear too frequently) and too much material between prayer times. Work your way through the entire Psalm in this way.

It may take you more than one session of prayer to complete praying through one Psalm. Keep a journal handy to record any insights you gain about the meaning of the Scriptures you are praying, any specific relevance to your life situation, any persistent impressions, and any other reactions you have. It is this practice, more than anything else, that has *"awakened my ear to listen as one being taught"* and by which I have been the gracious recipient of *"an instructed tongue to know a word that sustains the weary"* (Isaiah 50:4).

- *Repeat the process with each Psalm* until you become familiar with using the guides. Once you finish the entire book, it may be a good idea to go back and pray through the guides again until the ten Psalms/Psalm medleys become part of your prayer language.

- *Then try praying through other Psalms* that I have not included in this book, but which command your attention for whatever reason. Develop your own Prayer Guides using the ones in this book as a starting point.

The process may appear somewhat stilted and formal at first. If you are not accustomed to letting Scripture shape your prayers at all, you may be able to do no more, in the initial stages, than repeat the very words of the psalmist. "But shouldn't prayers be spontaneous and original?" you might ask. At the time I was writing this chapter, I was also taking a course on prayer at Regent College. In a small-group discussion that followed each class, the leader asked each of us to share a bit about how we had started on our prayer journeys. I was struck by the number of people who said they had begun by mimicking others – presumably more experienced Christians. That's how they learned the "lingo." (I suspect that's how so many of us learned to ask God to "be with them in a very special way.") We can only learn to pray by mimicking – exactly the way we learned our native tongues. The only question is this: Whom should we mimic? Since the Psalms were inspired by God and have been used by the Church for millennia as prayers, we could do worse than mimic them.

At any rate, reading the entire exposition of the Psalm first will allow you to pour more content into these expressions than you might otherwise have been able to do, even at the mimicry stage. Stay with it, and slowly but surely, you will find the psalmist's language becoming your own. In fact, the guides will increasingly become launching pads for your own prayers. To borrow the words of the Swiss Roman Catholic theologian Hans Urs von Balthasar, "the aim of the guides is to become superfluous. Whenever the person at prayer feels he can leave this crutch aside, whenever his own wings bear him aloft, he can dispense with them without the slightest regret."[8]

Is it worth the effort? Eugene Peterson's answer can't be bettered. Commenting on Jonah's prayer from deep inside the belly of the great fish, he notes that both the content and the form of Jonah's prayer were shaped by the Psalms. Then he gives us this application: "If we want to pray our true condition, our total selves in responding to the living God, expressing our feelings is not enough. We need a long apprenticeship in prayer. And then we need graduate school. The Psalms are that school. Jonah in his prayer shows himself to have been a diligent student in the school of the Psalms. *His prayer is kicked off by his plight but not reduced to it.* His prayer took him into a world far larger than his immediate experience. This contrasts with the prevailing climate of prayer. Our culture presents us with forms of prayer that are mostly self expression – pouring ourselves out before God … Such prayer is dominated by a sense of self. But prayer, mature prayer [shaped by the Psalms] is dominated by a sense of God. [Such] prayer rescues us from a preoccupation with ourselves and pulls us into adoration of, and pilgrimage to, God [emphasis mine]."[9]

The result: an increasingly ordered inner space. In recent years, we have known the conquest of outer space, because of the astounding technological breakthroughs of the NASA (National Aeronautics and Space Administration) space program and the COBE (COsmic Background Explorer) satellite. Compared to the conquest of inner space, however, these victories are totally irrelevant and impotent, no matter how effective they may have been in unlocking mysteries in the regions beyond this earth. No wonder the hymn writer cried out:

> Drop Thy still dews of quietness
> Till all our strivings cease;
> Take from our souls the strain and stress,
> And let our ordered lives confess
> The beauty of Thy peace.

Breathe through the heats of our desire
Thy coolness and Thy balm;
Let sense be dumb, let flesh retire;
Speak through the earthquake, wind, and fire,
O still small voice of calm![10]

An Unpayable Debt

I began this chapter with a reference to one of Calvin Miller's books. Here is another comment from that same book, which struck me with equal force: "The one thing people will not forgive in a pastor," he says, "is unfamiliarity with God."[11] I have attempted to take this charge seriously. While I have written this book in the fervent hope that it will indeed lead you to familiarity with God, I cannot guarantee that will happen. What I can assure you is that I have tried to put into practice everything I am suggesting you do in this book. These expositions came out of my own attempts to pray through the Psalms, a few of them for several years, before I dared to preach them.

In this pilgrimage, and in the writing of this book, I have also had many helpers, encouragers, and mentors. An exhaustive list would be prohibitively long, but there are some whom I must mention.

- I owe an incalculable debt to the pastoral staff, boards, and people of my beloved Rexdale Alliance Church in Toronto. My colleagues on staff have quietly and determinedly assumed the extra load that was their lot during the six-month sabbatical I took to write this book. I am especially grateful to my former Senior Pastor, Bud Downey, who shielded me from a lot of "flack" throughout the sixteen years of our ministry together so I could study, pray, and preach without hindrance. The board members have always been my friends in ministry – "yea" sayers who are committed to helping me become all that God has intended me to be, by allowing me to use every God-given opportunity for strategic ministry. They gave me gifts of sabbaticals so I could have measured, unhurried blocks of time to study, pray, and write.

  As for the congregation, they sent us away, not reluctantly, but with their evident blessing, love, and continued support. They have sat through the initial expositions of these Psalms, and their feedback has been invaluable in making them practical and relevant. My thanks especially to Grace Bird, who transcribed the sermons to a computer disk, which made the writing task that much more efficient. I am also grateful for the network of thoughtful and generous individuals in Toronto and Atlanta who provided me with restful places to live that were most conducive to study, meditation, prayer, and writing.

- The idea of a self-made man is a delusion, even when referring only to the human dimension of life. I owe an equally unpayable debt to my many mentors. When it comes to the topic of this book, no one has influenced me more than Eugene Peterson. You will see his stamp on my life and thinking in the many quotations from his books. If these excerpts inspire you to read them for yourself, I would be delighted. One special blessing during the sabbatical I took to write this book was the opportunity to study under him at Regent College. I am also grateful to him for giving me a block of his valuable time each week so I could mine the riches of his spirit and mind further.

    Others have served as "mentors in absentia" through their writings. Though I have tried to reference every explicit quote and acknowledge every idea that was not my own, I am aware that, over the decade in which I have grappled with the Psalms, I have unconsciously absorbed perspectives, insights, and even phrases of numerous authors – Alexander MacLaren, Klaus Westerman, John Goldingay, Ray Stedman, Stuart Briscoe, Lloyd Ogilvie, Leonard Griffith, Ron Hembree. Some readers may even recognize their individual influences where I cannot. I am a man in debt.

- I never cease to thank God for my family. Almost thirty-one years of marriage continue to fill my heart with gratitude to God for my wife Shyamala. Her love for people, her vitality of spirit, and her joy in living bring colour to my own life, characterized as it is by routine, schedules, and the entirely predictable. Her service to my aging parents, who have lived with us for several years, and especially to my father during his last months on earth, leave me in her eternal debt. She also provided an intuitive, and hence invaluable, "bird's-eye" evaluation of every chapter in this book. As for my children, not too many days pass by without my lifting my voice heavenward in gratitude to God for our daughter,

Sheila, and her husband, Duncan; our son, Vijay, and his wife, Jennifer – all of whose walks with God and whose increasing wisdom and maturity often bring tears to my eyes. Our two grandchildren, Rebecca and Matthew, have opened up new dimensions of love, life, and joy that we did not even know existed prior to their birth.

As for my parents, I owe them a debt that I can repay only before the throne of God. Writing a book takes discipline, logical thought, and perseverance – all three of which they instilled in me during the formative years of my life, often at considerable personal sacrifice.

• Finally, I want to thank my editor, Kathryn Dean, whose sharp eye, agile mind, and language skills have made this book so much more readable. Any residual confusions are entirely my own. Thanks also go to Warren MacDonald for his desire to see such material made available to the reading public and for his elegant book design. It is largely because of his initiative throughout the process that you now have this book in your hands.

When a man owes so much to so many, to whom does he dedicate a book? Surprisingly, the choice was easy. On October 6, 1994, my father went home to his Lord shortly after his eightieth birthday. What was remarkable is that Jesus became his Lord only three days before his death. A witness of thirty-one years finally bore fruit. While God alone gets the glory for this, I will never ever forget the handful of individuals in the congregation of Rexdale Alliance Church who stormed heaven and hell with fasting, weeping, and prayers for his soul long after my own passion had abated. They know who they are, and it is to them that I gladly dedicate this book. May it help them be architects of many more such divine conquests.

Sunder Krishnan
Toronto, Ontario
September 2002

Chapter 1

Who Speaks First?

In his book *The Christian Family*, Larry Christensen[1] recalled an incident involving his young niece. At mealtime one day, she said without warning, "Jesus, Jesus, that's all I hear in this house. But He don't say nothing!" With the unerring instinct of children, she had put her finger on the "nub" of a fundamental, practical problem in the Christian life. Jesus is a person, but He is unlike any other person we know. He is not visible, tangible, or audible. So we can't see, touch, or hear Him. Christensen did not say whether or how they answered his niece, but one thing is certain. After thirty-nine years as a Christian attempting to follow Jesus, twenty-one of which I have spent trying to help others in the same pilgrimage, I can say with reasonable confidence that most adult believers have never quite broken through to a satisfactory answer to the problem presented so unexpectedly at that breakfast table. Yes, we grow up hearing and believing that prayer is a two-way conversation, but if the truth were to be told, for many of us, it has been mostly one-way in practice – from us to Him. So whenever we read about listening to God or hear testimonies of people who have heard from God, we react. Some of us avoid the topic: What can we offer that is intelligent and honest? Others feel our antennae shoot up instantly: We've heard too many crazy things said and done in Jesus' name by people who claimed to have heard from Him. "God told me" sends out all the wrong vibes. Yet others develop theological defences. After all, the canon of Scripture is closed. God has said all He intended to in His Word. He doesn't need to say anything more. Our job is to study Scripture in order to accurately interpret what He has said and apply it with understanding. When we've finished, we will have discovered the text has one meaning. To say that it can have more than one meaning is to skirt dangerously close to "those neo-orthodox theologians" who tell us that the Bible isn't the Word of God; it only becomes the Word of God to us. (For those who don't like fancy labels and phrases, it's like saying, "If a certain passage in the Bible makes you tingle, it's the Word of God. Until then, it's just like any other word.") With one or more of these reactions, we quickly move on to other topics.

It has become something close to a life calling for me to persuade people that there is another way. Yes, the road is strewn with the wreckage of those who have "obeyed" a voice that they thought was God's. Marriages have been strained, even dissolved; family finances have been devastated; children have been disillusioned; faith and belief in God have been held up to mockery by unbelievers. But if ever we should avoid throwing out the proverbial baby with the bathwater, it's in this whole matter of listening to God. God is speaking, He intends us to listen, and He has made it possible for us to listen. And those who have heard can say with Augustine, "Behold thy voice surpasses the abundance of my treasures. Give that which I love."[2]

The Voice of the Lord

What is the first thing that usually comes to mind when we hear the phrase "The Word of God"? Usually we think of our Bibles, and more specifically, the words of Holy Scripture that we find written therein. And according to the customary use of the phrase, we would be right. But it wasn't always so; in fact, it was seldom so until very recent times. To the Hebrew, the phrase "The Word of God" was associated predominantly with something other than a book. It was, for them, a Voice. Consider what the Word of God says about itself.

- In Genesis, the Word of God was the Voice of God speaking Creation into being: "*In the beginning God created the heavens and the earth ... And God said, 'Let there be light,' and there was light*" (Genesis 1:1, 3). The subsequent verses in Genesis 1 show the Voice of the Lord shaping that which was formless and filling that which was empty (Genesis 1:2).

- Then in Psalm 19, we are told that this shaped and filled Creation itself becomes a powerful Voice that knows no barriers. It declares the glory of Him who created it. *"The heavens declare the glory of God; the skies proclaim the work of his hands. Day after day they pour forth speech; night after night they display knowledge. There is no speech or language where their voice is not heard. Their voice goes out into all the earth, their words to the ends of the world"* (vv. 1–4). The second half of the Psalm then tells us that what the Voice did in Genesis 1 for inanimate Creation, it also did for human life. Having created human life, the Law of the Lord (the Word of God) shaped that life: restoring, stabilizing, illuminating, preserving, warning, and searching the human heart (vv. 7–11). All of which calls forth the following response from the human being thus shaped: *"may the words of my mouth and the meditation of my heart be pleasing in your sight, O Lord, my Rock and my Redeemer"* (v. 14).

- Psalm 29 introduces us to a different aspect of the Word. It is a Voice that not only creates but also destroys what it has created: *"The voice of the Lord breaks the cedars; the voice of the Lord strikes with flashes of lightning. The voice of the Lord shakes the desert. The voice of the Lord twists the oaks and strips the forests bare. And in his temple all cry, 'Glory!'"* (vv. 5, 7–9). So even this destroying Word calls forth a response from the spectator, a shout of glory.

- This Voice that creates (the Creation itself echoing that Voice) and the Voice that destroys also invades human beings. Several times in the Old Testament we hear the prophets proclaim that the Word of the Lord came to them. They were hardly describing a mechanical process of dictation, a gentle tap on the shoulder, an apologetic request to take up a pen and write down several paragraphs so others could read at leisure. Nothing of the sort. The Word of the Lord coming to them was an event precipitating a conversation with the Speaker that totally overturned the normal course of their lives. Moses' quiet, domestic life in Midian was shattered forever when he was commissioned as a spokesman for Jehovah before Pharaoh; Jeremiah was an ordinary priest going about the ordinary business of a priest when the Word of the Lord came to him. It was a Voice that ran rough-shod over all his objections; it became a Word that burned inside him and had to be spoken. He couldn't not speak: *"But if I say, 'I will not mention him or speak any more in his name,' his word is in my heart like a fire, a fire shut up in my bones. I am weary of holding it in; indeed, I cannot"* (Jeremiah 20:9). In Hosea's case, the coming of the Word was an invasion of his whole domestic life so that his marriage, his wife, their children, and their names all became vehicles for the ongoing proclamation of what the Voice had told them. The Word, to the prophets, was an event that took total control of their lives.

- Then, as *they* spoke, *their* words proved to be as dynamic as the Voice that had commissioned them to speak. Their words created (oil and flour in the case of Elijah [1 Kings 17:14]) and destroyed (Jeremiah spoke Hananiah's doom [Jeremiah 28:16]). And just as God's Voice drew them into a conversation with Him, so their words constantly drew people into dialogue with them and shaped them, sometimes by softening their hearts, but more often by hardening their hearts. In fact, the confrontation of the true prophet by heart-hardened false prophets was a standing feature of Israel's life, becoming thematic in Jeremiah. The Word of the Lord always provoked people into conversation with the speaker.

- Then, suddenly, four hundred years of silence. No Word from God, no Voice after the prophet Malachi. Equally suddenly, the silence is broken. Luke's Gospel describes it for us: *"In the fifteenth year of the reign of Tiberius Caesar – when Pontius Pilate was governor of Judea, Herod tetrarch of Galilee, his brother Philip tetrarch of Iturea and Traconitis, and Lysanias tetrarch of Abilene – during the high priesthood of Annas and Caiaphas, **the word of God came to John** son of Zechariah in the desert. He went into all the country around the Jordan, preaching"* (3:1–3). And how did John characterize his ministry? *"A **voice** of one calling in the desert."* Four hundred years and not one change in the "Word = Voice" equation!

- But all of this was preparation for the "real thing," as one Coke commercial has been fond of saying. The Voice that created, the Voice that shaped and filled Creation so that it became an echo of the Voice, the Voice that destroyed Creation, the Voice that invaded the lives of prophets as an event that pulled them into dialogue with the Speaker, the Voice that, through them, shaped life, hardening and softening hearts through dialogue, was now about to take human form and enter Creation as an audible Voice. The Word was to become flesh in the incarnation. Hans Urs von Balthasar has described this phenomenon well: "Certainly, the Word of revelation did not simply fall from heaven in the person of Christ; the single, rushing torrent was fed, as it were, by many already existing streams. There is a period of preparation, a kind of crescendo, up to the full volume of the divine voice in the world."[3]

- And when He spoke, the Voice incarnate did everything the Voice of the Lord had done for centuries. His Voice brought forth life (bread and fish [Matthew 14:18]) and destroyed life (the fig tree cursed [Matthew 21:20]). He also did the same for humans, giving life (the raising of Lazarus [John 11:43]), shaping life with His words (no man ever spoke with such authority [Luke 4:36]), and drawing people into dialogue with Him, dialogue that often shaped life by hardening hearts (recall Jesus' dialogues with the Pharisees, Sadducees, and Herodians during the last week of His life [Matthew 21:23ff]). Finally, His Voice invaded human beings and commissioned them to speak the Word (the two words "follow me" were enough to permanently change the lives of several fishermen and a tax collector [Mark 1:17, 18]). And after Jesus ascended to the Father and the "Spirit-anointed" apostles continued to proclaim the message, that Voice, through them, did exactly the same things. It created, destroyed, and shaped lives by pulling people into dialogue with the speakers, softening or hardening their hearts in the process.

When we look at what the Word of God says about itself, we are left with this unmistakeable conclusion. *The Word of God is, and always was, intended to be the Voice of God that pulled hearers into dialogue with Him, permanently affecting them in the process, by either hardening or softening their hearts.* That's how the Word of God was regarded by the Church for the first fifteen centuries after Christ. So how did we get to the status quo, where the Word is more readily associated with a printed page and less, if at all, with a Voice to be heard and a person to be related to?

Two Critical Shifts

I believe that the most illuminating answer to this question is found in Eugene H. Peterson's book *Working the Angles*.[4] It is well worth reading in its entirety, but let me sum up the argument. Peterson traces the above shift in perspective to two causes: *the invention of the printing press* and a change in the *way we think of education.* Before the printing press, books had to be copied by hand. Large books like the Bible obviously took more time to copy, and hence, were more expensive, less available to the masses, and less widely read. So most people encountered the Scriptures by hearing them read aloud, usually in public. This certainly had its disadvantages, but people in those days couldn't easily lose sight of the fact that the Word of God was a Voice to be listened to, not just a printed word to be read. With the onset of the printing press and the many blessings that came from it (mass availability of the Scriptures, for example), attention inevitably shifted from listening to reading. Peterson also notes several major differences between listening and reading. In reading, for instance, we are in control, while in listening, the speaker is in control. In reading, we take the initiative; in listening, the speaker takes the initiative. In reading, the book cannot know when our attention wanders; in listening, the speaker can usually tell when we aren't paying attention. The implications for the way we encounter the Scriptures are obvious.

As for the shift in the way we think of education, Peterson points out that until recent times, education was something that went on in the context of a relationship between teacher and student. Dialogue, disputes (argument), and modelling were the main tools that the teacher used. Today, education is seen largely in terms of transferring information from the teacher's head to the student's notebook, usually bypassing the student's head. A relationship between the teacher and the student is almost impossible, with class sizes so large as to make any dialogue and disputation practically impossible, if not unthinkable. Thus the emphasis shifted, not only from "listening" to "reading," but also from "relating to the speaker" to "acquiring information." Hence, the Scriptures are no longer a Voice that pulls us into relationship with the Lord, but something to be read to obtain data. Given what the Word says about itself, we have to reverse the shift. Reading the Scriptures must somehow be seen as a means of listening in order to relate to the speaker. But what does all this have to do with prayer? Let's take a closer look at how Jesus, the Voice incarnate, strategized and detailed His mission on earth.

The Servant of the Lord

A careful reading of the Gospels will show us that Jesus saturated His ministry on earth with prayer. After a day of intense ministry involving teaching, healing, and battling demons, we might have expected Jesus to take it easy, but Mark tells us that on the next day, *"Very early in the morning, while it was still dark, Jesus got up, left the house and went off to a solitary place, where he prayed"* (1:35). Other times He did not even bother to go to sleep; He spent whole nights in prayer. What was He praying about? Why did He need to pray? After all, He was the Son of God, who already knew why He had been sent to earth. The answer is perhaps mysterious but not at all obscure. Let's begin with Isaiah's prophecy eight hundred years before Jesus came to earth.

Serious students of Scripture have long recognized that the "Servant of the Lord" section in Isaiah's prophecy (Chapters 42–53) refers not only to Israel as a nation but also to the Representative of Israel – the Messiah, Jesus Christ. As such, it contains certain passages that are autobiographical and which offer rare insights into the Messiah's thoughts and ways. Here is a remarkable example, one that is directly pertinent to our purposes: *"The Sovereign LORD has given me an instructed tongue, to know the word that sustains the weary. He wakens me morning by morning, wakens my ear to listen like one being taught. The Sovereign LORD has opened my ears, and I have not been rebellious; I have not drawn back"* (Isaiah 50:4–5). Jesus, as we have already noted, was the Voice of the Lord personified. How did He know what to say? According to the passage above, the Sovereign Lord woke Him up morning by morning, then awakened/opened His ears to listen. That's how His tongue was able to utter words to sustain the weary (His mission on earth).

And to assure you that we are not reading too much into this Old Testament passage, here's another insight into the mind of Christ, this time in His incarnate form. We read in Hebrews: *"Therefore, when Christ came into the world, he said: 'Sacrifice and offering you did not desire, but a body you prepared for me; with burnt offerings and sin offerings you were not pleased. Then I said, "Here I am – it is written about me in the scroll – I have come to do your will, O God"'"* (10:5–8). In this passage, Jesus tells us why He came into this world – to do God's will. How would He know God's will? Notice the phrase *"A body you have prepared for me."* This is a quotation from Psalm 40, but there the corresponding phrase is *"my ears you have opened."* Why? So that I can hear what is written about me in the Scroll. So what's implicit in Isaiah 50 is explicit in Jesus' own words. His mission was to listen with divinely opened ears to the Father's personal and specific will (it is written about me) revealed in the written Word. That's why Jesus prayed. That's what He was doing when He prayed: listening to the Voice in the written Word concerning Him. That Voice, clearly heard, then released the prodigious energy, concentration, and perseverance that characterized His mission. Listening prayer was at the heart of Jesus' mission.

I will never forget the way Henri Nouwen summarized it in a lecture he once gave at the University of Toronto. For Jesus, the order was always *communion* with God, which drew a *community* around Him and through which He accomplished *ministry*. We, however, usually follow the opposite order. We desperately try to accomplish something (ministry). When we fail, we try to get people to help us (community), and when that fails, we pray (communion). No! Jesus' entire ministry began with, and was sustained by, regular daily listening to God with opened ears and, metaphorically, an open Scroll. It is no surprise, therefore, that He taught his disciples to do exactly that. Let's look at the Lord's Prayer, or, as has been pointed out by many, the disciples' prayer, which begins with the familiar "Our Father, who art in heaven."

Our Father in Heaven

Here, familiarity has bred, not contempt, but too rudimentary an understanding of these opening words that Jesus taught us to pray. We know that the first word, "Abba," was a radical departure from tradition. It was a term of endearment, which little children used to address their father ("Daddy"). It speaks of the incredible privilege of intimacy with the awesome Jehovah, something unthinkable to an Israelite at prayer until Jesus articulated it. That much we probably know, intellectually if not in experience.

What of the other half – "in heaven"? Is it there to balance the first half, to keep intimacy from degenerating into brash presumption? This is plausible and almost certainly intended. But a few years ago, a not-so-familiar passage in the Old Testament gave me a fresh insight into the phrase "in heaven": *"Guard your steps when you go to the house of God. Go near to listen rather than to offer the sacrifice of fools, who do not know that they do wrong. Do not be quick with your mouth, do not be hasty in your heart to utter anything before God. God is in heaven and you are on earth, so let your words be few. As a dream comes when there are many cares, so the speech of a fool when there are many words ... Much dreaming and many words are meaningless. Therefore stand in awe of God*" (Ecclesiastes 5:1–3, 7). If God is in heaven and we are on earth, this passage tells us that we should be approaching Him to listen before we speak.

This is proper silence, not the kind that encourages our minds to wander in prayer. Without this listening silence, our speech is not likely to be prayer as much as the speech of a fool, the many words of the babbler we spoke of earlier. Was this passage in Ecclesiastes in our Lord's mind when He taught us to pray, "Our Father in heaven"? Was He saying, "God is in heaven, so go near to listen. Let your words be few. Otherwise you will babble"? It fits the context of the Lord's Prayer perfectly. For, in the preamble to His teaching, one of the two dangers Jesus warned His disciples against was babbling like the Gentiles, who trusted in the length and volume of their prayers.

But like so many other things that Jesus taught them, the disciples did not learn. Months, perhaps years, later, Jesus took Peter, James, and John with Him to pray. There, He was temporarily stripped of the veil that clothed His Divine radiance. He shone with the intrinsic glory of God in heaven. Peter was so overcome with this sight that he began to babble: "*As the men were leaving Jesus, Peter said to him, 'Master, it is good for us to be here. Let us put up three shelters – one for you, one for Moses and one for Elijah.' (He did not know what he was saying.) While he was speaking, a cloud appeared and enveloped them, and they were afraid as they entered the cloud. A voice came from the cloud, saying, 'This is my Son, whom I have chosen; listen to him'*" (Luke 9:33–35). God had to stop Peter's babbling, telling him to listen rather than talk when confronted with God's glory. (Peter did finally learn – after the Holy Spirit was poured out on him. But that's described in Part 2 of this book.)

Many of us have also not learned to stop babbling – though we can recite the "Our Father" in our sleep. Peterson comments on this eloquently: "In language silence is as important as sound. But more often than not, we are merely impatient with silence. Mobs of words run out of our mouths, non-stop, trampling the grassy and sacred silence. We stop only when breathless. Why do we talk so much? Why do we talk so fast? Hurry is a form of violence practiced on time. The purpose of language is not to murder the silence but to enter it cautiously and reverently. Silence is not what is left over when there is nothing more to say but that aspect of time that gives meaning to sound. Silence is restored to language so that words, organic and living, once again are given time to pulse and breathe."[5] Like Peter, we, too, must stop babbling so we can listen.

Let's step back and look at what we have learned so far. I have been building a biblical case for listening to God (through His Word) as the indispensable, first movement in all prayer. The case has unfolded in three parts:

1. For most of biblical history, God's people have thought of the Word of God not in terms of the printed page, but as a Voice to be heard so the listener can enter into a relationship with the Speaker through dialogue, disputation, and imitation.

2. The ministry of Jesus, both as prophesied by Isaiah and as portrayed in the Gospels, was characterized by such listening prayer, shaped by what was written in the Scroll (the Scriptures) concerning Him.

3. The opening lines of the Lord's Prayer, which Jesus gave in explicit response to the disciples' request to be taught how to pray, demonstrate the importance of listening before speaking.

Case closed, isn't it? Well, not quite. Before we can end this chapter, I need to put to rest two popular objections that might still prevent some people from beginning the journey into listening prayer.

Is It Really for Everyone?

So far, the New Testament case for listening has dealt with the experience of Jesus and His instructions to His chosen disciples. What evidence is there that the call to listen applies to "ordinary believers"? A detailed exposition is beyond the scope of this chapter, but here are some observations indicating that such evidence exists:

• Jesus taught the common people in *parables*. According to Him, the most important one is the parable of the sower, whose seed fell on four kinds of soil: *"Then Jesus said to them, 'Don't you understand this parable? How then will you understand any parable?'"* (Mark 4:13). What is the recurring emphasis of this parable? It is this: how various people heard the Word. And what is Jesus' application of the parable? *"Then Jesus said, 'He who has ears to hear, let him hear'"* (Mark 4:9) – an exhortation to listen, intended for all who follow Him.

• The letter to the Hebrews opens with a declaration that Jesus is God's final Word to all people. As Son and High Priest, He supersedes the prophets, the angels, Moses, Joshua, and Aaron. The key application of this greater revelation through Jesus is this: *"Therefore, brothers, since we have confidence to enter the Most Holy Place by the blood of Jesus, by a new and living way opened for us through the curtain, that is, his body, ... let us draw near"* (Hebrews 10:19–22a). The whole point of Hebrews is to exhort every believer to draw near in order to enter the Holy of Holies, the immediate presence of God, something unthinkable under the Old Covenant. And why do we need to enter? God has spoken; we must listen. This is the climax toward which the entire epistle builds. It is driven home by way of a contrast between Mount Sinai (the Old Covenant) and Mount Zion (the New Covenant). Of Sinai the author writes: *"You have not come to a mountain that ... is burning with fire ... **or to such a voice speaking words** that those who heard it begged that no further word be spoken to them"* (Hebrews 12:18–19). But of Zion, he writes, *"But you have come to Mount Zion ... the city of the living God ... the church of the firstborn, ... to God, the judge of all men ... to Jesus the mediator of a new covenant, and to the sprinkled blood **that speaks a better word** than the blood of Abel."* The Holy Spirit directed an entire book of the New Testament to drive home to every believer that it is their unbelievable privilege to be able to approach God and to hear Him speak without being terrified by His holiness.

• The last book of the Bible, Revelation, begins with this exhortation: *"Blessed is the one who reads the words of this prophecy, and blessed are those who hear it and take to heart what is written in it, because the time is near "* (1:3). The word for "read" means, literally, "to read aloud," showing that the emphasis is on hearing and not on mere reading. This assertion is followed in Chapters 2 and 3 with warnings to the seven churches in Asia Minor, and each of these ends with an essentially identical invitation: *"He who has an ear, let him hear what the Spirit says to the churches"* (3:6). Peterson sums it up well when he writes, "The Revelation is the Spirit's emphatic declaration that the written word has not done its work until we hear the words in a personal act of listening. This last word on Scripture is therefore primarily a work ... by which letters on paper are converted to voices ... in us."[6]

Apostle or not, the calling to listen is for every believer. But what if ...

I'm Not the Type, Pastor

Though everyone may not articulate it in this way (and some may not be able to articulate it at all), I often hear objections that, in composite, run something like this: "Sunder, all this contemplation bit is fine if you are that type of person – quiet, somewhat on the passive side, having mystical tendencies, more comfortable in a study locked up with a book than with people. Me, I'm active. I feel close to God when I'm doing something – not when I'm investigating my 'inner space.' Besides, if I'm going to be really honest, I can't help thinking that contemplation can sometimes be a substitute for action, a cloak for laziness, even unbelief. So why don't you listen and I'll act? Besides, I don't have the time."

If there is a single chapter in the Bible that seems to have been tailor made to address this objection, it is Isaiah 55. Consider the first three verses: "'Come, all you who are thirsty, come to the waters; and you who have no money, come, buy and eat! Come, buy wine and milk without money and without cost. Why spend money on what is not bread, and your labor on what does not satisfy? Listen, listen to me, and eat what is good, and your soul will delight in the richest of fare. Give ear and come to me; hear me, that your soul may live'" (Isaiah 55:1–3). Verse 2 is pivotal. Bread nourishes us; satisfying labour bears lasting fruit. To spend money on what is not bread and labour on what does not satisfy refers to work that brings neither internal nourishment nor external fruit. Sounds suspiciously like burnout, doesn't it? The solution is found in the two verses (vv. 1 and 3) that sandwich the problem presented in verse 2. Four times we are invited to come and four times to listen (give ear, hear). And if we do, the promise is that our souls will live. How? "'I will make an everlasting covenant with you, my faithful love promised to David ... For my thoughts are not your thoughts, neither are your ways my ways,' declares the LORD. 'As the heavens are higher than the earth, so are my ways higher than your ways and my thoughts than your thoughts. As the rain and the snow come down from heaven, and do not return to it without watering the earth and making it bud and flourish, *so that it yields seed for the sower and bread for the eater, so is my word that goes out from my mouth: It will not return to me empty, but will accomplish what I desire and achieve the purpose for which I sent it. You will go out in joy and be led forth in peace; the mountains and hills will burst into song before you, and all the trees of the field will clap their hands. Instead of the thornbush will grow the pine tree, and instead of briers the myrtle will grow. This will be for the LORD's renown, for an everlasting sign, which will not be destroyed'"* (vv. 3, 8–13).

He makes our souls live by renewing His Covenant with us. He exchanges His thoughts and His ways for ours through His transforming, life-giving Word. Thus, we are given both bread and seed: bread for nourishment and seed to sow and harvest later as grain or fruit. These correspond exactly to the two things our former work did not give us: bread and satisfying labour. The Lord does this by rooting our work in His covenantal purposes, by showing us how to do His work in His ways. The result: we go out with a joy that is contagious. Those who work for, and with, us are no longer intimidated by us or driven by us; they are now sharers in our joy. And God gets the glory. What an incredible contrast to the plight of verse 2: money spent on what is not bread and labour that does not satisfy. The single secret to this transformation? Stopping long enough to listen so He can replace our thoughts and ways with His as we listen to His life-giving Word.

Could it be that burnout, as we know it, is not so much a matter of too much work as it is working without listening to God, so that our work is not rooted in His covenantal purposes for us and the world? Isaiah 55 answers with a resounding "Yes." Listening to God, therefore, is not just for those who are temperamentally cast as "contemplatives." It is for all of us, because our vocational sanity depends on it. Listening to God is not a "cop-out" from hard work. On the contrary, as Peterson says, it "generates and releases an enormous amount of energy into the world – the enlivening energy of God's grace, rather than the enervating [weakening] frenzy of our pride."[7] Not listening to God is "laziness at the center, while the periphery is adazzle with a torrent of activity and talk."[8] Or as von Balthasar puts it, "Contemplatives are like vast underground rivers, at times causing springs to gush forth where least expected, or revealing their presence simply by the vegetation which is secretly nourished by them."[9]

Author and pastor Gordon MacDonald tells the story of a traveller making a long trek deep in the jungles of Africa. "Natives had been engaged from a tribe to carry the loads. The first day they marched rapidly and went far. The traveller had high hopes of a speedy journey. But the second morning these jungle tribesmen refused to move. For some strange reason they just sat and rested. On inquiry as to the reason for this strange behavior, the traveller was informed that they had gone too fast the first day and that they were now waiting for their souls to catch up with their bodies."[10] That just about sums up most of us, doesn't it? We have gone so fast for so long that our souls have been left far behind. The tragedy is that while it took the Africans one day to realize their plight, we remain ignorant for years, if not decades. We must stop, all of us. We must learn to listen, all of us, to the Divine Voice in the written Word so that we can work within a God-glorifying, soul-satisfying, covenantal framework.

And if we still will not heed the call, let this climactic warning from Hebrews speak for itself: "*See to it that you do not refuse him* **who speaks**. *If they did not escape when they refused him who warned them on earth, how much less will we, if we turn away from him who warns us from heaven? At that time* **his voice** *shook the earth, but now he has promised, 'Once more I will shake not only the earth but also the heavens.' ...Therefore, since we are receiving a kingdom that cannot be shaken, let us be thankful, and so worship God acceptably with reverence and awe, for our 'God is a consuming fire'"* (Hebrews 12:25–29).

With theological and temperamental objections out of the way, let us turn our attention to the rediscovery and recovery of one of our most neglected faculties, one that I have found an essential complement to becoming a listener.

Chapter 2

Just Imagine

For a large part of my Christian life, I was either a practising engineer or training to be one. I was in my first year of undergraduate engineering studies in New Delhi, India, when I heard the Gospel and responded to the invitation to follow Jesus Christ. I continued to study engineering even as my faith life was nurtured, first through the ministry of Youth for Christ in India and then through Campus Crusade for Christ in Boston (where I did my graduate work). I finally put down roots in a local church in Toronto, Canada, where I was employed as an engineer with Atomic Energy of Canada. During this time, others helped me identify, clarify, and develop my primary spiritual gift of teaching. Not surprisingly, given my engineering background, my approach to the Scriptures throughout this period of my life was totally analytical, with a focus on understanding the structure and meaning of revelation as a means of breaking through to answers for the many theological and practical problems that are part of our lives as followers of Jesus.

Study was the primary route, both to energize my will to obey God and to shape the content of my gradually developing prayer life. When I left my engineering career in 1980 to join the pastoral staff of Rexdale Alliance Church, my preaching ministry was based largely on the same principle: an appeal to the will through the intellect. All this time, I never hesitated to disparage my abilities in matters requiring creativity or imagination. This was no "Uriah Heep-ishness" on my part – just an honest and quite ready acknowledgement of what I thought I was not.

But God had His own agenda. All along, almost undetected

by me, the Spirit of God was slowly weaving another strand into my spiritual makeup, gradually revealing another element of my inner space. Initially, these new developments came mostly in the form of observations and challenges, sometimes one-liners, sometimes whole paragraphs in books and magazine articles I would read. Since I wasn't aware of what was happening, I did not keep track and hence have no chronological record of these gracious intrusions. One of the earliest that I recall, however, came when I read a study by Reginald Bibby and Don Posterski on three thousand Canadian teenagers. When asked to rate various "values" in order of importance, they placed imagination and creativity alarmingly low on the scale.[1] What's more, those who esteemed these values the least were from evangelical Christian homes. "What a tragedy" was my instinctive response. Hypocritical, I suppose, since these were the two characteristics most conspicuous by their absence in my own life and ministry. Reading these statistics also gave me my first inkling that I was going to have to do something about this lack.

I was confronted a second time by a "one-liner" in a sermon preached by my brother-in-law Ravi Zacharias. As he unfolded the various strategies of Satan in his temptation of our Lord, he said (with respect to Satan's offer of the kingdoms of this world in all their splendour): "Imagination has the power to bypass the intellect and get directly at the will." The application to me as a preacher was self-evident. A preacher's goal is to effect life change in his or her listeners. This won't happen unless their wills are mobilized. If, indeed, imagination can get directly at the will, to neglect it in my preaching was not only foolishness but an abrogation of my calling. Although this was the second time the Lord had prodded my conscience regarding my neglect of this critical faculty, I never "got around to it" – at least not until one man's writings began to so challenge and reshape my theology of pastoral ministry that I began to earnestly desire what the great Scottish preacher Peter Marshall called "a sanctified imagination."

A Sanctified Imagination

In the first chapter of his spellbinding treatment of the puzzling and mystifying, yet magnetic, Book of Revelation, Eugene Peterson writes about the threefold makeup of the author of Revelation, St. John. He is a theologian, a poet, and a pastor. As a *theologian*, he "takes God seriously and makes it his life work to think and talk of God in order to develop a knowledge and understanding of God in his being and work. He offers his mind in the service of saying 'God' in such a way that God is not reduced or packaged but known, contemplated and adored."[2] To that I said, "Amen." It's what I hoped I'd been doing reasonably well for years; it's what I loved to do. As a *pastor*, he "is the person who specializes in accompanying persons of faith 'in the middle' – facing ugly details, the meaningless routines ... all the while insisting that this unlovely middle is connected to a splendid beginning and a glorious ending. A pastor takes actual persons seriously as children of God and faithfully listens to them in the conviction that their life of faith in God is the central reality to which all else is peripheral."[3] To this I could also say, "Amen," for even though pastoring didn't come naturally to me, I had begun to learn to be more of a pastor in my ministry in my local church. But St. John was also a *poet*. And poetry "is not the language of objective explanation but the language of imagination. We do not have more information after we read a poem, we have more experience. It is not an examination of what happens but an immersion in what happens. A poet takes words seriously, as images that connect the visible and the invisible, and becomes custodian of their skillful and accurate use."[4] This time the "Amen" was definitely muffled, barely audible. I knew now that I had no choice. If I was to be obedient to my calling as a preacher of the Word, it was not enough that I take God seriously as a theologian and offer my mind to Him; it wasn't enough to take people seriously and listen carefully; I had to take words seriously and begin to exercise my imagination.

I have never regretted that decision. Not that I have abandoned intellect. It will remain my primary forte. But it is being increasingly empowered by the imagination. Elsewhere Peterson writes, "We have a pair of mental operations, Imagination and Explanation, designed to work in tandem ... Explanation pins things down so that we can handle and use them – obey and teach, help and guide. Imagination opens things up so we can grow into maturity – worship and adore, exclaim and honor, follow and trust. Explanation restricts, defines and holds down; Imagination expands and lets loose. Explanation keeps our feet on the ground; Imagination lifts our heads into the clouds. Explanation puts us in harness; Imagination catapults us into mystery."[5] I am only a few years along the road in this particular pilgrimage, and already my life and ministry have been enriched beyond anything I could have predicted or hoped.

An Objection

"Ah! But I'm not a theologian, poet, or pastor," I can hear you saying. "Why should I bother with sanctifying the imagination?" For two very good reasons. We have an enemy who is skilled in the use of imagination, our imagination, to bypass our intellect and get to our wills. This was not merely the "ace up his sleeve" in his attempts to veer our Lord off His chosen path of obedience to His Father's will. It's the way he operates on all of us – and he began way back in Eden. What was it that finally broke through Eve's defences? Satan appealed directly to her imagination with this promise: "*For God knows that when you eat of it your eyes will be opened, and you will be like God, knowing good and evil.*" And through her imagination, he also encouraged her to contemplate the aesthetic delights of the forbidden fruit: "*When the woman saw that the fruit of the tree was good for food and pleasing to the eye, and also desirable for gaining wisdom, she took some and ate it*" (Genesis 3:5– 6). This appeal to our imagination to tempt us to disobedience is a critical part of his strategy for all of us, and multimedia (especially its visual component) is his most effective instrument. Thus, an unsanctified imagination, either by benign or willful neglect, merely becomes that much "easier pickings" for the Devil.

But, praise God, our imaginations are double-edged swords. Recall that Satan never has made, and never will make, a single original contribution, not even in the field of temptation. He can only twist and pervert the good that God has made, in order to accomplish his destructive ends. Imagination is, after all, part of us as creations made in God's image. And the Spirit, too, uses our imaginations to energize our wills. That's the second reason an exercised imagination is for all of us. Two sentences that have had a greater impact on my life in the last four years than almost anything else I have read should remove any remaining doubt: "If we want to change our way of life, acquiring the right image is far more important than diligently exercising will power. Will power is a notoriously sputtery engine on which to rely for internal energy, *but a right image silently and inexorably pulls us into its field of reality, which is also a field of energy* [emphasis mine]."[6] Reality speaks of truth and energy of power. Thus, the right image not only reinforces our conviction of the truth behind it; it also empowers the appropriate response.

Imagination and Prayer

I find I am most decisively convicted of truth and able to respond appropriately when these right images become fuel for my prayers. That's when the "discipline" dimension of prayer is progressively swallowed up in the delight of a communion of partnership with the Sovereign God in accomplishing His purposes. Listen to yet another insightful, almost lyrical, passage from Peterson's pen on the indispensability of imagination to prayer: "A lot of people reject the word of God ... and turn their rejection into a world power. These people command most of the armies of the world, direct the advances of science, run school systems, preside over governments, and rule in the market places. If these people are in active conspiracy against the rule of God, if the movers and shakers of the earth are conspiratorially aligned against it, what difference can prayer make? What is at issue here is size, size that intimidates. And intimidation is fatal to prayer. So we require an act of imagination that enables us to see that the world of God is large – far larger than the world of kings and princes, prime-ministers and presidents, far larger than the worlds reported by newspapers and television, far larger than the world described in big books by nuclear physicists and military historians. We need a way to imagine – to see – that the world of God's ruling word is not an afterthought to the worlds of stock exchange, rocket launchings and summit diplomacy but itself contains them ... If we fail here, prayer will be stunted; we will pray huddled and cowering. Our prayers will whimper."[7]

A Second Objection

But once we begin to bring images into our prayers, aren't we skirting dangerously close to idolatry? After all, that's what the pagans do, don't they? Make images of their gods so they have something concrete to pray to, something they have fashioned out of their imaginations. And doesn't that encourage walking by sight, instead of faith? In fact, look what happened to Israel soon after Moses led them out of Egypt. When God detained Moses for an unexpectedly long time up on Mount Sinai, the crowd below murmured impatiently. And what did they do? They created a golden calf and exclaimed, *"These are your gods, O Israel, who brought you up out of Egypt. Tomorrow there will be a festival to the* LORD*"* (Exodus 32:4–5). We don't make physical images, some will say, but mental images are just as real, aren't they? The objection is valid and the danger is there, but as with learning to listen to God, we cannot afford to "throw out the baby with the bathwater."

The Holy Scriptures contain much that is didactic in nature (material that is explicitly doctrinal, containing specific instructions that govern thought and behaviour and spell out consequences of conformity or rebellion). A good example of such instruction is found in Titus 3:9–10: "*But avoid foolish controversies and genealogies and arguments and quarrels about the law, because these are unprofitable and useless. Warn a divisive person once, and then warn him a second time. After that, have nothing to do with him.*" However, other verses in the Bible are totally "image." Here's one that portrays the purifying effect of God's righteous judgement on His people: "*Moab has been at rest from youth, like wine left on its dregs, not poured from one jar to another – she has not gone into exile. So she tastes as she did, and her aroma is unchanged*" (Jeremiah 48:11). Wine left to sit undisturbed apparently develops neither aroma nor flavour. But if it is distilled by being poured out from one vessel to another (with the settled impurities left behind), it becomes fragrant and smooth tasting. Jeremiah compares the impending Babylonian exile of Judah to wine being made aromatic and flavourful. Almost makes one want to be judged, doesn't it, rather than being ignored? That's the power of image.

Yet other parts of Scripture, while not entirely imagery, are cast in the form of a story (a history, a parable, an allegory). Certainly, stories teach "lessons" and principles, but they do so by appealing first of all to our imaginations and then to our intellects. Consider this amazing allegory of God's grace in granting us the gift of salvation that makes us His children: "*On the day you were born your cord was not cut, nor were you washed with water to make you clean, nor were you rubbed with salt or wrapped in cloths. No one looked on you with pity or had compassion enough to do any of these things for you. Rather, you were thrown out into the open field, for on the day you were born you were despised. Then I passed by and saw you kicking about in your blood, and as you lay there in your blood I said to you, 'Live!'*" (Ezekiel 16:4–6). If you read the rest of the passage, you will find even more explicit imagery.

In light of the above, imagine how little of the Scriptures would be left if we removed from them all history, story, parable, and poetry. God has ordained the written record of His revelation to us in such a way that the majority of it is directed to our imaginations so it can work in tandem with our intellects. And this empowers us to obey the explicitly doctrinal and ethical prescriptions of the Word. God evidently thought the danger of idolatry a risk well worth taking. The benefit must indeed be significant. Practically speaking, the most effective, perhaps the only, way to avoid the slide into idolatry is to make sure the images that stimulate our imaginations in prayer are those found in Scripture, or awakened by Scripture. Commenting on one specific category of biblical images (the metaphors rooted in the Creation), Peterson writes, "The Hebrews who insisted strenuously on the holiness of matter and the divinity of creation knew, by commandment and through the practice of prayer, the difference between an idol and a metaphor [we can substitute "image" for "metaphor" and his point is unchanged]. An idol reduces and confines; a metaphor expands and connects. An idol starts with a mystery and fashions it into something that can be measured; a metaphor begins with something common and lets it expand to immeasurable glory. An idol gathers divinity into a lump – sometimes a very elegant and finely crafted lump, but a lump nonetheless – that can be controlled; a metaphor puts materiality into speech – the moment the word is spoken it is no longer under control, but is subject to the spontaneous dynamics of conversation in which the living God is the partner."[8]

A number of biblical images and metaphors have served to galvanize my prayers, pulling me into their field of energy and reality and working in tandem with my intellect to energize my will and help me persevere in obedience. I will describe them in some detail in the next sections and hope that this will encourage you to discover the biblical images and metaphors that speak most powerfully to your "inner space."

1. Why the Bush Did Not Burn
(an image for His personal dealings with us)

Anyone who has grown up in a Judæo-Christian home has almost certainly heard the story of Moses and the burning bush. One day while tending his sheep, he saw a bush that seemed to be on fire, yet remained intact. He reacted just the way we would. *"Moses saw that though the bush was on fire it did not burn up. So Moses thought, 'I will go over and see this strange sight – why the bush does not burn up'"* (Exodus 3:2–3). The same mystery that had intrigued Moses had formed my primary reaction for many years: How come the bush wasn't being consumed?

Nearly twenty years ago, however, a collection of devotions

by Arthur Matthews[9] forever changed the way I would look at this story. Let's move back to an earlier time in Moses' life when he had to flee from Egypt. The Bible tells us that while he was a prince in Egypt, Moses had been well trained in all the wisdom of Egypt: he was powerful in speech and action; he was a leader who got things done. One day, undoubtedly stirred by the Holy Spirit, he began to sense that his destiny was bound up in the welfare of the Hebrew slaves. Specifically, he knew he was to be the one who would deliver them from their present bondage in Egypt. Though right about his role, he initially carried it out in the wrong way. He saw an Egyptian overlord beating a Hebrew slave and killed the overlord. He did God's work Egypt's way, running rough-shod over people to accomplish his ends. That murder was witnessed and came to Pharaoh's attention. Moses, knowing his life was in danger, then fled to Midian, where he came to a well. There he sat, tired and discredited by both God's people and their enemy Egypt. Moses then married and settled down in Midian, where he soon forgot his mission of delivering his people and accomplishing God's work. Moses was a man with a *lost vision*, a *faded passion*, and a *waning sense of purpose*. In such a state, he saw the bush.

As he came closer, he heard God speak to him: *"I am the God of your father, the God of Abraham, the God of Isaac and the God of Jacob. I have indeed seen the misery of my people in Egypt. So I have come down to rescue them from the hand of the Egyptians … So now, go. I am sending you to Pharaoh to bring my people the Israelites out of Egypt"* (Exodus 3:6, 7, 10). God's vision was unchanged. He was (and is) the Covenant-keeping God of Abraham through whom all nations (including the Egyptians) would learn of Jehovah's greatness. *God's passion* (His compassion for the Israelites' suffering) was aroused. And *God's purpose* was still unchanged for Moses and His people (their deliverance from captivity through Moses, an event that served as the dominant illustration throughout the Old Testament of the Christian's deliverance from the bondage of sin). Therefore, God appeared to a man whose own vision, passion, and purpose were nearly extinct and said to him, "So now, go." Moses put up a fight at first, but eventually he went. And he would never be the same again. His vision, passion, and purpose were all fickle and vacillating, an easily quenched fire. But God's vision, passion, and purpose in him were an unquenchable fire. Arthur Matthews' electrifying conclusion: *It could not be quenched because it did not need Moses for fuel.*

The miracle of the burning bush was not that the bush was not consumed but that the fire did not need the bush for fuel. It was more accurately the miracle of the "fuelless fire." The bush went on burning without being consumed, not because the bush was remarkable but because the fire was. That's why any old bush would have done. When I realized this, I became excited. I, too, have *a vision*: seeing the nations of the world honour and worship Jesus as Lord. I have *a purpose*: to work out the vision in and through the local church I serve. But my passion, that is another matter. It is as fickle and vacillating as Moses'. What keeps me going is this image of the "fuelless fire" that can start burning in the heart of a disillusioned woman or man; a fire that does not need me for fuel but is fed by His vision, passion, and purpose. It is this image that fuels believing prayer, in times of optimism and otherwise. Imagination works in tandem with intellect to energize the will and secure perseverance in obedience.

God called Moses and ignited this holy flame in his heart, not merely for Moses' sake, but to redeem a whole community and to form them into His unique people. So it is with us under the New Covenant. Jesus saves us not merely as individuals, but in the very act of salvation, He organically unites us with the Church, the community of the redeemed. In *The Body*, a powerful and moving call to live as members of this community, author Charles Colson quotes John Calvin and then comments, "So highly does the Lord esteem the communion of His Church that He considers everyone a traitor and apostate who perversely withdraws himself from any Christian society which preserves the true ministry of the Word and sacraments … Those are stern words. But if it is impossible to fulfill the great commission apart from the Church particular, if apart from the Church particular, one can't participate in the ordinances or sacraments, then one cannot claim to be a Christian and at the same time claim to be outside the Church. To do so is at least hypocrisy and at worst blasphemy; the Christian life must be rooted in community for the kingdom to which it points is itself community."[10] In our society, characterized by what M. Scott Peck and earlier thinkers have termed "rugged individualism," I have found that intellect and explanation alone have not been sufficient to drive Colson's and Calvin's truths home far enough to actually change lives. Perhaps imagination working in tandem with intellect stands a better chance. Let's consider some images of the Church that the Spirit has given in Scripture.

2. The Bride of Christ
(an image for His corporate dealings with us)

Not surprisingly, our most fruitful source for images of the Church as the bride of Christ is Paul's letter to the Ephesians – the one book in the New Testament that has been written explicitly to portray the glory of the Church. I have chosen five words and phrases from Ephesians that have proved most effective in stimulating my imagination and strengthening my commitment to the local church.

- **An Adoption**: *"He predestined us to be adopted as his sons through Jesus Christ, in accordance with his pleasure and will"* (Ephesians 1:5). In our society, the word "adoption" has one dominant usage: to describe how a child not biologically our own becomes legally ours. In biblical times, however, it had other familiar uses. It referred, for example, to the public ceremony staged when a Roman son came of age. In the novel *The Robe*, a young Roman, Marcellus, described this ritual in a letter: "When a Roman of our sort comes of age, Paulus, there is an impressive ceremony by which we are inducted into manhood. Doubtless you felt as I did that this was one of the high moments of life. Well do I remember – the thrill of it abides with me still – how all our relatives and friends assembled that day in the stately Forum Julium. My father made an address welcoming me into Roman citizenship. It was as if I had never lived until that hour. I was so deeply stirred, Paulus, that my eyes swam with tears. And then good old Cornelius Capito made a speech about Rome's right to my loyalty, courage and strength. They beckoned to me and I stepped forward. Capito and my father put the white toga on me – and life had begun."[11] There is coming a day when we, individually, and particularly as a Church, will come of age; when we will be publicly declared to be the sons and daughters of God in a ceremony that will leave the principalities and powers (our heavenly audience) gasping. This adoption, Paul writes elsewhere (Romans 8:19–23), is what all of Creation is awaiting and for which we, too, are groaning. The Church will be the centrepiece of God's finished work of redemption. That's the day that we, like Marcellus, will say that life has begun.

- **A Poem**: *"For we are God's workmanship, created in Christ Jesus to do good works, which God prepared in advance for us to* *do*" (Ephesians 2:10). Scholars tell us that the word "work-manship" has the same root from which our English word "poem" derives. The Church is thus compared to a poem that God has composed, individual lines of which (in this imagery) are individual believers. So just as poets use their command of the language to combine words in hitherto "unthought-of" patterns and juxtapositions, in order to capture our minds and stir our emotions, God has combined and juxtaposed His spiritual sons and daughters into a beautiful poem, the Church.

• **A Stone Cathedral**: "*Consequently, you are no longer foreigners and aliens, but fellow citizens with God's people and members of God's household, built on the foundation of the apostles and prophets, with Christ Jesus himself as the chief cornerstone. In him the whole building is joined together and rises to become a holy temple in the Lord. And in him you too are being built together to become a dwelling in which God lives by his Spirit*" (Ephesians 2:19–22). In this passage, the word translated as "*joined together*" is a compound word that seems to have been coined by St. Paul. The component words mean "to choose," "to join," and "together," but the force of the compound is best understood by an illustration. Imagine building a wall with bricks. You have a pile of bricks close at hand and also the cement. Once you get the hang of it, the process flows easily. You reach out for a brick (any one from the pile will do, since they are all identical), slap on the cement, and align it with the brick you put in place previously. You repeat that process until the wall is as high and wide as it is meant to be.

Now imagine that you have to build the wall not out of bricks but out of stones. The process is considerably more involved. After you've positioned the first stone, you can't simply grab the next one from the stone pile. Since the stones are not all the same shape or size (as the bricks were), you have to choose the second stone carefully so its size and shape match the contours of the first stone. The third stone, which goes on top of the first two, has to be chosen and prepared even more carefully, because it has to match the contours of both the first and the second stones. The process thus involves "choosing," "joining," and "togetherness" – precisely the three words that Paul used to create a term describing how God sees and builds up the Church. It is a building, but not a plain brick unit. It is a magnificent cathedral built of specially dressed stones, each one unique and perfectly fitted to the others. The first stone, the all-important cornerstone, from which the whole building gets its bearings, is Jesus Christ Himself. Next to Him, and forming the foundation, is the first set of stones, the apostles and the prophets. And then it's our turn. Each individual Christian is a uniquely cut and dressed living stone, chosen to match the others perfectly. As the GM commercial says of its auto parts, "Our parts don't just fit; they match." So does each believer – into the grand edifice called the Church, a holy dwelling for the Holy Spirit.

- **An Embroidered Carpet or a Gem**: *"His intent was that now, through the church, the manifold wisdom of God should be made known to the rulers and authorities in the heavenly realms"* (Ephesians 3:10). This image of the Church is built around the word "manifold," a term used to denote the visual variety of a magnificently woven multicoloured carpet or garment. Paul applies this image to the Church to help us see Her as an exquisitely embroidered carpet or garment or even a jewel. The sparkle from every facet of this jewel reveals to an awestruck audience of heavenly beings yet another aspect of the "manifold" wisdom of God. (Paul does not say explicitly that the Church is "manifold" in its beauty; it is a reasonable inference, however, because, in order to demonstrate God's "manifold" wisdom through the Church, She has to be "manifold" in some way. At any rate, it is a licence well within the purview of a sanctified imagination.)

- **A Bride**: *"Christ loved the church and gave himself up for her to make her holy, cleansing her by the washing with water through the word, and to present her to himself as a radiant church, without stain or wrinkle or any other blemish, but holy and blameless"* (Ephesians 5:25–27). This image of the Church (one that subsumes all the preceding images) is set in a wedding banquet in which Christ is the bridegroom and the Church is the bride. As a pastor, I have performed many weddings, and I have often pondered the incredible difference in the bride's appearance at the rehearsal and at the wedding. On the rehearsal night, a casual observer would not likely be able to identify the bride. She is often dressed in jeans, her hair somewhat out of place, her face drawn and tired. She is usually irritable with her fiancé or anyone else who may have forgotten an errand or two. She is merely one of the crowd. The next afternoon, however, no one has any difficulty knowing who the bride is. All eyes are on her. So it is with the Church. We have seen Her only on rehearsal night. But a day is coming when She will be a radiant and holy bride, and again the heavenly audience will gasp.

These five images – an adult son's adoption, a poem, a stone cathedral, an embroidered carpet or a gem, and a radiant bride – rekindle my love for the Church and help me persevere in my prayers for Her and in my service to Her, when a lecture on the theology of the Church may have left me cold and unmoved.

This passage in Ephesians also tells us that it is the bridegroom, Christ, who makes His bride so beautiful. The Scriptures provide us with a magnificent image for this divine courtship.

3. The Courting Bridegroom

"I slept but my heart was awake. Listen! My lover is knocking: 'Open to me, my sister, my darling, my dove, my flawless one. My head is drenched with dew, my hair with the dampness of the night.' I have taken off my robe – must I put it on again? I have washed my feet – must I soil them again? My lover thrust his hand through the latch-opening; my heart began to pound for him. I arose to open for my lover, and my hands dripped with myrrh, my fingers with flowing myrrh, on the handles of the lock. I opened for my lover, but my lover had left; he was gone. My heart sank at his departure. I looked for him but did not find him. I called him but he did not answer. The watchmen found me as they made their rounds in the city. They beat me, they bruised me; they took away my cloak, those watchmen of the walls! O daughters of Jerusalem, I charge you – if you find my lover, what will you tell him? Tell him I am faint with love. How is your beloved better than others, most beautiful of women? How is your beloved better than others, that you charge us so? My lover is radiant and ruddy, outstanding among ten thousand. His head is purest gold; his hair is wavy and black as a raven. His eyes are like doves by the water streams, washed in milk, mounted like jewels. His cheeks are like beds of spice yielding perfume. His lips are like lilies dripping with myrrh. His arms are rods of gold set with chrysolite. His body is like polished ivory decorated with sapphires. His legs are pillars of marble set on bases of pure gold. His appearance is like Lebanon, choice as its cedars. His mouth is sweetness itself; he is

altogether lovely. This is my lover, this my friend, O daughters of Jerusalem" (Song of Songs 5: 2–16).

Interpreting this book as an allegory of Christ's love for his Church has a long and distinguished history. It is not a recent, prudish attempt to cover up embarrassment at its explicitly sexual language. Its vivid imagery of a bridegroom wooing his bride is an accurate depiction of Christ's love for the Church.

- Verse 2 portrays the groom outside the house, knocking on the window, wanting to be let in while the bride is asleep. His drenched head implies that He has been outdoors for a while. Eventually, she does wake up. The repeated "must I" in verses 3 and 4 underlines the reluctance of the bride to leave the warmth of her bed when she does awake. What a picture of how Jesus sees us (my dove; my flawless one) and His desire for us, even when we slothfully neglect to pursue intimacy with Him. What will He now do?

- Verse 4 sounds more like the description of a two-bit burglar trying to break in. He breaks the glass, thrusts his hand through the broken pane, and tries to unlock the door. Christ will use whatever route is open to pursue intimacy with His beloved. And if none is open, He will create a route. Now her awakened heart (v. 2) becomes a pounding heart (v. 4), for she has heard His Voice (v. 6). All the "must I's" vanish as she gets up to open the door for Him.

- Suddenly, she finds her hands dripping with myrrh (v. 5). How did myrrh (a rare perfume) come to be on her hands? Verse 13 offers a clue (remember this is poetry, not history). The lover is dripping with myrrh, and could it be that when He tried to unlock the door by thrusting his hands through the shattered glass, He touched the latch? If so, it is then marked with the fragrance of myrrh, and the bride picks up some of this fragrance as soon as she touches the latch to open the door. To the intellect, this sequence seems far-fetched, but to the imagination, stimulated by poetry, it paints a thrilling picture. Whatever the lover touches is forever marked with His fragrance, and that perfume becomes part of us once we stop slothfully neglecting His call to commune with us. We can no longer remain the same.

- But it seems too late, doesn't it? For when the bride finally opens the door, her lover is gone. (His absence, if she only knew it, is an integral part of His wooing.)[12] Yet the touch of myrrh makes sleep impossible. So the bride pursues her bridegroom – without much initial success. Her subsequent pleas for help fall on deaf and mocking ears. The absent lover and the bride's rough treatment at the hands of the watchmen (v. 7) underline both the difficulty of the pursuit of intimacy with God and the reality that the world is no friend to this process. It can be a lonely pursuit. Calls for help are often met with an unbelieving challenge (v. 9). So why bother pursuing intimacy with our lover, the groom?

• Answer: the beauty of the bridegroom (vv. 10–16). Notice the emphasis on the groom's eyes, cheeks, lips, and mouth (vv. 11–13). As for the bridegroom's words, they are sweetness itself (v. 16). The beauty of His character and the irresistible words of His mouth are what set the bride's heart pounding and keep her pursuing Him. Then comes the climax: this is my lover, this is my friend. There's the goal of our conversion: to know Jesus as our lover and friend. And this is how He pursues us – with His persistent knocking, with the tantalizing fragrance of His presence. Even His absences make us pant after Him and desire Him so much that we will not take "no" for an answer.

There is enough imagery here to keep us pouring our hearts to God without babbling or giving up in pessimism when He seems elusive and/or when those closest to us attempt to dissuade us with exhortations to be "practical" (or even mock our attempts at intimacy).

A "Warm-up" Exercise

In this chapter, I've attempted to build a case for the need to develop a sanctified imagination. Let's review the main assertions. I began with a personal testimony of the beginning and continuation of my own journey toward this objective. After this came two reasons why developing a sanctified imagination is an essential exercise for all of us. The *negative* reason is that Satan will not hesitate to appeal to our imaginations in order to bypass our intellects to get to our wills. Therefore, we need to work on sanctifying our imaginations to guard against these invasions. The *positive* reason is that acquiring the right image is far more effective in energizing our wills to obedience than mere concepts and commands that try to tap directly into our willpower. In the next section, we looked at the danger of imagination degenerating into a mental version of idolatry, but the conclusion was that the Scriptures deem the risk to be well worth taking, because of the benefits. The key is to ensure that the images we focus on are biblical in origin and are used primarily as moulds to shape our prayers, not as ends in themselves. For this reason, I developed three biblical images (or sets of images) to serve as illustrations:

- an image for God's personal dealings with us (the fuelless fire and the burning bush)
- an image for how He sees us corporately (an adoption, a poem, a stone cathedral, an embroidered carpet or a gem, a bride on her wedding day)
- an image for how Jesus woos and purifies His bride so she is radiant and holy (the Song of Songs)

But the final proof of the pudding, as the cliché goes, is always in the eating. So to drive home the lessons of this chapter, to remove any final traces of doubt as to whether this is really for you, and to serve as a warm-up for learning to pray through the Psalms, here is an exercise.

- Look at your calendar right now and set apart a place and a "one- to two-hour" block of time that you know will be uninterrupted. (Spouses with young children will need to help each other to manage this.) Take your Bible, a notebook, and this chapter along with you.
- Then slowly work your way through the above images, recording every fresh insight that the Spirit grants you, every truth that is reinforced, every act of obedience that comes with new urgency, and so on. (If you are at a loss as to know where to start, use the suggestions in the Prayer Guide on the next several pages.)
- If you run out of time (you may need more than one session to pray through all the images I have outlined), schedule another block of time as soon as possible. I hope and pray that by the time you've finished, you'll have such an appetite for prayer that you'll turn to the next section of this book with eager anticipation. Then we will be ready to heed this clarion call to the Church: "A major and too little remarked evil in our time is the systematic degradation of the imagination. The imagination is among the chief glories of the human. When it is healthy and energetic, it ushers us into

wonder and adoration, into the mysteries of God. When it is neurotic and sluggish, it turns people, millions of them, into parasites, copycats and couch potatoes. The [North] American imagination today is distressingly sluggish. Most of what is served up to us as the fruits of imagination is, in fact, the debasing of it into soap operas and pornography … It is time to get aggressive, for the Christian community … to join our poets, singers and storytellers as partners in evangelical witness. How else [will we] hear Isaiah's poetry and Jesus' parables, see John's visions and Jonah's plight?[13]

Prayer Guide

The Fuelless Fire

1. Take a few moments to answer these three questions about your life as a Christian: What is my purpose in life? What am I passionately concerned about? What do I have a vision for?

2. Read Exodus 3:1–14 and review the comments about Moses and the burning bush in this chapter.

3. How do your answers to the questions in (1), above, fit with the passion and compassion of the God who spoke to Moses? How do they need to be modified? Whenever you hit a wall, stop and pray. Turn your perplexity and your need for insight into prayer.

4. List the major obstacles you see as standing in the way of your vision, purpose, and passion. Acknowledge them specifically before God. (If you want a model for such a dialogue, read the rest of Exodus 3 and 4.)

5. If God were to light a fire in your heart that did not need you as fuel anymore, what would that mean? What would happen to these obstacles? Use your answers to shape your prayers. Ask Him to light a "fuelless fire" in your heart. He is the God of Abraham, Isaac, Jacob, and Moses, and He is your God, too.

6. What if He were to light a fire like this in the hearts of the members of your family? Use the insights gained up to this point to shape your intercessory prayers for them.

7. To make sure we do not forget the "nations," think of a missionary or missionaries that you know. (The closer your connection with them, the better.) What if God were to light

such a fire in their heart(s)? What might that do for their
ministry? Again, use your answers to pray for them.

The Church

1. What do you think of the local church of which you are a part?
   Be honest!

2. Read through each of the images that Paul uses to describe
   how God sees your church. Take some time to let it sink in: This
   is how God sees your church and each true believer in it. It
   might help to actually reword my description of the various
   images of the Church (adoption, etc.) by inserting the name of
   your church where the term "Church" now appears. Read your
   rewritten descriptions aloud.

3. Confess the sin inherent in the difference (if any) between how
   you see your church and how God sees it. This may become
   even more pointed when you think of specific individuals in the
   local church.

4. Pray that God will indeed make your church a poem, a stone
   cathedral, an embroidered carpet or a gem, a radiant and holy
   bride. Try to translate the ideas suggested by each of these
   images into specific requests for your church. (And remember
   that this includes that particular individual you like the least in
   your church. Name him or her as you pray.)

5. Now try the process for "that church" down the street which is
   always stealing your congregation. The confession list may
   grow a bit longer at this point.

6. Pray the same for the local church your missionary friend(s) is
   (are) planting or working with overseas.

The Wooing of the Bridegroom

1. Meditate on the description of the bridegroom in the Song of
   Songs 5:10–16. Have you ever thought of Christ in any of these
   terms? If so, respond in praise. Do any of these images suggest
   any favourite hymns or choruses? Then sing them. (Hymns like
   "Fairest Lord Jesus," "O Sacred Head, Sore Wounded," "Jesus,
   Lover of My Soul," "Jesus, Thou Joy of Loving Hearts," and
   "Jesus, the Very Thought of Thee" help me catch at least a
   glimpse of His beauty more easily than if I try to visualize His
   beauty without poetry and music.) If none of this helps, ask
   Jesus to open your eyes so you can see Him as the "beloved"
   did.

2. Read and reflect on the process of wooing and refusal in the Song of Songs 5:2–6. How has Christ knocked on your door? What are the "Must I" statements you make as you ignore that knocking? Offer your "Must I's" to Him with brutal honesty, confessing your sin and accepting His forgiveness. Thank Him for His persistence and ask Him to keep knocking.

3. If you are struggling with the absence of God, read James Houston's comment in this chapter's endnote number 12. Use those insights to cry out to God. Pour out your heart to Him, express your longing for intimacy and even the dryness that makes longing seem useless.

4. Read the entire Song, marking out other passages that you can use as fuel for future conversations with your lover.

Chapter 3

Psalm 84:
The Highway to Zion

1 *How lovely is your dwelling place, O* Lord *Almighty!* 2 *My soul yearns, even faints, for the courts of the* Lord*; my heart and my flesh cry out for the living God.* 3 *Even the sparrow has found a home, and the swallow a nest for herself, where she may have her young – a place near your altar, O* Lord *Almighty, my King and my God.* 4 *Blessed are those who dwell in your house; they are ever praising you.*

Selah

5 *Blessed are those whose strength is in you, who have set their hearts on pilgrimage.* 6 *As they pass through the Valley of Baca, they make it a place of springs; the autumn rains also cover it with pools.* 7 *They go from strength to strength, till each appears before God in Zion.* 8 *Hear my prayer, O* Lord *God Almighty; listen to me, O God of Jacob.*

Selah

9 *Look upon our shield, O God; look with favor on your anointed one.* 10 *Better is one day in your courts than a thousand elsewhere; I would rather be a doorkeeper in the house of my God than dwell in the tents of the wicked.* 11 *For the* Lord *God is a sun and shield; the* Lord *bestows favor and honor; no good thing does he withhold from those whose walk is blameless.* 12 *O* Lord *Almighty, blessed is the man who trusts in you.*

A Holy Jealousy

It was November 1962, about two months before I was to hear the life-changing Gospel message for the first time ever. I was a seventeen-year-old, first-year undergraduate student at the Indian Institute of Technology in New Delhi, India. This particular Sunday afternoon, I, along with a few friends, was at a tea party at the home of an American missionary. As part of the afternoon's entertainment (that's what I ignorantly termed it at that time), a gifted baritone soloist sent chills down my spine with a magnificent rendering of a song that I had never heard before. How was I to know that the lyrics were taken from a Psalm I would use countless times in my own meditations, one that was destined to become a lifelong cry of my heart before God, for myself and for others. The song I heard that afternoon? "How Lovely Are Thy Dwelling Places" – based on the opening verse of Psalm 84.

The dominant mood of the psalmist as he penned this song is clear from a benediction that appears three times in the Psalm: "*Blessed are those who dwell in your house; they are ever praising you*" (v. 4); "*Blessed are those whose strength is in you, who have set their hearts on pilgrimage*" (v. 5); "*O LORD Almighty, blessed is the man who trusts in you*" (v. 12). The word "blessed" is thematic in the Psalms and, interestingly, appears in the first phrase of the first Psalm: "*Blessed is the man ... .*" Of the many possible nuances of meaning that could be assigned to this word, the appropriate one is the most obvious: "O happy man! O lucky woman! I envy you ... ." And what is there about this blessedness that arouses such envy? It is not the beautiful boats, houses, bodies, cars, careers, etc., of "blessed people." Envy of that type is debilitating and divisive, estranging us from those who possess what we don't have, but that we would like to have. The psalmist's envy, on the other hand, is holy and purifying. Apparently, the word "blessed" comes from a root which carries the idea of going forth, advancing, leading the way. So the adjective "blessed" can refer to those who are pressing on in a life with definite goals and purposes. Theirs is a life worth living because it is going somewhere.[1] That's the kind of life the psalmist covets, and by describing it to us, seeks to make us covetous, too. Specifically, he thinks about three groups of blessed people and one thing about each group that makes their lives directed and purposeful, and hence, enviable. There are those who have arrived, those who are on the way, and those who trust God.

Those Who Have Arrived

The first blessed group consists of *"those who dwell in your house; they are ever praising you"* (v. 4). In the summer of 1965, two years after I had become a follower of Jesus Christ, Youth for Christ, India (the organization through whom I heard the Gospel), conducted an All Asia Youth Congress in Hyderabad, a large city in southern India. A delegation of forty youth from Delhi YFC were heading down there for a week of fun, music, and preaching. I desperately wanted to go, especially since I had been selected to represent the city of Delhi in the youth preachers contest. But I also had to complete an industrial training program that summer as part of my engineering education. My most persuasive efforts to get permission for a week-long break were denied. Several times during the week of the Hyderabad congress, my mind would wander to my friends in that city as I found myself musing, "Right now they must be marching through the city in the inaugural parade. By now, the opening rally must be well under way. I wonder what new truths they are learning from the speaker. Oh, how I wish I could be there with them."

The psalmist found himself in a similar situation. For some reason, he could not go to worship at the temple in Jerusalem. Wherever he was, his thoughts would periodically flit to the worshipping throng. He might look at the sun to check what time of day it was and think, "Right about now they must be in the temple praising You, O God, in joyful song." Perhaps his mind went to the temple singers who would be leading the people in this worship. They were even better off than the pilgrims. Their job was to stay at the temple praising, singing, and leading others in worship all the time. Imagine having that as a life calling. The psalmist envied them as much as I envied my friends who had gone to Hyderabad.

But the psalmist's longing went beyond companionship with the worshippers. We find a clue to this in verse 1: *"How lovely is your dwelling place, O LORD Almighty!"* In going to the temple, the worshippers would be drawing near to God. Sure, God's intimate presence could be encountered only in the innermost chamber of the temple known as the Holy of Holies, and no ordinary worshipper could ever enter there. But just to come that physically close to where the Ark of the Covenant resided, that quintessential symbol of God's presence among his people, that was a privilege the psalmist sorely missed. And the more he thought of this holy privilege, the fiercer his heart burned: *"My soul yearns, even faints, for the courts of the* LORD; *my heart and my flesh cry out for the living God"* (v. 2). Note the comprehensiveness of his passion: his soul (referring to his mind, will, and emotion), his heart (referring to the very core of his being, his essence), and his flesh (referring to his humanness and its associated needs and weaknesses) are all part of this expression. Then note the intensity of his desire: he yearns, faints, and cries out – and all for the living God. This was the nerve centre of his longing cry. The idols of the nations were lifeless hunks of wood and stone, but his God came down in smoke and fire, and rattled the earth beneath his feet. He was alive, and it was the aliveness of their God that the worshippers, and the singers who led them, relived in the temple celebration. This living God is what the psalmist longed for. To get close to Him was to get everything. That is why he envied those who were even now at the temple, and especially those who got to stay there as a life calling.

How do we stack up when measured against this comprehensive, intense cry of the psalmist for coming near to the living God? How easily are we satisfied with less than such an encounter? Rituals satisfy us, whether it is going to church on Sunday, putting in an appearance at mid-week prayer services, or even getting our daily devotions over with. Rules satisfy us: as long as we do or don't do certain things and exhort others to do or not do the same, we feel satisfied. And those of us who are intellectually inclined are gratified by theological niceties, catch phrases, and statements about God, tightly woven arguments for His existence and brilliant answers to the most commonly recurring questions of the skeptics.

Certainly, all of these have a place in the outworking of our Christian lives, but overarching and integrating all of them, do we, like the psalmist, insist on regular encounters with the living God, one who speaks to us and is relevant to our whole being – mind, will, emotion, and body? After all, if God became man, lived among us, and died and rose again as a man so that there is a "man in glory," we can expect this resurrection life to flow through us and infuse our humanity with His Divine life, can't we? We can cry out and demand that the living God motivate us, free us from guilt, and quicken us to obey Him because that's what we want to do from the very depths of our being and not because someone else expected it of us. Such a desire for, insistence on, and expectation of an encounter with the living God will drastically change the attitude with which we come to church, to corporate prayer meetings, and to our private prayer times – not as rituals to be performed but as occasions to express our hunger for an encounter with the living God.

Note also that the psalmist does not tell us exactly how God communicates this Divine life in answer to our prayer. His focus is on the hunger itself, to encourage us by his example to cry out to God and insist on experiencing the reality of His resurrected life, refusing to be satisfied with dead substitutes, religion that has a form without any power. I can add from my own experience, though, that while God sometimes answers such prayers in a dramatic way, He usually imparts it through less obvious, almost silent, channels. As Phillips Brooks put it so well in one of our favourite Christmas hymns: "How silently, how silently / The wondrous Gift is given! / So God imparts to human hearts / The blessings of His heaven. / No ear may hear His coming, / But in this world of sin, / Where meek souls will receive Him, still / The dear Christ enters in."[2] What's more, every taste of the living God that He allows in answer to our prayers only serves to increase the hunger. A thirst slaked in His presence only intensifies the thirst for more.

Now precisely because we are looking at a process, merely reading these observations on the psalmist's frame of mind will not be enough to bring us to the point where we cry out with the comprehensiveness and intensity shown in the opening verses of the Psalm. But we can begin wherever we are. And let's not be put off by the inevitable warnings not to go overboard on this matter of experiencing the living God. Sadly, these warnings often come from people within the Church. Ironical, isn't it? If someone wants to become a doctor, no one says to them, "Now don't go overboard on this matter of understanding the human body." If a professional teacher decides to take night courses to improve their teaching and their promotability, no one rushes to warn them against too much professional development. Yet as soon as someone wants to go all out in the pursuit of the living God, these same people become alarmed about possible excesses. If God is stirring your heart, soul, and flesh for an encounter with Him, don't be put off by such warnings. Instead, follow the psalmist's example and be sustained in your determination by the lives and words of those who have gone ahead of you on this journey:

"those who are ever praising Him." Self-taught American pastor and modern-day "prophet" A.W. Tozer provides an encouragement that cannot be easily improved:

> Come near to the holy men and women of the past and you will soon feel the heat of their desire after God. They mourned for Him, they prayed and wrestled and sought for Him day and night, in season and out, and when they had found Him, the finding was all the sweeter for the long seeking. Moses used the fact that he knew God as an argument for knowing Him better. David's life was a torrent of spiritual desire and his Psalms ring with the cry of the seeker and the glad shout of the finder. Hymnody is sweet with the longing after God, the God whom, while the sinner seeks, he knows he has already found. How tragic that we in this dark day have had our seeking done for us by our teachers. Everything is made to centre upon the initial act of "accepting Christ" (a term, incidentally, not found in the Bible) and we are not expected thereafter to crave any further revelation of God to our souls. We have been snared in the coils of a spurious logic which insists that if we have found Him we need no more seek Him ... Thus the whole testimony of the worshipping, seeking, singing church on that subject is crisply set aside. The experiential heart theology of a grand army of fragrant saints is rejected in favor of smug interpretations of Scripture which would certainly have sounded strange to an Augustine, a Rutherford or a Brainerd. [But] in the midst of this great chill there are some, I rejoice to acknowledge, who will not be content with shallow logic. They will admit the force of the argument, and turn away with tears to hunt some lonely place and pray, "O God show me Thy glory." They want to taste, to touch with their hearts, to see with their inner eyes the wonder that is God.[3]

Now from this growing experience of the living God comes a sense of security, adding to the psalmist's envy: *"Even the sparrow has found a home, and the swallow a nest for herself, where she may have her young – a place near your altar, O* LORD *Almighty, my King and my God."* It is highly unlikely that sparrows and swallows were literally building nests and hatching their eggs near the temple altars, although we can't absolutely rule it out. But the psalmist's line of thought probably runs something like this: he thinks of the humble sparrow, to which first-century traders in Palestine didn't attach much value (two sparrows are sold for a penny and five for two, etc.). He also includes the swallow, a restless, darting bird, and thinks of them both, secure in their nests. These two pictures lead him to exclaim, "Lord, even the restless swallow and the worthless sparrow have found homes, their nests, which you taught them to build for themselves. In the same way, Lord, let me find rest and peace in the home You have designed for me – that is, a place near your altar."

Just as the nests of the sparrow and swallow represent their natural habitats, what they were made for, so, too, nearness to the altar of God (representing a life of worship, thanksgiving, and sacrifice) is our natural habitat, what we have been made for. Augustine captured a similar thought in these often-quoted words from his *Confessions*: "Thou hast made us for Thyself and our hearts are restless until they find their rest in Thee." And God has fully answered this prayer in Jesus Christ. In and through Him, we do have access to that which was unthinkable for the psalmist; we have an open door through the torn curtain into the Holy of Holies, the innermost sanctum of the temple, the very presence of God – and that without the intermediary work of any human priest. Jesus' present ministry as our High Priest is all that we need to guarantee this access. We can build our nest there. It can become our natural habitat. Worship can become the air we breathe most naturally.

One further observation: this picture of the sparrow and swallow nesting at the altar and hatching their eggs at the place of worship and sacrifice has always fascinated me. Since it seizes my imagination and not just my intellect, it convinces me as nothing else can that the altar is also the most natural place to raise our young. Twenty-one years of ministry and counselling have only deepened my conviction that one of the most urgent tasks of Christian parents is to communicate to our children that the Christian life is at heart a communion with the living God. Without this, all the rituals, rules, and even the theological niceties are irrelevant and can even be damaging. Family devotions have to go beyond a few hasty bedtime stories (whether or not they are Bible stories) to help children see God alive in the men, women, and circumstances of these narratives. These need to be read and recounted at the altar (i.e., in an atmosphere of worship and prayer), for answered prayer is one of the most dynamic means of communicating the reality of the living God to our children.

One December many years ago, our church was facing a major financial challenge. With two weeks left, we needed several tens of thousands of dollars to meet the budget. One Tuesday night after the conclusion of the regular mid-week prayer meeting, five people stayed to pray for another hour and a half, asking God for His miraculous intervention and provision. One mother went back from that time of prayer, gathered her three young children around her, and told them of the situation. Together they read the story of Jesus feeding the multitudes by multiplying five loaves and two fish. She then asked them if they had any money they could contribute toward the church's finances. They returned with whatever change and small bills they'd been able to find in their piggy banks.

Their mother then led them in a prayer of thanksgiving as they offered their small collection to the Lord Jesus, asking Him to multiply it into whatever the church needed. As God provided miraculously over the next two weeks, you can imagine the effect this had on the three kids. Each Sunday, as they read the amount that God had led His people to give the previous week, their eyes opened wide in astonishment and wonder.

That's how we let our children know that God is alive: at the altar, and in an atmosphere of prayer, as we make the Bible stories come alive in contemporary application. And what is true of a multi-thousand-dollar need can also be true of a whole range of life situations. The routines of daily living need to be saturated with prayer – brief and extended, personal and intercessory, financial or spiritual. In this way, we will bear and raise our young near the altar of the living God.

A question that immediately comes to mind is this: What if God doesn't answer our prayers? Won't it damage my children's faith? The subject of unanswered prayer would probably take up an entire book in itself. However, if my experience with my children is any indication at all, they seem to have far fewer problems accepting the mysteries and paradoxes of God's ways with human beings than we adults do. What's more, nothing is ever gained by shrinking from a step of faith (prayer) out of fear (no answer). Finally, unanswered prayers provide natural opportunities for theological conversations with children at a level they are capable of understanding.

The psalmist concludes this part of his prayer with a cry to the *"LORD Almighty, my king and God."* The triumphant commander of innumerable hosts is also his personal God. He who runs the universe has plenty of time for each individual child – something no pastor can manage, no matter how noble his or her intentions to care for the flock. Unless we learn to encounter the living God ourselves, we are almost certain to be disappointed at some time or another with our human shepherds. Their job is to lead us to the living God, but we as individuals must also work to encounter Him "whom to know is life eternal" (John 17:3).

Prayer Guide

1. Take a few moments to reflect on the rituals, rules, and intellectual / theological affirmations that bring you satisfaction in your Christian life. To what extent are they based on encounters with the living God? To what extent do they stimulate comprehensive and intense longing for further encounters with the living God? How might these rituals, rule-keeping activities, and affirmations change to better bear the stamp of the living God? Use your reflections to shape your longings for the "courts of the Lord."

2. Is a place near His altar – the place of worship, thanksgiving, and sacrifice – your natural habitat yet? Would you like it to be so? At this stage, don't worry about how this might happen. Simply express your desire that it be so and tell God that you are willing to be led and taught by Him.

3. Do you envy those "who are ever praising God" – those who have arrived, our prayer masters from history? Have you settled for an easy "acceptance" of Christ? Do you feel no need to seek Him more? Reflect on Dr. Tozer's observation to evaluate your own "conversion" experience. Ask God's Spirit for a new work of grace to either create or rekindle a hunger for more, to lead you to men and women whose writings in prose and poetry can fuel the flame of hunger for the living God.

4. Conclude this phase of your prayer with a favourite hymn or chorus expressing your longing for the living God. "How Lovely Are Thy Dwelling Places" is a chorus based on this very Psalm.

Looking at those who are "ever praising God," who have gone on before us to Zion, who have arrived, so to speak, can and often does inspire hunger and thirst in us. But it can also discourage us, especially if they are much further along the road than we are. Their achievements may seem unattainable to us. That's one reason the psalmist turns his attention from them to the next group of enviable people.

Those Who Are on the Way

"Blessed are those whose strength is in you, who have set their hearts on pilgrimage" (v. 5). The way to Jerusalem was hard, tiring, and dangerous. Pilgrims had to pass over rough terrain and could easily be waylaid by robbers and wild beasts. Why would anyone envy a person who had decided to make this trip? Why does the psalmist show holy envy here? The reason is simply this: trusting and sharing in God's strength, these pilgrims have determined to get to Zion, no matter how difficult the journey. They have made a critical choice and there is no turning back. It is their irrevocable decision, their determination, and their trust in God's strength that the psalmist envies.

I well remember my first solo trip in my tiny Volkswagen beetle along an eight-lane highway, from the east end of Toronto, where I lived, to the west end, where I worked. No sooner had I gingerly pulled into the highway traffic than it began to rain. I panicked, but there was no turning back. I was driving alone on the highway to work, no matter what. (I found out later that my brother-in-law, who had taught me to drive, was praying for me that morning.) Determination in spite of our own limitations is needed as we make key decisions in the life of faith. In Elijah's immortal words to the errant people of Israel: *"'How long will you waver between two opinions? If the LORD is God, follow him, but if Baal is God, follow him"* (1 Kings 18:21).

I recall the conversion testimony of a young man in our church. The preacher at a camp he was attending sent the campers away one night with the challenge to either choose God or choose against Him. No one had ever set the latter option that bluntly before him. As it is in conversion, so it is in Christian service. A single missionary from our church illustrated this for us when she outlined, in one of her letters, the many routine acts of service she was expected to perform as bookkeeper for the mission. "It doesn't bother me to have to serve people," she said, "because, before I came here, I made the decision to be a servant."

The pilgrims of Psalm 84 had made just such a decision – to embark on the difficult journey to Zion so they could meet the living God, trusting in His strength to get them there. The Apostle Paul gives us the New Testament equivalent of this exhortation when he writes to the Colossians, *"Since, then, you have been raised with Christ, set your hearts on things above, where Christ is seated at the right hand of God. Set your minds on things above, not on earthly things"* (3:1–2). So set your hearts today and make the critical decision to adopt a lifestyle that will enable you to pursue the living God until His life is actualized in you. And make it an irrevocable decision – facing the fact that the journey is difficult and hazardous, yet daring to believe that God's strength will be available and sufficient to enable you to complete the journey. These are the results of such a choice:

- *"As they pass through the Valley of Baca, they make it a place of springs; the autumn rains also cover it with pools"* (v. 6). The road to Zion led through some barren, arid places. One valley, in particular, was nicknamed "Thirst Valley," or the "Valley of Weeping." (The word "Baca" could refer to either, perhaps because the valley reduced people to tears through the ravages of thirst.) Yet, surprisingly, the determined pilgrims passing through this valley transformed it into a spring. Not literally, of course, but because God was their strength, they were able to find refreshment even in the thirsty valley, not just for themselves but for others who had succumbed to the rigours of the valley. Hence the psalmist's envy.

  Applied metaphorically to our spiritual journey, the pictures evoke a different application. In our journey toward an encounter with the living God, we, too, will go through the Valley of Weeping. There, we may very well encounter some who are struggling in their walk. They may be so battered that they have almost decided to give up on the journey. They began well, they intended it to be an irrevocable commitment, they didn't intend to stop along the way, but now they aren't even sure they want to continue. That's our opportunity to stop long enough in our journey to Zion to make the Valley of Weeping a place of springs as we draw on the strength of our God, this time not for our sake alone but for the thirsty pilgrim who has almost thrown in the towel. We slow our walk to their pace and journey with them until their feet become strong enough again to pick up the pace.

Ah! you exclaim. What can we say to thirsty, weeping pilgrims who have gone so long without water that the prospect of an encounter with the living God in joyful worship seems a sheer impossibility? Notice the latter part of verse 6: *"the autumn rains also cover it with pools."* Scripture elsewhere refers to the autumn rains as the "former" rains and the spring rains as the "latter" rains. With the hindsight of the New Testament, we know that both "former" and "latter" rains can be legitimately interpreted as powerful images of the eventual outpouring of the Holy Spirit on all believers. That's why we can dare to stop in the Valley of Baca to help the weary pilgrim who has almost quit. The living God, who is our strength, has given us the Holy Spirit. Through the Spirit's power and influence, our listening ears and encouraging tongue are baptized and instructed to speak words of wisdom that put a new spring in the step of flagging pilgrims so they can recover their vision of Zion and resume their journeys.

- The second result of the irrevocable choice to make the pilgrimage to Zion is found in verse 7: *"They go from strength to strength, till each appears before God in Zion."* That's paradoxical. What we would expect is that the longer they'd been on the road, the closer they'd come to their destination, the weaker they would be from the rigours of the journey. Instead, these pilgrims go from strength to strength. There are at least two reasons for this surprising development. As Old Testament pilgrims got closer to Zion, they were joined by pilgrims arriving from other parts of the country and heading to the same destination. Meeting these fellow travellers would boost their morale. Besides, it was customary for pilgrims to sing the Psalms of Ascent (Psalms 120–134), which were written especially for this purpose: to keep them moving, filling their minds with anticipation of the joyful prospects that awaited them in Zion. So the closer a pilgrim came to Zion, the more he or she would become aware of other pilgrims making the same journey, sustained by the same irrevocable choice not to stop till they arrived at the city. And the singing would keep getting louder. What was earlier a faint attempt at optimism would now reverberate in a thousand throats as a triumphant declaration that Jehovah reigns in Zion in the midst of His Enemies. Faith would well up in their hearts, their feet would find new strength, and their pace would quicken. And once they actually came close enough to catch a glimpse of the magnificent temple, this invigorating effect would be multiplied.

Again, the application to our spiritual pilgrimage is obvious. In this journey, we are sustained not only by those who have arrived and those who have gone on before us; we are also encouraged by the presence of our fellow pilgrims. At first, we are aware of them more by faith than by sight; but then, as we see and hear others, we find strength to continue. That's one reason I have made it my life work to stir as many believers as I can to travel this road to Zion with me. Often the thought of these "disciples" and what they are learning as they encounter the living God keeps me on the road to Zion when my own zeal would otherwise flag.

Writing this book is one of many ways in which I hope to broaden that effort to recruit disciples beyond my own congregation. As the Spirit leads more of you to respond, we will all go from strength to strength. We will all get better at making the Valley of Baca a place of springs. We will all become more skilled at drawing on the strength of our God. We will all encourage each other with the glad prospect of standing before God in Zion. No wonder the psalmist prays in verse 8, *"Hear my prayer, O LORD God Almighty; listen to me, O God of Jacob."* Make me like these pilgrims who have set their hearts on pilgrimage.

Prayer Guide

1. Will you make an irrevocable commitment to keep moving until you meet God in Zion? Will you commit to working your way through the Prayer Guides in this book until you have learned a new language, until imagination starts to work in tandem with intellect, until the written Word becomes a living Voice that speaks a personal word to you? Write out a prayer expressing this commitment, pray it out loud, stick it in the front of this book and in your Bible, and use it until it becomes embedded in your memory. Ask God to teach you to draw on His strength to maintain your commitment.

2. Is there anyone you know who is currently going through the Valley of Baca? Pray for them right now, using the insights you

have gained from this Psalm. Mark down a time when you can pray with them. Your private prayers for them, shaped by Psalm 84, will teach you how to pray effectively with them. One of the most powerful ways to minister to people weeping in the Valley of Baca is not to lecture them in theology but to pray Scripture with them. Your cry for the living God will make the omnipresent God manifest to them in a way that mere lecturing can never accomplish. Then pray for at least one missionary who, in their cross-cultural ministry, is going through the Valley of Baca, a very familiar experience for almost all first-term missionaries who have left home and family.

3. Who are your fellow pilgrims on this journey to Zion? Take time to share and pray through this Psalm with them. If you don't know any, ask God to lead you to someone with whom you can share the journey.

Those Who Trust in God

The psalmist envied the first group for the fact that they had made it to Zion, living in an atmosphere of praise and worship and enjoying the security of knowing God as their natural habitat. He envied the second group, for they were fortunate enough to have set their hearts on pilgrimage. They also knew how to draw on the strength of God for themselves and for those flagging in the Valley of Baca. He now directs his envy at a third group of people for their ability to trust the living God for a sufficient provision for all their needs: "*O LORD Almighty, blessed is the man who trusts in you*" (v. 12). This sufficiency is portrayed in two contrasting ways:

- "*Better is one day in your courts than a thousand elsewhere*" (v. 10). This is not a statement to be evaluated arithmetically; it is the psalmist's way of emphasizing quality of life, rather than quantity. What's the theology behind this conviction? If we look in the New Testament, we will find the Apostle Peter modifying the psalmist's words as he writes, "*But do not forget this one thing, dear friends: With the Lord a day is like a thousand years, and a thousand years are like a day*" (2 Peter 3:8). The latter assertion is easy to understand. A thousand years will obviously be like a day when the reference point is an eternal, infinite God. But what about the former statement: a day is like a thousand years? That is not an obvious metaphor for eternity. But taken together, both phrases underline the fact that God stands outside of time. Therefore, when we encounter the living God in spiritual Zion, eternity invades our part of chronological time and expands it. While we may have less quantity of time after we have spent time worshipping God, its quality has been transformed and so has the person entering that time – namely, us. The net result: we end up accomplishing more of value and worth in less quantity of time than if we had tried to free up more time by "skipping out" on God because we were "too busy."

Our usual rationalization is "I'm so busy; God will understand." He will, but that is to miss the point altogether. We are the losers; we have lost out on yet another opportunity to allow our time to be invaded by eternity, thus transforming both the time remaining and ourselves, who have to work and live in it. That's why time spent encountering the living God is the only thing that can liberate us from the tyranny of the urgent. Then we can afford to stop in the Valley of Baca beside a weeping pilgrim without fretting over the resulting interruption of our busy schedules.

Martin Luther understood this well. It was said of him that, whereas he normally spent three hours a day in prayer, he wrote in his journal one day that, since he had so much to do that day, he needed to take four hours alone with God. Luther wasn't making bargains with God along the lines of "If I give You one more hour, will You help me with … !" On the contrary, he knew that unless eternity touched his part of chronological time, the resulting work would be useless. That's why overloaded pastors, busy businessmen and women, "assignment- and exam-harassed" students, and even frenzied mothers of young children can dare, indeed must dare, to take the time to pray in God's courts and alone, even when schedules do not seem to permit it.

- The second contrast that emphasizes the sufficiency of the living God is found in the other half of verse 10: "*I would rather be a doorkeeper in the house of my God than dwell in the tents of the wicked*." In this passage, "doorkeeper" means, literally, the "keeper or guard of the threshold," which divided the outside of the temple from the inside. A loose paraphrase of the psalmist's sentiment might read something like this: "I would rather take a humble job that would allow me at least a foot into the presence of the living God than to have the most prestigious, lucrative job that would interfere with my pilgrimage to Zion to encounter the living God." Takes us right back to the issue of critical choices, doesn't it? What makes such a criterion for appropriate employment reasonable or wise (especially since our intuitive reaction is to reject it as impractical, if not downright foolish)? Answer: the sufficiency of God to provide what the world cannot.

The psalmist summarizes this in verse 11: "*For the Lord God is a sun and shield; the Lord bestows favor and honor; no good thing does he withhold from those whose walk is blameless.*" God is the *sun*, the light that dispels the darkness of our minds; He is the *shield* that protects us from the flaming arrows which the enemy of our souls constantly rains on us; He grants us *favour* (grace) and *honour* (glory) – true glory, rather than the transient honour we might seek and find in the tents of the wicked.

Does it really work that way, you might wonder? Is it really better to be a doorkeeper in the house of God than to dwell in the tents of the wicked? In 1980, the same year that I resigned from my job at Atomic Energy of Canada after eleven years as a nuclear engineer, I received an invitation to join a "two-man" company that specialized in teaching communications to industry executives. I would only have had to work a hundred days every year to be paid nearly 50 percent more than what I was earning as an engineer. Five years later, that company hit rock bottom. Instead of thrashing around in that quagmire, I have enjoyed twenty-one wonderful years as a pastor, heir to spiritual riches no amount of money could buy – my fellow pilgrims en route to Zion.

- The assertion that God will not withhold any good thing from those who walk blamelessly isn't a carte blanche promise of unlimited prosperity. It is an assurance that God will not refuse the very things the psalmist has been crying out for throughout the Psalm – that is, an encounter with the living God, strength for the journey to Zion, and the rain of the Holy Spirit to help him through the dry stages of the pilgrimage and to refresh the heart of weary fellow pilgrims almost defeated by the Valley of Baca. A slice of eternity will invade time and release him from the tyranny of the urgent, and finally, he will have vocational holiness, a job that will not get in the way of the pursuit of God. Can any greater good than this be imagined? This is precisely what the psalmist says God will not withhold from those who set their hearts on pilgrimage.

Prayer Guide

1. Where do you feel time pressure the most acutely? Bring that area of your life to Him in prayer, asking the God of eternity to touch your time. Ask for the faith to believe that on days when you have "so much to do," you need to pray more, not less. Be alert for the first time He will test you with respect to this prayer.

2. Does your present job enhance or interfere with the pursuit of the living God? Are you pursuing any honour or favour in your work that dulls your appetite for God? What changes do you need to make in your approach to your present job? Do you need to look for another one that is more consistent with your irrevocable commitment to making a pilgrimage to Zion? Again, use your answer to these questions to shape your prayers to the living God.

An Invitation

The rest of this book is an attempt to provide the "nuts-and-bolts" kind of help that we will need in our pursuit of God. It will present the rich variety of language that we need to shape our cries to God so our prayers do not become monotonous, repetitive, and cliché-ridden. But the journey begins here. Will we refuse to be satisfied with nothing less than the living God? Will we set our hearts on pilgrimage? Unless that issue is settled, I doubt if the remaining pages will make any lasting impression or lead to any permanent transformations in anyone's life and being. But if we do make that critical choice, this pilgrimage to Zion will increasingly become the joy of our hearts and our reason for living. A powerful illustration of this possibility is suggested by an alternate translation of verse 5 in the New American Standard Bible: *"Blessed are those in whose hearts are the highways to Zion."*

Within three days of my arriving in North America, I was taken by car along one of the major highways in the city of Toronto, Canada. Although I realized that I would eventually have to learn to drive, I vowed to myself that I would always hug the inside lanes and never venture into the passing lane. And that's exactly what I did the first few times I drove on the highway. Eventually, however, the endless succession of cars whizzing by me, all of them reaching their destinations much sooner than I, "got to me." So, setting aside my fears, I ventured out into the passing lanes, accelerating as required. You guessed it! Not too many weeks passed before I made a beeline for the passing lanes every time I got onto a highway – so much so that now I prefer driving on the highway, especially in the passing lanes, and I travel as fast as I legally can. Any time I am confined to the inside lanes, I chafe. The highway has become home.

So it will be with the pilgrimage to Zion to meet the living God. As we persevere in it, we, too, will become like those "in whose hearts are the highways." Meandering country lanes that once seemed so attractive and inviting will lose their charm. Everything will be measured and evaluated in terms of our journey to Zion and what will get us there quickly and unhindered. It will be the highway we want to travel on, and in the passing lane at that!

Chapter 4

Psalm 48:
A Tale of Two Cities

1 *Great is the* LORD, *and most worthy of praise, in the city of our God, his holy mountain.* 2 *It is beautiful in its loftiness, the joy of the whole earth. Like the utmost heights of Zaphon is Mount Zion, the city of the Great King.* 3 *God is in her citadels; he has shown himself to be her fortress.* 4 *When the kings joined forces, when they advanced together,* 5 *they saw her and were astounded; they fled in terror.*
6 *Trembling seized them there, pain like that of a woman in labor.*
7 *You destroyed them like ships of Tarshish shattered by an east wind.*
8 *As we have heard, so have we seen in the city of the* LORD *Almighty, in the city of our God: God makes her secure forever.*

Selah

9 *Within your temple, O God, we meditate on your unfailing love.*
10 *Like your name, O God, your praise reaches to the ends of the earth; your right hand is filled with righteousness.* 11 *Mount Zion rejoices, the villages of Judah are glad because of your judgments.*
12 *Walk about Zion, go around her, count her towers,* 13 *consider well her ramparts, view her citadels, that you may tell of them to the next generation.* 14 *For this God is our God for ever and ever; he will be our guide even to the end.*

An Excited Janitor

Driving back from a family vacation in Florida one summer, we stopped overnight at a city in Tennessee. The following day, my customary early morning walk took me past a church, a massive complex of buildings set in perfectly manicured, well-maintained grounds. A sign outside proclaimed that the city had chosen it for the "City Beautification Award" – and I am sure that if I had come a few hours later, the janitor of that church would have been quite willing to take me around the place, excitedly pointing out the various features that had swayed the decision of the judges in its favour. As it was, I had to make my own guesses. But there is another sacred building, also dignified with an award for beauty that is well worth our reflective examination. This time we have a janitor; in fact, his family have been janitors for a long time in this "church." The building he watches over is Mount Zion – the destination of the pilgrimage we had learned to set our hearts on as we prayed Psalm 84.

Zion was the name of the fortified city that David captured from the Jebusites, whereas Jerusalem referred to the broader area around Mount Zion. But in the Old Testament Scriptures and especially in the Psalms, the names "Zion" and "Jerusalem" are used almost interchangeably. So let's get into our time machines, zip back about 2,500 years, and visit Zion, the City of God. As our tour guide, the janitor, meets us at our destination, he hands us a pamphlet containing a succinct description of everything he is going to show us. It's entitled "Psalm 48." Our first stop is still some distance from the city, yet close enough to form an overall impression. Our guide points out some general features of the city. In verse 2, he says, *"It is beautiful in its loftiness, the joy of the whole earth. Like the utmost heights of Zaphon is Mount Zion."* So the first thing he draws to our attention is Zion's loftiness, or height.

There are usually two ways in which we are impressed by heights. First of all, they give us a spectacular panoramic view of the surrounding territory. I will not easily forget the view of the Swiss Alps that unfolded before my eyes as an alarmingly small cable car, suspended from equally small cables, slowly swayed its way up the side of Mount Grindelwald in Switzerland. "Beautiful for loftiness" would have been a perfect description of the scene. The psalmist probably had some such idea in mind when he used the phrase, for north of Mount Carmel on the Mediterranean coast, there apparently runs a road along the mountain ridge that not only affords a beautiful view of the city of Haifa sprawling below, but also of the harbour and the bay. The name of this road is captured in the psalmist's phrase *"beautiful in its loftiness."*[1] But heights also affect us through the view from "the bottom." Whenever I come close to the base of something that is really tall, it draws my eyes upward rather than around. Natural objects like huge mountains do that; so do objects made by humans – such as very tall buildings. I remember the first time, thirty-five years ago, when I walked in downtown Toronto. Even though it did not yet have the gigantic office towers owned by the banks and insurance companies or the famed CN tower, I was still walking most of the time with my head craned upward because hardly any building in my home city of New Delhi, India, was more than five or ten storeys high at that time. Some church buildings – majestic cathedrals with their massive ceilings, huge arches, and magnificent stained-glass windows high up on the side of huge stone walls – have the same effect. On my first visit to Paris, France, in 1975, I remember being affected that way by Notre-Dame Cathedral – even more than by the Eiffel Tower.

The psalmist has described a similar double view – not only the view from the top that Mount Zion afforded, but also the view from the bottom. In verse 12, he exhorts us to *"Walk about Zion, go around her, count her towers, consider well her ramparts, view her citadels."* He obviously doesn't want us to miss anything, because he uses five different exhortations: walk about her, go around her, count her towers, consider her ramparts, and view her citadels. As tourists, we can imagine him saying to us, "Now, please, folks, don't just snap a few quick pictures and then run off to the curio shop or the fast-food outlet; take some time to drink in the beauty of the towers and the citadels." It's apparent that this guide was totally enraptured with Zion.

But here's the catch. Those who have been there tell us that Mount Zion and Jerusalem were not at all impressive in terms of their actual height. They did not look like Grindelwald or the highway overlooking Haifa. So why is the psalmist so excited about Zion? Why does he refer to its loftiness? What is his perspective? In verse 1, he says, *"Great is the LORD, and most worthy of praise, in the city of our God, his holy mountain."* It is God's city, therefore, that is *"beautiful in its loftiness, the joy of the whole earth"* (v. 2). Then, in verse 3, we read, *"God is in her citadels; he has shown himself to be her fortress."* How has He shown Himself to be her fortress? In verses 4 to 7, the psalmist writes, *"When the kings joined forces, when they advanced together, they saw her, and were astounded; they fled in terror. Trembling seized them there, pain like that of a woman in labor. You destroyed them like ships of Tarshish shattered by an east wind."* This is likely an historical reference to the invasion of Judah in King Hezekiah's time by King Shalmaneser of Syria. In that situation, God showed Himself to be "a present help in the midst of trouble" by killing 185,000 of Shalmaneser's army overnight and panicking the rest of them early in the morning. That act of God is celebrated in Psalm 46, in which the psalmist calls out to the besieged people of Zion to "Come on out and see the works of the Lord." There, he pointed to the desolations that God had caused among the enemy, their shattered bows and arrows. Here in Psalm 48 he is asking them to come out and look at something else. "Come on out and walk around your city," he says. "Count all the towers, not one of them is missing. He not only shattered the enemies. Zion has also been preserved untouched; it is still an impregnable fortress." I am sure that our guide would recount this great story from Israel's history as our tour proceeded.

Then, as we were completing our walk around Zion, zipping up our camera cases, and heading for the buses, he would probably say, "Just a minute, we haven't finished yet. You've only seen the outside. I want you to go inside the temple in Zion and take a look at what's happening there as well." Verse 9 tells us what we will see if we follow his advice: *"Within your temple, O God, we meditate on your unfailing love"* – the covenant loyalty of God. Inside we see a worship service in process. We see worshippers meditating.

- First of all, on *the faithfulness of their God*, who made covenants with their fathers and who kept faith with them, of which the dramatic deliverance from Shalmaneser's army is but one instance.

- Then they meditate on *the effects of that dramatic deliverance* on the people in the surrounding areas. In verses 10 and 11, we read, *"Like your name, O God, your praise reaches to the ends of the earth; your right hand is filled with righteousness. Mount Zion rejoices, and the villages of Judah are glad because of your judgments."* When the surrounding nations, and not just the villages of Judah, heard about the dramatic deliverance of the God of Israel, they, too, were amazed. Here is one example from Israel's early history in Canaan: the news of how God delivered the Israelites by parting the Red Sea found its way into Rahab's ears and heart in Jericho long before Israel ever got there. It put the fear of God into her heart and made her respect and fear the God of Israel. The nations couldn't help but notice the contrast between the power of Israel's God and the impotence of the gods of wood and stone that they worshipped.

- Yet another focus of the meditation of Zion's worshippers is found in verse 10: "*Your right hand is filled with righteousness.*" Not only did the surrounding villages of Judah and the pagans notice the contrast between the power of Israel's God and the powerlessness of the pagan gods, but they were also struck by *the moral beauty of the God of Israel* (reflected in the law that He had given to His people) in contrast with many of the immoralities that characterized their own worship. (That contrast was one vehicle through which the sensitive Gentiles of those days were drawn to worship Jehovah.)

As the congregation inside Zion meditated on these things, a huge shout of praise welled up from within them – as described in verse 1: "*Great is the* LORD, *and greatly to be praised, in the city of our God.*" We can capture the towers and ramparts of Zion in our photographs, but no camera known to man can capture the exuberant worship being experienced and expressed inside. How can you put worship on film, even if it is ASA 1000? We cannot, but we leave with the "film" of our hearts indelibly impressed by what we saw there, and we go away saying, as the psalmist did in verses 8 and 14, "*As we have heard so have we seen in the city of the* LORD *Almighty, in the city of our God: God makes her secure forever … For this God is our God for ever and ever; he will be our guide even to the end.*" For the Israelite pilgrims of the psalmist's time, who literally went to see the city, these parting words can be paraphrased in this way: "Wow! We'd always heard about the glory of Zion, but now we've finally seen it with our own eyes. And it's every bit as good as we've been told. What's more, we have met our God and we leave convinced that this God of Abraham, Isaac, and Jacob; this God of Hezekiah; this God who has so magnificently preserved Zion in the past, is our God. He will also be our Guide, not only on the long and dangerous journey back home, but even as we go back and tell our children about the beautiful things we've seen and the uplifting, faith-building worship we've known here. He will then be our guide as we declare His greatness in Zion and as we describe the beauty of Zion to our children."

Now we can see why the psalmist considered the building to be beautiful in its loftiness. It had nothing to do with physical height; it was lofty because God met the people there. In its majestic spaces, He entered the inner space of their hearts. You can't get a building taller than the one that bridges the gap between God and people, can you? Our tour guide delighted in Zion, the building, because of what went on inside it.

Prayer Guide

Since this Psalm begins with a shout of praise, it is appropriate to begin our prayer time with a joyful song. Of the many Zion songs in Christian hymnody, one of the most eloquent is "Glorious Things of Thee Are Spoken." If you know the melody, sing it; if you don't know it, but would like to, look it up in a hymn book. If you can't sing it easily, read it aloud as poetry. Linger over the many phrases and images, most of which are drawn from God's intimate presence with, and provision for, Israel in the wilderness as they journeyed from Egypt to Canaan. Use the many images of the hymn to fuel and shape your prayers.

> Glorious things of thee are spoken,
>   Zion, city of our God;
> He whose word cannot be broken
>   Formed thee for His own abode:
> On the Rock of Ages founded,
>   What can shake thy sure repose?
> With salvation's walls surrounded,
>   Thou may'st smile at all thy foes.
>
> See, the streams of living waters,
>   Springing from eternal love,
> Well supply thy sons and daughters,
>   And all fear of want remove:
> Who can faint, when such a river
>   Ever flows their thirst t'assuage;
> Grace, which like the Lord, the giver,
>   Never fails from age to age.

Round each habitation hovering,
  See the cloud and fire appear
For a glory and a covering,
  Showing that the Lord is near;
Thus deriving from their banner
  Light by night, and shade by day,
Safe they feed upon the manna
  Which he gives them when they pray.

Blest inhabitants of Zion,
  Washed in the Redeemer's blood;
Jesus, whom their souls rely on,
  Makes them kings and priests to God.
'Tis His love His people raises
  Over self to reign as kings;
And as priests, His solemn praises,
  Each for a thank offering brings.

Saviour, if of Zion's city
  I, through grace, a member am,
Let the world deride or pity –
  I will glory in Thy name.
Fading is the worldling's pleasure,
  All his boasted pomp and show;
Solid joys and lasting treasure
  None but Zion's children know.[2]

- Thank God that He, the God of Abraham – who is faithful to His Covenants with His people, who is able to instill fear into the hearts of those who would attack His people and who is able to open the hearts of men and women of other nations – is your God.

- Thank Him that, in Jesus Christ, the gap between a Holy God and a sinful human has been bridged so thoroughly that intimacy with Him is a glorious privilege.

Our tour is over. We are ushered back into the time machine. The pilot flips a switch and we find ourselves back in twenty-first-century North America – wherever you happen to be reading this paragraph. Today, the people of God are not part of one small nation. There is no centralized place of worship like Zion, and there is no fortress. Instead, we have hundreds of thousands of church buildings, old and new. What are we to make of the janitor's comments? How can we, today, delight in Zion in the way that they did? What does it mean to view Zion's towers and the ramparts? What is the City of God and what is its practical significance?

To answer these questions, we need to step back from Psalm 48 and see it in the larger context of the Scriptures as a whole. From Genesis to Revelation, God has distributed many major themes that function like large skeletal bones, giving structure to His Word. One of these, pertinent to the questions raised by our tour of Mount Zion, is the contrast between the "City of God" and the "city of man." Let's begin with the city of man (Augustine's famous phrase for humanity's efforts apart from God).

The City of Man

Do you remember who built the first city? Cain, infamous for murdering his brother, Abel. The reason he built the city was to name it after his son, Enoch. Thus, the designer and builder of the very first city of man was a murderer who built in order to proclaim the glory of a human name. The second builder of cities in the Bible, Nimrod, appears in Genesis 10. He built the city of Babylon as the centre of his expansionist, violent enterprise to capture other neighbouring cities. The purpose of that city was also to establish his name. Then he led the people in the building of the Tower of Babel, once again to establish a name for the people. A detailed study of the significance of the Tower of Babel is beyond the scope of this chapter; suffice it to say that the fundamental purpose of Babel was to centralize both the government and the worship of the people, thus representing the control of the "many" by the "few."

Millennia have passed. Yet the nature of the cities of man remains unchanged. Our cities bear the marks of Cain's and Nimrod's efforts – vying for a name for themselves. Several years ago when Toronto (the city where I live) was experiencing an incredibly meteoric rise in house prices, a "real estate" article in one of the city newspapers quoted someone as saying, "Look, if we are going to be a big city like Los Angeles and San Francisco, it is about time our houses cost the same as houses there cost." That's what he was concerned about – not the hardship to thousands who would now be even further away from owning reasonable accommodation, but whether Toronto would be in the same league as Los Angeles and San Francisco. What a price we pay for this name.

Now, in the Scriptures, Babylon typifies the city of man, so her ultimate destiny also typifies that of the city of man. In Revelation 18 we read, *"Woe! Woe, O great city, O Babylon, city of power! In one hour your doom has come … Woe! Woe, O great city, dressed in fine linen, purple and scarlet, and glittering with gold, precious stones, and pearls! In one hour such great wealth has been brought to ruin! … Woe! Woe, O great city, where all who had ships on the sea became rich through her wealth! In one hour she has been brought to ruin! … With such violence the great city of Babylon will be thrown down, never to be found again"* (vv. 10, 16, 19, 21). Three times this phrase appears: *"… in one hour … in one hour … in one hour."* And if that seems like an impossibility, think of how much damage an earthquake can do to lives and property in a city in much less than an hour. And the effects are not always limited to one city. A few weeks after an earthquake in Kobe, Japan, in 1995, I read a cover story in a major newsmagazine about a bank that was bankrupted of assets. The institution lost more than $2 billion because one employee traded wildly on the financial markets. The employee's cardinal mistake: not taking into account the effects of the Kobe earthquake on the value of the Japanese stock exchange's key economic indicator.

To summarize the biblical assessment of the city of man: it is anti-God, self-centred, and destined for destruction. Interwoven with this description, we also find a fascinating portrayal of a totally different kind of city – the City of God.

The City of God

Right after Nimrod's attempts to build Babel had been frustrated by God through the confusion of languages, He called out an insignificant man named Abram and said, in effect, "What you can't do for yourself, I will do. I will make your name great and I will also make the name of your progeny great." Then He sent Abram to Canaan, the land He had promised to give him and his descendants. In Canaan, however, Abram – now "Abraham" (Genesis 17:5) – owned no real estate. Instead, his life was characterized by two things: a tent and an altar. Unlike cities, which are permanent, tents are readily dismantled, moved, and set up again. As for the altar, it signifies a life of worship and submission to God, moving at His direction. From the very beginning, the man who the Bible says *"looked for the City whose builder and maker [was] God"* was characterized by two things: he was loosely attached to real estate and he moved where and when his God told him to move.

Centuries later, when Abraham's descendants had indeed become a numerous people and a nation, God delivered them from bondage in Egypt and led them back to the Promised Land just as He had done with Abraham. As He led them through the wilderness, He gave them detailed instructions as to how to build their tabernacles of worship. Their key feature was their portability. Neither the people of God nor the temple of God was rooted in one place; they moved and stopped at God's command – the tent-and-altar principle again. Centuries later, when the nation of Israel had settled in Canaan, it was a man's idea to change this moveable tabernacle into a fixed dwelling place. After building his palace, King David wondered why he should live in a palace and God in a tent. So he decided to build an equally impressive, permanent temple. That's when God sent the prophet Nathan to correct a few false notions in David's thinking but accommodated Himself to David's desire anyway. "Go ahead," He said, "build me a building and I will dwell in it, but remember I am not limited to it." As for Mount Zion, the special place chosen by David for the permanent temple, God agreed to that, too, saying, essentially, "Okay, I will put My name there; I will call it the City of God."

Further centuries passed before the dangers of this development became apparent. False prophets and corrupt priests led the people of Judah into believing that, because of the temple's presence and because Jerusalem was the City of God, they were safe from the Babylonians, even though they were living in open disobedience to the commands of God. The result: Babylon, the city of man, swallowed up Jerusalem, the City of God. As for the temple, it was ransacked and destroyed.

After the exiled people of Judah returned to Canaan, a modest attempt was made to rebuild the temple under Ezra and Nehemiah, encouraged by the preaching of Haggai and Zechariah. But it was not until the days of King Herod (who ruled Palestine when Jesus was born) that a magnificent temple was built. Herod's motive was not to glorify God, but to pacify the Jews so he could rule them more easily. It was this temple that formed the scene of much of Jesus' ministry. Then came Jesus' denunciation as He left the temple saying, "*Behold, your house is left to you desolate*" (Matthew 23:38). The foolish and short-sighted disciples challenged Him by saying, essentially, "Master, wait a minute, don't You see these beautiful decorations, don't You see these massive stones?" (Mark 13:1) and Jesus shocked them with His reply: "Not one stone here will be left on another" (Matthew 24:2).

To leave no doubt about the significance of Jesus' words, the Holy Spirit caused a whole book of the Bible to be written to drive home this one point. In this book, Hebrews, a main theme is this: Forget the earthly temple and focus your attention instead upon the heavenly tabernacle, where true worship is being led by Jesus, the supreme and only High Priest. As for the ultimate destiny of the City of God: just as Revelation 18 spelled out the ultimate destiny of the city of man, Revelation 21 does the same for the City of God. What is that? "*'Come, I will show you the bride, the wife of the Lamb.' And he carried me away in the Spirit to a mountain great and high, and showed me the Holy City, Jerusalem, coming down out of heaven from God. It shone with the glory of God, and its brilliance was like that of a very precious jewel ... I did not see a temple in the city, because the* LORD *God Almighty and the Lamb are its temple. The city does not need the sun or the moon to shine on it, for the glory of God gives it light, and the Lamb is its lamp. The nations will walk by its light ... on no day will its gates ever be shut, for there will be no night there*" (vv. 9–11, 22–25). God Himself will dwell with and in His people. They will become the temple. It is this City of God that Abraham, the patriarch, looked for, by faith.

Let's summarize what we have learned about the two "cities." Just as the city of man was anti-God, self-centred, and destined for destruction, so the City of God is primarily the community of faith that is loosely rooted to this world. Wherever the community of faith is, God is present, whether or not there is a building to house that community's worship. In fact, the clear intent of Scripture in intertwining these twin themes is to destroy, once and for all, our love affair with buildings – a love affair into which we, in North America, have sunk billions of dollars, out of all proportion to what we invest in overseas missions – and instead to drive home to us the truth that the real beauty of Zion lies in the people of God and in what the community of faith does. So, regardless of what the city thought about the church building I visited in Tennessee, I wish I could have been there for the Sunday morning service. I wish I could have been in the homes of the people after they left the worship service. I wish I could have been with them in their places of work during the following week, for that's where the real beauty (or the ugliness) of the church would have been revealed, regardless of how many awards the building earned from the city.

Prayer Guide

Choose one inner-city ministry (e.g., Teen Challenge, a rescue mission, etc.) that you know is active in your city. Choose the nearest city if you don't live in one. If you know the people involved, that would be even better.

- Use the images of the Psalm and the hymn to pray for their protection and that they will truly be kept and nourished as the City of God in the midst of the city of man.
- Pray for the leaders of these ministries that they will be free from the temptation of building "a name" for themselves like Cain and Nimrod.
- Conclude this phase of your prayers by asking God to raise up leaders and workers for other areas where the city of man needs to be penetrated by the City of God. (You will find many examples of such work in Charles Colson's book *The Body*.)[3]

With a good grasp of the biblical themes of the City of God and the city of man, we can return to Psalm 48 and consider how to apply its principles to our own lives. Let's begin with the injunction to walk about Zion.

Walk about Zion

Since Zion no longer refers to building materials and architecture, but to "living stones" – the men and women of God who make up the building – we need to know more about those people. Who are the towers? Who are the ramparts? What are the citadels? Obviously, some sanctified imagination, disciplined by the fruit of our study of the Scriptures, is necessary to supply the answers. Anglican minister and author Leonard Griffith helped bring these ideas alive in my imagination. I hope his words inspire you as well.[4]

- **Towers**. If a building has a tower, it's the first thing you see; it is the building's most prominent part. In spiritual Zion, towers might reasonably refer to those in the Church of Jesus Christ who are prominent and visible: its great leaders. "Take a good look at them," says the psalmist. It is a much-needed exhortation. Griffith writes, "Indeed our culture seems almost to discourage qualities of leadership. Educational systems cater to the average mind and force all students into the same mould of mediocrity. Politics, labour unions, business, industry, the arts and the media promote a monotonous egalitarianism. A comic cartoon shows a father and son walking down a city street and looking at an unusual statue, a group of stone figures huddled together on a stone pedestal. The father is saying, 'You see my boy, there are no more great men, only great committees.' That could be one reason why Christians have lost their sense of pride in the Church. They can tell the committees, but not the towers thereof."[5] We may have to walk around a bit longer and look a little more intently to find them, but the Church has had its towers all along. In practical terms, this means that all of us as Christians are to attempt at least a rudimentary understanding of the history of the Church and the great men and women that God has used to preserve the City of God from being engulfed by the city of man.

I will never forget a comment made by Dr. Victor Adrian, former president of Ontario Theological Seminary, when he was teaching a course on historical theology. "We should all know," he said, "what the great fights in the Church have been about." There are some things that are worth fighting about, and we are inspired by the men and women whom God has used to lead these fights. I think of *Athanasius*, who led the fight for the deity of Christ against the heresy of Arianism; *Augustine*, who wrote his classic *City of God*, to defend Christianity against the charge that it was responsible for the sack of Rome by pagans in the fifth century; *Wycliffe*, who led the early fight to have the Bible translated into the vernacular; *Luther*, who took on the massive organization of the Church to recover the cardinal doctrines of justification by faith, the priesthood of all believers, and the authority of the Scriptures over the Church. I also think of the towers of more recent times: the Church's theologians, its writers (like *Solzhenitsyn*), its musicians, and its artists, who have kept before us the vision of the City of God and kept it from being engulfed by the city of man. Finally, don't forget the leaders in your local church; they are towers, too. Sure, they are not necessarily famous, like those I have named above, but the Bible tells us to remember our leaders, to consider their way of life, and to imitate their faith. Let's pitch our tents close to the towers, unlike Lot, who pitched his tent close to Sodom and ended up engulfed by the city of man.

- **Ramparts**. Again I am indebted to Leonard Griffith for a helpful distinction between the towers and the ramparts. He says that "the ramparts refer to the defence structures of Jerusalem. They are not as impressive as the towers, but they are just as important, perhaps more so. You can do without towers, but you cannot do without ramparts. They keep the city strong and secure, they hold off the invaders. The towers would fall if it weren't for the ramparts. Neither are the church's ramparts all that impressive or even noticeable, but we should notice them quickly enough if they were suddenly removed. They are the strong defenders of the church, the servants of the church, the quiet people who, by their love and loyalty and devotion, hold up its structures."[6]

So we are not only to look at the impressive and prominent leaders of the Church, past and present, but also at how every member of Zion contributes to making it a beautiful body. On one of our many trips to India, some friends from Canada accompanied us. Naturally, we visited the famous Taj Mahal in the northwestern state of Rajasthan. It is located in such a spot that the first complete sight of it is framed only by blue sky; there is not even a tree on the horizon, just its towers and its ramparts. Pointing to this, our guide said, "Shah Jahan [the Moghul emperor] built it that way to show us that beauty doesn't come from ostentation, but from simplicity and proportion." That's how the ramparts in a church work. They are responsible for the beauty that comes from a simple, proportionately functioning body.

One Sunday evening, after most of the congregation had gone home after the service, a friend and I were putting the finishing touches on our own backyard beautification program in the parsonage. One of our elders drove up, and observing us amateur landscape artists at work, he recounted a delightful story that was a perfect illustration of a proportionately functioning body. He told me how he had spent the last four days helping another elder build a portable air-conditioning system for that man's elderly mother, to protect her from the heat in her apartment, which was sometimes higher than 100 degrees Fahrenheit. This elder may not have known that this very same woman could often be found late at night working on some beautiful flower beds around the side of the parsonage and the front of the church. When I put these two "ministries" together, I was excited at this very simple demonstration of the proportionate functioning of the body. Two men skilled with their hands and minds minister to a senior citizen by providing for her physical needs, and she comes right back and uses her skills to beautify the church. Every time I saw those flower beds that summer, I was reminded that their outer beauty flowed from an expression of inner beauty that came from a rightly proportioned and functioning church.

- **Citadels**. Here we are not left to our imaginations or to speculative exegesis, for verse 3 reads, "God is in her citadels." To consider the citadels is to ask, " Is God in the citadel or has Jesus Christ left the place desolate?" To make the question even more pointed, does our reflection on the towers and ramparts of our church inspire us to meditate on the Covenant loyalty of our God or does it lead us to give credit to our own human efforts alone? Does our commitment to holiness flow out of an increasing appreciation for the moral beauty of a God whose right hand is filled with righteousness, or is it just a legalistic attempt to obey some external constraint to satisfy human prescriptions? Does the righteous judgement of God and the spread of His Kingdom among the nations cause so much joy to well up within us that, as Psalm 48 says, the glad celebration inside Zion (our churches) engulfs the surrounding villages of Judah and His praise reaches the ends of the earth? This contagious gladness has made Africa, and now Asia, the geographic centres of Christianity. In 1987, the number of Christians from non-white nations exceeded the number of Christians from white nations. The issue is not one of colour, but that many different races and nations have been totally engulfed by the living organism that is spreading out from the Spiritual Zion.

Is that enough to make us shout, *"Great is the LORD, and greatly to be praised, in the City of our God"*? In short, is the worship of the people a response to a God who is present and active? If not, if it is mere formalism, it doesn't matter how beautiful our temple is, it doesn't matter how brilliantly crafted the preachers' sermons are, it doesn't matter how aesthetically pleasing the music is, God is not in her citadels.

We can also approach the citadel issue from the other end, as it were. God may be in the citadels, but are we there where He has promised to be, and is? Three aspects of this problem came to mind as I considered the congregation of which I am a part. I have included them here to illustrate and stimulate your own reflection on this question.

1. What happens to the *attendance* in your church when your pastor (or some other tower) is away on vacation? Is God not in the citadels when the pastor isn't there? God's warning to Ezekiel is timely: "*As for you, son of man, your countrymen are talking together about you by the walls and at the doors of the houses, saying to each other, 'Come and hear the message that has come from the LORD.' My people come to you, as they usually do, and sit before you to listen to your words, but they do not put them into practice. With their mouths they express devotion, but their hearts are greedy for unjust gain. Indeed, to them you are nothing more than one who sings love songs with a beautiful voice and plays an instrument well, for they hear your words but do not put them into practice*" (Ezekiel 33:30–32). It is not enough to rhapsodize over good preaching and strong, charismatic leadership. The congregation must be vital with or without a pastor. (One of my greatest joys during both my sabbaticals has been to hear of the way my own congregation is flourishing in my absence. Not that I was under any illusions of indispensability, but it is gratifying to know that God is in her citadels and so are her people, whether I am there or not.)

2. Then evaluate your congregation's attitude to *Communion services*. (The specifics of what follows apply to churches that do not celebrate the Lord's Supper every Sunday, but the principles apply, regardless of frequency.) Sunday evening services in our fellowship draw typically 30 to 50 percent of the average morning attendance. There may be good

reasons for not attending an evening service, but the pattern holds even on Sunday evenings when the Lord's Supper is scheduled. Celebrating Communion is one of the two ordinances that God has explicitly commanded. It was the high point of the liturgy of the early Church. The Scriptures teach us that Christ is present in the "Sacraments" in a mysterious way that has defied the understanding and definitions of theologians for two thousand years. They've fought over the issue, but they don't know exactly what it means to eat and drink of His body and blood; all they know is that He said, *"Take and eat; this is my body ... Drink from it, all of you. This is my blood of the covenant, which is poured out for many for the forgiveness of sins"* (Matthew 26:26b–28). They don't know exactly how He is present in the elements representing His suffering and death; all they know is that He is, that He meets His people and ministers the power of His risen life to them. God is especially "in the citadels" when we celebrate the Lord's Supper. Are we?

3. Finally, consider the attitude of your people to *singing*, as opposed to preaching and listening. Is it a time for them to participate or is it a time to tune out? A comment from *Leadership* magazine may help put the issue in perspective: "Somehow, about 40% of church goers seem to have picked up the idea that 'singing in church is for singers.' The truth is that 'singing is for believers.' The relevant question is not 'Do you have a voice?' but 'Do you have a song?' As one well-known Zion hymn puts it, 'Let those refuse to sing who never knew our God ... .'"[7]

What's the purpose of all this walking around the towers, ramparts, and citadels? The psalmist answers that question in verse 13, *"Consider well her ramparts, view her citadels, so that you may tell of them to the next generation."*

Prayer Guide

- Consider the *towers* of your local church (pastoral staff and elders). Pray that they will love the church like the janitor of Mount Zion; that they will know what to fight for; that God would put in them the spirit of an Augustine, an Athanasius, a Luther; that they would be free from the spirit of a Cain or a Nimrod, not loving buildings and fame more than the people they lead; that they will be able to lead their congregations in worship that magnifies the God who keeps Covenants, who is more than able to handle the Church's enemies, and who will glorify His name among the nations.

- Then focus on the *ramparts* (the behind-the-scenes contributors). Thank God for their faithfulness, pray that they may be encouraged (ask God how you can be part of the answer to that prayer yourself); ask God to raise up many more such workers and for an atmosphere in the church that will release people to use their spiritual gifts for ministry; and pray that leaders will not be threatened by gifted individuals.

- Finally, is God in the *citadels*? Pray for genuine revival that will destroy formal, lifeless religion and infuse a spirit of worship, holiness, and love into those who have not heard the Gospel, so "His praise can reach the ends of the earth." Pray for the leaders as well as the people. What signs are there, if any, in your church that God may be in the citadel but the people are not? Where are they resisting godly leadership and quenching the Holy Spirit and possibilities of revival? Tear down these strongholds.

Tell of Them to the Next Generation

In Chapter 6, we will explore in greater detail this matter of handing the baton over to the next generation, but Psalm 48 underlines one critical principle in accomplishing this task. We not only teach God's truth by our words; we communicate it by our attitudes as well. To borrow the phrases of experts in communication, the non-verbal dimension of our teaching is critical. Do our children sense our delight in Zion? How do we speak about the towers and ramparts of Zion at lunch on Sunday afternoon? What kind of priority do they sense us assigning to worship and to the sacredness of Communion? As for those of you who are involved in children's ministries in the church, does your delight in Zion, in her towers and ramparts get through to your young charges so they go home saying, "We want to come to church. We love the gates of Zion"? Finally, what level of commitment do our children sense in us to the mission of the local church? Do the things happening inside our Zion spill over into "the villages of Judah" around us? Do they reach the ends of the earth?

Anglican minister Leonard Griffith tells this story: "Some years ago, a newspaper in Britain offered a prize for the best essay on the subject 'What is wrong with the Church?' There were plenty of entries because plenty of people were prepared and are still prepared to answer that question at great length. In fact, they will answer without being asked, they will tell you what is wrong with the Church. But the prize was won by a clergyman from Wales who gave this answer. 'What is wrong with the church is our failure to realize the wonder, the beauty, the mystery and the glory and the greatness of God.'"[8] Let us recapture the wonder of God and the Church as we pray Psalm 48. Then let us convey that wonder to our children.

Prayer Guide

Examine your own home. What attitude and priorities toward
Zion are you communicating to your children? Do they love the
Church more or less because of you?

- Pray appropriately, as indicated by honest answers to the above
  questions.
- Ask God to guide you in passing on your enthusiasm for Zion to
  your children.
- Finally, pray for those who work with children and young
  people in your church – including the attitude they convey by
  their non-verbal messages and priorities demonstrated by the
  choices they make.

Chapter 5

Psalm 92:
Getting Ready for Church

1 It is good to praise the LORD and make music to your name,
O Most High, 2 to proclaim your love in the morning and your
faithfulness at night, 3 to the music of the ten-stringed lyre and the
melody of the harp. 4 For you make me glad by your deeds, O LORD;
I sing for joy at the works of your hands. 5 How great are your
works, O LORD, how profound your thoughts!
6 The senseless man does not know, fools do not understand, 7 that
though the wicked spring up like grass and all evildoers flourish,
they will be forever destroyed. 8 But you, O LORD, are exalted
forever. 9 For surely your enemies, O LORD, surely your enemies
will perish; all evildoers will be scattered. 10 You have exalted my
horn ["horn" here symbolizes strength] like that of a wild ox; fine
oils have been poured upon me. 11 My eyes have seen the defeat of
my adversaries; my ears have heard the rout of my wicked foes.
12 The righteous will flourish like a palm tree, they will grow like a
cedar of Lebanon; 13 planted in the house of the LORD, they will
flourish in the courts of our God. 14 They will still bear fruit in old
age, they will stay fresh and green, 15 proclaiming, "The LORD is
upright; he is my Rock, and there is no wickedness in him."

A Surprising Survey

In early 1989, *Christianity Today* conducted a survey among 475 randomly selected subscribers, asking them to rate their level of interest in several questions concerning the Christian faith and life. The list included topics like "The trustworthiness of the Bible," "The role of women in ministry," "Heaven and Hell," and "Knowing God's will for your life." The results held one colossal surprise. About 64 percent of the respondents rated as "high" or "very high" their level of interest in the question "Should Christians take the Sabbath more seriously?"[1]

What does it mean to take Sabbath, or Sunday (I will use the words interchangeably) more seriously? Reorganizing our priorities so that Sunday morning worship becomes a non-negotiable item in our life? Attending church twice on Sunday? And what does seriousness about the Sabbath entail in between Sundays, when we are not in church?

There are two approaches to answering questions like these. The first one is to sift through the mass of biblical, historical, and sociological data on the subject, weigh the pros and cons on each issue pertaining to Sabbath keeping, and come to a reasoned conclusion. However appropriate and necessary such a procedure may be, it is not pertinent to the purpose of this book. We're going to follow the second approach and pray about the Sabbath – not in the traditional, cliché-istic, "Brother, sister, seek the mind of the Lord and do what He tells you" sense, but as God Himself has taught us. Of the 150 Psalms in the Bible, only one, according to its title, is devoted explicitly to the Sabbath: Psalm 92. As we learn how the psalmist thinks about the subject, we will be able to turn those thoughts into our prayers, and through that process, find answers to our questions. So, having set our hearts on a *pilgrimage to Zion*, having understood what constitutes the *beauty of Zion*, let us learn how to get ready for the *celebration in Zion*.

A Necessary Affirmation

He begins with an affirmation: "*It is good to praise the* LORD *and make music to your name, O Most High, to proclaim your love in the morning and your faithfulness at night, to the music of the ten-stringed lyre and the melody of the harp. For you make me glad by your deeds, O* LORD; *I sing for joy at the works of your hands*" (vv. 1–3). Three activities involved in this affirmation are worth noticing: *hands* extended toward heaven (the meaning of the Hebrew word for "praise"), musical *instruments* like the lyre and the harp being played, and *words* being proclaimed. ("Proclaim" here conveys the idea of standing before a group of people and speaking out.) Taken together, it becomes evident that the activity is corporate, rather than individual. People are raising their hands, others are playing instruments, and yet other people are singing and proclaiming. But because in the Hebrew text the word "good" begins the sentence, the dominant phrase is "It is good." We might paraphrase the psalmist's affirmation this way: "Good it is to praise the Lord with extended hands, to proclaim His love and His faithfulness in words accompanied by music."

It is a much-needed affirmation, addressing one of the many debilitating flaws of our culture. Eugene Peterson describes it eloquently: "What I saw was not attractive: an entire culture living on the edge of panic. A mind-boggling technology that could do almost anything in and with space, but fidgety, nervous, and spastic with time. I saw the people around me work masterfully with computers, organizations, and electronic equipment, but when presented with an unplanned or undefined ten minutes, hour, or day, they were suddenly overtaken with the St. Vitus' Dance. They could not stand still. They could not be still. And I began to observe the results ... The incredible shoddiness in personal relationships that characterizes our culture is more than anything a consequence of sins against time, for intimacy requires time, affection requires time. Without time, neither the best of intentions nor the highest standard of living penetrates the human relationships through which we realize our dignity and our worth. And the outrageous adolescence in religion that is the scandal of our churches in these days is more than anything else a consequence of sins against time. For maturity requires time, worship requires time. *Without time, rhythmic, unhurried, expectant time, neither the most sincere conversion nor the most ardent commitment penetrates our lives and becomes sane, mature and wise holiness* [emphasis mine]."[2] Psalm 92 begins by reminding us that the Sabbath is a gift of unhurried, rhythmic, and expectant time from God, in which it is good for us to praise God, and to proclaim and respond to words of love and faithfulness to the accompaniment of vocal and instrumental music.

Some believers, and even some Christian leaders, disapprove of music in worship; others allow for "a capella" singing only (with no musical instruments). The psalmist would disagree categorically with both these decisions. He affirms that it is not only good to praise God, but to do so to the accompaniment of instruments. I still remember the opening words of *Twelfth Night* in my Eleventh Grade introduction to Shakespeare: "If music be the food of love, play on ... ." And if Shakespeare's English doesn't "get to you," listen to this twentieth-century equivalent: "Music quickens something deep within us. Our bodies assimilate the sound and rhythm and experience an aliveness; melody and harmony draw us over the boundary of the tuneless grunts and groans of daily discourses, the demands and complaints that fence us into the corral of self. Surely it is significant that nearly all the prayers in the Psalms carry evidence within them of being played musically."[3]

When proclamation is wedded to music, it usually takes the form of poetry, not prose. And just as music becomes a powerful aid to lifting our souls in worship even as we proclaim His love and His faithfulness, so does poetry – because of its power to create images in our minds. "Poets," says Eugene Peterson, "recombine words in fresh ways so that old truth is freshly perceived. They take truth that has been eroded to platitude by careless usage and set it in motion before us in an animated and impassioned dance of ideas. [Poetry] makes an image of reality in such a way as to invite our participation in it. The poet is not trying to get us to think more accurately or to train us into better behavior, but to get us to believe more recklessly, behave more playfully – the faith-recklessness and hope-playfulness of children entering into the Kingdom of God. He will jar us out of our lethargy, get us to live on the alert, open our eyes to burning bushes and fiery chariots, open our ears to the hard steel promises and commands of Christ, banish boredom from the Gospel, lift up our heads and enlarge our hearts."[4] That's the function of poetry, especially when set to music.

Let's take all the above information and amplify the psalmist's affirmation. When we take the great scriptural affirmations about God – His love and His faithfulness, for example – and entrust them to skilled writers who can express them poetically, and when other skilled individuals set this poetry to music so it can be sung and accompanied by a symphony of instruments, the resulting product, because of its power to tap into our imaginations, bypasses the logical objections of the mind and gets right to the will. The notions that Satan keeps feeding into our minds to make us deny the great attributes of God – His love and His faithfulness – are thus effectively overwritten and defused. That's why "*it is good to make music … .* " Now if this were a piece of multimedia equipment rather than a printed book, I could give you a live illustration of the greater power of poetry set to music than the same message in prose. But since it isn't, a verbal illustration will have to do. Recall the familiar Gospel story of Mary of Bethany, who broke the alabaster box of expensive perfume and anointed Jesus with it. Here's how it sounds in the prose of John 12:

> *Six days before the Passover, Jesus arrived at Bethany, where Lazarus lived, whom Jesus had raised from the dead. Here a dinner was given in Jesus' honor. Martha served, while Lazarus was among those reclining at the table with him. Then Mary took about a pint of pure nard, an expensive perfume; she poured it on Jesus' feet and wiped his feet with her hair. And the house was filled with the fragrance of the perfume* (John 12: 1–3).

That's the prose. Here's how it sounds in poetic form – in a well-known song by Gloria Gaither and Bill George, recorded by Steve Green:

> One day a poor village woman,
>   driven by love for her Lord,
> Recklessly poured out her valuable essence,
>   disregarding the scorn.
> And once it was broken and spilled out,
>   the fragrance filled all the room,
> Like a prisoner released from his shackles,
>   like a spirit set free from the tomb.
>
> Broken and spilled out, just for love of You, Jesus,
> My most precious treasure lavished on Thee.
> Broken and spilled out, and poured at your feet
> In sweet abandon, let me be poured out
>   and used for Thee.[5]

Now imagine these verses sung by a gifted vocalist, and that to the accompaniment of music whose dynamics perfectly reflect the mood of the story – a sudden, unexpected welling up of strong emotion in a human soul, the fragrance of perfume permeating a whole room. I have heard my wife sing this song literally dozens of times in worship settings; yet each time, though I know every word in John's Gospel and the song, I am reduced to a tearful, silent humility before the magnificence of my Saviour's sacrifice on my behalf. Any skeptics still? Or will we acknowledge the truth of the psalmist's affirmation? Now to actually experience the goodness of what the psalmist affirms, we need one another, especially on Sundays. There, our own frail, inharmonious voices can be reinforced in the swell of other, more gifted voices around us. There, we have our minds directed to poetry in the hymns and choruses that we either do not sing when we are alone or have forgotten or don't have time to sing, because of the frenetic pace of our lives. Sundays allow us to do what the psalmist affirms is good.

It is not difficult to imagine the colossal difference it would make to our experience of corporate worship on Sunday mornings if most people in any congregation took time during the week, preferably on Saturday night, to remind themselves that Sunday is a Divine gift, which allows them to distill the quietness of God into the frenzy of their own lives. We would all benefit if we let the opening affirmation of the psalmist sink in – that it is good to proclaim the attributes of God with song and with musical instruments so that our very bodies, exemplified by extended hands, express the reaching out of our souls for the living God. And we should remind ourselves that we need other people for this to happen.

What would be the result if we took some time to anticipate what God intends for our Sunday and if we asked the Holy Spirit of God to accomplish His will through the entire congregation's participation? What if we took time to pray for members of the pastoral staff who are involved in putting the service together, that God would guide them in the selection of the hymns and the choruses and in the ordering of the services in such a way that His love and His faithfulness would be proclaimed in poetry and music? What if this prayer extended to include the instrumentalists, the choir members, and other worship leaders? It would be so much easier to commit ourselves to coming to church the next Sunday because we would already be there in our hearts and minds. Weather and other minor inconveniences would no longer be factors in "getting to church." What's more, we would be much more likely to come to church on Sunday morning in the psalmist's frame of mind: *"For you make me glad by your deeds, O LORD; I sing for joy at the works of your hands"* (v. 4). This doesn't happen automatically, but only as we take time to prepare, to remind ourselves what corporate worship on Sundays is all about.

Prayer Guide

1. Remind yourself that the Sabbath is a gift of rhythmic, unhurried, and expectant time from God to distill the quietness of God into the frenzy of our lives. Ask Him to do this for you and for the entire congregation next Sunday (tomorrow?), using the specifics of your own life circumstances (and those of your congregation) to shape these requests.

2. Reflect on the powerful images in this Sabbath hymn and pray as they stir longings and desires in your heart:

> Dear Lord and Father of mankind,
>   Forgive our foolish ways;
> Reclothe us in our rightful mind;
>   In purer lives Thy service find,
> In deeper reverence praise.
>
> In simple trust like theirs who heard,
>   Beside the Syrian sea,
> The gracious calling of the Lord,
>   Let us, like them, without a word
> Rise up and follow Thee.
>
> O sabbath rest by Galilee!
>   O calm of hills above,
> Where Jesus knelt to share with Thee
>   The silence of eternity,
> Interpreted by love!
>
> With that deep hush subduing all
>   Our words and works that drown
> The tender whisper of Thy call;
>   As noiseless let Thy blessing fall
> As fell Thy manna down.
>
> Drop Thy still dews of quietness
>   Till all our strivings cease;
> Take from our souls the strain and stress,
>   And let our ordered lives confess
> The beauty of Thy peace.

> Breathe through the heats of our desire
>   Thy coolness and Thy balm;
> Let sense be dumb, let flesh retire;
>   Speak through the earthquake, wind, and fire,
> O still small voice of calm![6]

3. Pray that the worship leaders, choir, and musicians will be guided by the Spirit in the selection and ordering of poetry and music, in such a way that they will help the congregation proclaim His love and His faithfulness, involving body, soul, and spirit in the process.

Embroidered Wisdom

The second major strand in the psalmist's thinking about the Sabbath is found in verse 5: *"How great are your works, O LORD, how profound your thoughts!"* Familiar words in English, while providing an adequate translation, sometimes mask the richness of meaning in the Hebrew. The word for "thoughts," we are told, is related to one used by weavers to describe intertwined threads in an embroidered fabric, or braided hair. Applied to God, it refers not just to His plans, but also to their interwoven intricacies which, taken together, form an embroidered, beautiful whole. And "profound" refers to the depth of wisdom reflected in the embroidery of God's thoughts. So the Sabbath is not only a time to stretch upward in worship to let the quietness of God distill into the frenzy of our lives. It is also a time to plumb the depths of God's thoughts (in His Word) to let them weave through the perplexities of our lives.

These two purposes of the Sabbath work together interactively. Just as worship prepares our hearts to reach up to God, so, too, reflecting on the profundity of His Word provokes and fuels our worship. A perfect description of the depth of God's Word is found in the Apostle Paul's doxology toward the end of Romans 11. Chapters 9 and 10 and the first part of 11 are probably three of the most mysterious, and sometimes the most "dispute-provoking," chapters in the Bible. Do you know why? Because they deal with the sovereignty of God in salvation – His absolute authority in influencing the hearts of men and women, either hardening or softening them. They discuss the mystery of God in election, in foreknowledge, in predestination, in justification, and in glorification. They grapple with the mystery of Israel's rejection of the Messiah and the consequent propagation of the Gospel among the Gentiles and what this might mean in terms of God's covenantal promises to His chosen people. The bottom line, according to Paul, is that God does not owe anyone any answers for the ways in which He works.

How does all of this affect Paul? He does not respond in frustration with a God who will not give all the answers. Paul is not irritated that God's ways will not fit into a tight theological system, and he is not angry that God is sovereign and therefore human beings are not! Instead, he worships the all-wise, all-knowing God: "*O the depths of the riches both of the wisdom and the knowledge of God, how unsearchable are his judgments and his ways past finding out*" (Romans 11:33). Plumbing the depths of the interwoven braided mysteries of God's dealings with us does not need to turn us into intellectual rebels. It can humble us before Him in submissive worship. Admittedly, we may never experience Paul's ecstasy, but the same process is at work.

I remember a day when, for various reasons, my early-morning schedule was out of control. I therefore decided to cut short the time I normally spent in reflection and worship at the beginning of each day. Well, I didn't get up from my desk for over two hours. A few paragraphs in the particular book I happened to begin reading gave me some brand-new insights into the mystery and wonder of God's ways and workings. I simply couldn't stop reflecting, praying, and worshipping at the time I had planned to end. An unexpected, though brief, insight into the profundity of God's thoughts changed an understandable reluctance to worship into a prolonged period of meditation and prayer.

This is what is meant to happen to us on Sunday morning as we listen to the exposition of the Word of God. The preacher's role and that of the congregation are both significant in making this possible. The preacher must expose the depth of God's thoughts in a way that people can understand, pressing imagery and poetry into service. Calvin Miller, in one of his inspiring books on preaching, gave me a priceless one-liner that I have never forgotten: "Image is the bait that keeps people snapping on the golden heels of dogma."[7] The expositor must hook the people onto theology by using vivid imagery. The people's job, meanwhile, is to listen carefully. Congregations today are accustomed to thinking of listening to the sermon as a passive activity. It is not. They desperately need to recover the Reformers' conception of listening to preaching as an active participation in worship. Further, they need to "go for the meat," snap on the golden heels of systematic theology, rather than resting content with all sorts of catchy phrases and sayings that abound in motivational sermons. These will prove to be "vanity" in the crucible of life; when the heat is turned up they will disappear in a wisp of smoke. But the profundity of God's thoughts, in the same crucible and the same heat, will provoke worship.

A few years ago, I was discipling a young man in my congregation. He thrilled my heart when he shared this story with me. He had been away on a business trip and ended up sharing a room with a colleague. One night he and this roommate talked until about two o'clock in the morning. "What did you talk about?" I asked. He said, "I just opened my Bible to Galatians, Chapter 2, and I re-preached to him the entire sermon that you preached on Sunday morning." That's active listening to the depth of God's thoughts. That's snapping on the golden heels of dogma. And to know that there are people listening so intently, that even one person can be gripped to such an extent, makes all the work involved in unlocking God's thoughts worthwhile. What would happen if large segments of a congregation followed this person's example, exited to the marketplace, and re-preached the sermons they heard on Sunday morning?

It's time to ask ourselves once again how our Sabbaths might be transformed if we continued to remind ourselves in our Saturday night prayer that the Sabbath is good, not only for stretching upward in worship, but also for confronting ourselves with the profundity of God's thoughts – that this attention to our inner space is necessary for living wisely in the face of life's perplexities. What if we took time to yield our minds to God, asking the Holy Spirit to unstop our ears and illumine our eyes so we'll be able to hear and understand the "deep things of God" and listen actively? What if we then prayed for those charged with the responsibility of proclaiming God's Word, that the Spirit would anoint them with a vivid imagination, clear intellect, and dogged determination, so they will keep us snapping at the golden heels of dogma and provoke us to a worship that engages body, soul, and spirit?

Prayer Guide

1. Remind yourself that the Sabbath is also given to distill the wisdom of God into the perplexities of your life. So yield your mind to Him and ask the Spirit to teach you on Sunday, unstopping your spiritual ears and illumining your spiritual eyes to the truth of His Word. Ask Him to help you take in the "meat" and not settle for "milk." Then pray the same for your entire congregation. Again use your specific circumstances to shape the details of your prayer.

2. Pray that the preacher will do the hard work of studying and communicating with imagery that will keep people snapping on the golden heels of dogma and that people will listen actively.

3. Review with gratitude the profound thoughts of God that He has already shown you in the past and use them to pray for specific perplexities in your life, those particular issues in life that you are not able to understand. Put your intellect aside and bow down in worship before God because of the mystery of His ways and the unsearchable nature of His judgements.

Of Grass and Palm Trees

In the Sabbath we celebrate *the heights of God's greatness* in joyful music. We are confronted with the *depths of His embroidered wisdom* and we respond with a doxology. Not surprisingly, the third dimension of the Sabbath is the *breadth of life with God*. The psalmist addresses that aspect in verses 6–7 and 12–15: "*The senseless man does not know, fools do not understand, that though the wicked spring up like grass and all evildoers flourish, they will be forever destroyed … The righteous will flourish like a palm tree, they will grow like a cedar of Lebanon; planted in the house of the LORD, they will flourish in the courts of our God. They will still bear fruit in old age, they will stay fresh and green, proclaiming, 'The LORD is upright; he is my Rock, and there is no wickedness in him.'*"

In this section, the psalmist paints a vivid contrast between two groups of people. On the one hand, there are the "senseless," the "fools," and the "wicked"; on the other hand, there is the psalmist himself and the group of people he calls "the righteous." The adjectives he uses to describe the former group are not pejorative, harsh, critical, "holier-than-thou" judgements. Notice his emphasis. *"The senseless man does not know, fools do not understand … ."* The word "know" in Hebrew is more than intellectual, rational knowledge. It is a knowledge that comes from intimacy with a person – in this case, God. "Understanding," of course, has to do with intellect. The psalmist is merely describing the consequences when we do not take time to extol the majesty of God in worship, or put in the mental effort required to plumb the profundity of His thoughts. The inevitable result is foolishness and senselessness. And it is during Sabbath worship that we see how right the psalmist is, because the wisdom of the world is then put in its proper perspective.

All through the week, we are battered by the opinions and pronouncements of specialists, experts in the media, experts among our colleagues at work, expert authors of articles in professional magazines and journals, the very quantity of which is sufficient to overwhelm us, even if the quality is unimpressive. What is the result of this bombardment? We rethink our Christian convictions; we doubt and reel like drunks between two opinions. We become two different people: one kind in the world and another in church. We speak one kind of wisdom among our professional colleagues and neighbours; we speak another kind in church. But, praise God, on Sunday morning, an accurate perspective is restored as all the so-called wisdom of the experts, apart from God, is shown to be foolish and senseless.

Since the psalmist chooses to amplify one particular aspect of the difference between these two categories of people, I suspect this is where the change in our perspective is most needed. It is the difference between a temporal and an eternal perspective on life as a whole. And being a good preacher, the psalmist hooks us, not with bare theology, but with two beautiful images that reinforce this contrast. He talks about the difference between grass and palm trees. Let's amplify this contrast using other biblical data. A quick survey of the metaphorical usage of "grass" in the Bible reveals that it is used to drive home three things. Grass springs up quickly, spreads everywhere, and is short-lived. According to the psalmist, that's what the wisdom of fools and the senseless is like: it springs up quickly and it is pervasive in its influence, but it is short-lived. That's why popular theories in psychology, sociology, and philosophy follow one another in rapid succession. Their momentary success, judged in terms of the number and prestige of those who espouse them, belies their imminent demise. "Here today and gone tomorrow" is an apt label for them. Contrast that with the following characteristics of the palm tree:[8]

1. It flourishes even in difficult seasons because it sends its roots deep into the ground.

2. Unlike other trees, which are dead at the centre and alive on the surface, the palm tree's life is at the heart, so it is protected from external abuse.

3. Palm trees are storm-resistant. Their leaves do not catch wind like a sail and their roots are not tapered, which makes the tree difficult to uproot.

4. The palm tree's fruit improves with the age of the tree.

No wonder the psalmist uses palm trees as an image for the life of the righteous. They will stay fresh and green, bearing fruit in old age. The key to this is the living heart and roots that go deep into the ground. So what keeps the heart of the righteous alive? What nourishes the root? Consider verses 12 and 13: "*The righteous will flourish like a palm tree, they will grow like a cedar of Lebanon; planted in the house of the* LORD, *they will flourish in the courts of our God.*" The "house of the Lord" and "the courts of our God" are synonymous with the temple of God. So it is a life of worship in God's presence, to which Sabbath worship is central; it is a life yielded to the pursuit of intimacy with God, which will keep the heart, or the centre, of our lives alive, so that life's perturbations, while scarring the outside, cannot penetrate to the interior and thus interfere with the process of bearing fruit. Sabbath worship reminds us of this fundamental difference in perspective between the wisdom of the world and God's wisdom. We are in it for the long haul, while they, the senseless, are in it for a short time. As our hearts are becoming alive, their hearts are shrivelling up. For us, the best is yet to come; for them, the best they will have is the way it is now – it's downhill from here on. These are the perspectives that can be restored on the Sabbath.

The psalmist is not finished yet. He gives us some clues as to the kind of fruit the righteous will bear. One is implied in the declaration "*They will stay fresh and green*" (v. 14). A few years ago, on a Saturday morning, I was reviewing my sermon for the next day when the phone rang. It was an eighty-one-year-old woman whom I knew quite well. After the customary pleasantries had been exchanged, she said, "I am coming to your church tomorrow morning." More chit-chat and then I asked, "How are you getting here?" She said, "Oh, I still drive. Mind you, I have a cane with me, but I tell my younger friends that the cane is just for style."

That comment took my mind back almost ten years earlier when my wife and I, along with our children, who were then eight and five, went down to Florida for a week. We'd stayed at this woman's home for three days. The last Sunday night, after worshipping in their church, she and her husband took us out to a nearby restaurant called "Freddy's." We'd barely got settled at our table when a host of teenagers from that same church who happened to be at Freddy's left their parents, pulled up their chairs to our table, and gathered around the woman and her husband. For the next half-hour, I observed these two people in their seventies holding their own in conversation with the young kids. Of course, they could no longer match the physical vitality of teenagers, but when it came to vitality of spirit, they didn't yield an inch. They were as fresh and green as palm trees, with a *vitality of spirit* that mere age could not dull. That's one kind of fruit we can expect in the righteous.

Not only will the righteous stay fresh and green, but they do so proclaiming. The word "proclaim" is the same one we encountered in verse 2, which we know means "to stand before people and speak." Palm trees have precious truths to declare to the next generation. Whether their voices are strong or whether they can still carry the proverbial tune is beside the point; they have a song and a message in their heart that they will still speak until their very last days. As for the content of that message – "*They will proclaim that the LORD is upright; he is my Rock, and there is no wickedness in him*" – why does the psalmist stress the fact that they will proclaim that there is no wickedness in Him? If the righteous are like palm trees, their fruit, at least the best of it, is not going to appear until much later in life. Part of the process of bearing sweet fruit will also involve having the trunk scarred by abuse and being lashed by strong winds. Meanwhile, the wicked will be springing up everywhere like grass, and their instantaneous freshness and popularity will be "oh so" attractive. This creates a real temptation to draw wrong conclusions about God, but it is precisely this temptation that the palm trees don't yield to.

Instead, they proclaim to the younger palm trees: "It's okay. He's still righteous. There's no wickedness in Him."

Two weeks before I completed my initial studies of this Psalm, I had an unexpected encounter with another "palm tree" – a sixty-eight-year-old man who preached the first sermon that began my journey toward Christ. (He was, at that time, the director of India Youth for Christ, and he was passing through Toronto, so we met for lunch. Since I had been meditating on this Psalm, I shared what I'd been learning about palm trees and asked him, "Victor, it's been thirty years since I first heard you preach and you're almost seventy right now. What advice do you have for me?" He gave me three specific lessons which, taken together, were a magnificent illustration of a "palm tree proclamation": (1) the older you get, the harder the battle gets; (2) temptations that you thought you'd licked as a young man resurface with new power later on, but a fresh infilling of the Holy Spirit is still the answer; and (3) you'll see the fruit of your earlier ministry only later in life. Then he offered this grand summary: "Life is rough, but Jesus is tough." That's the *proclamation of a palm tree* that the Lord is righteous and in Him is no wickedness.

Not only are palm trees fresh in spirit and not only do they have good news to proclaim about God's faithfulness and righteousness, but *the proclamation itself remains fresh*. "Old" truth comes alive in newly packaged forms. This, too, happens as a result of a life of worship. Recall that the palm tree flourishes in the courts of God. And there is a depth that only experience can lend to truth, depth without which truth cannot resonate in the listener's heart with the ring of self-authentication that we call unction or authority.

Prayer Guide

1. Ask God that, on Sunday, He will restore your perspective by heightening the contrast between His wisdom and that of the world – that the "wicked" are like grass destined for perishing, while you are destined to become like a palm tree. Pray for specific areas in your life where the rapid, temporary flourishing of the foolish and senseless seems more attractive than the slow maturing of the palm tree, which will bear fruit only in later years.

2. Use the characteristics of the palm tree (printed again below) as springboards for specific prayer requests.

   (a) It flourishes even in difficult seasons because it sends its roots deep into the ground.

   (b) Unlike other trees, which are dead at the centre and alive on the surface, the palm tree's life is at the heart, so it is protected from external abuse.

   (c) Palm trees are storm-resistant. Their leaves do not catch wind like a sail and their roots are not tapered, which makes the tree difficult to uproot.

   (d) The palm tree's fruit improves with the age of the tree.

3. Pray for mature palm trees in your congregation, that they will continue to bear fruit and proclaim God's attributes, willing to be mentors of the young. Pray for the younger palm trees, that they will be willing to learn from the older ones in their midst. Pray that the young will recover a respect for the wisdom of age and seek to combine it with the vitality of their youth.

Oxen, Oils, and Enemies

By now the perceptive reader will have noted that I have so far said nothing about verses 8–11 of the Psalm: *"But you, O LORD, are exalted forever. For surely your enemies, O LORD, surely your enemies will perish; all evildoers will be scattered. You have exalted my horn like that of a wild ox; fine oils have been poured upon me. My eyes have seen the defeat of my adversaries; my ears have heard the rout of my wicked foes."* In these verses, we find two more images to go along with palm trees: a "wild ox" and "fine oils." At first, the relationship between the two is not at all obvious. I have discovered six references to wild oxen in Scripture. Taken together, they convey the idea of unrestrainable strength, combined with exuberance, demonstrated by activities such as skipping and dancing. As for fine oils, my Eastern background lends some valuable and relevant insight. In India, it is customary for young children to have what is termed a weekly "oil bath." In our home it took place on Saturdays. Mothers would heat some peanut oil in an iron skillet and rub down their children's entire bodies. The head in particular would be soaked as the remaining oil would literally be poured out on it and massaged into the hair. Kids stayed in this "soak" stage for about two hours, after which a thorough bath would wash away the oil, leaving the skin supple and, according to folktales, the body free from any disease. (At least one exegetically sound interpretation of the command in James 5 to "anoint with oil" suggests the restoration of a weakened body by rubbing with oils.) If the image of the wild ox signifies unrestrained strength and exuberance, that of fine oils signifies a more supple strength.

How are we to apply the meaning of these images in the larger context of a Sabbath Psalm? If the palm tree planted in the house of the Lord is a symbol of people at prayer and worship, the wild ox rubbed down with oil symbolizes the same people at exuberant play. Really! Prayer on the Sabbath makes sense, but play? For many, that is "*verboten*" on the Sabbath. But Eugene Peterson's comments are helpful and thought provoking here. He points out that the two Scripture passages which explicitly command us to keep the Sabbath (Exodus and Deuteronomy) give different reasons for the commandment. In Exodus, we are told to keep the Sabbath because God rested from His work of creation on the seventh day. This is a *Sabbath for praying* and reflecting on God and His work. In Deuteronomy, the reason given for the Sabbath is that Israel had been slaves in Egypt for four hundred years, subject to constant dehumanizing labour. They had no time to refresh body and soul in play of any kind. So here the *Sabbath is for playing*, though playing doesn't mean vegetating in front of the television or playing to win in competitive sports. He summarizes thus: "Keeping a Sabbath is simple and easy: we pray and we play, two things we were pretty good at as children, and can always pick up again with a little encouragement if we can only find the time. But we don't have to find the time; it is given to us. A day a week. A Sabbath. A day to pray and play – God's gift. Christian practice orients the first element of the day around the act of worship – praying. This is *the great act of freedom in relation to heaven*. This is the exercise of our minds and bodies in acts of adoration and commitment, supplication and praise, ventures of forgiving and giving. We explore, enjoy and share it in our assembly for worship. For most of you this praying will start out in [y]our sanctuary when I [or your pastor] call[s] you to worship. Simple. The second element of the day is for playing. This is *the great act of freedom in relation to earth*. We exercise our minds and bodies in games and walks, in … reading, in visiting and picnicking, in puttering and writing. We take in colors and shapes, the sounds and smells. We let the creativity of the creation nudge us into creativity. We surprise ourselves by creating a meal, or a conversation or an appreciation, or some laughter that wasn't in our job description."[9]

And lest we think this kind of Sabbath keeping is really escapism – a "Nero fiddling while Rome burns" sort of spirituality – note that all these sabbatical principles are set in the context of enemies, evildoers, adversaries, and foes (all featured in verses 8–11). The real world has enemies – God's enemies – who therefore can easily become our enemies (and often do). To counter them effectively, we need to have the endurance of palm trees as well as the exuberance of wild oxen and the suppleness of strength that comes from being "rubbed down with fine oils." This is not to enable us to extract revenge for harm done to us (that's God's business) but to strengthen us for fearless forays into enemy territory, in order to carry out God's purposes. It is Sabbath prayer and play that makes us ready for such weekday forays into a world largely controlled by the enemies of God. We set aside the Sabbath for prayer and play, resisting the clamour to do something practical and, to our surprise, we discover it was the most practical thing to do. Thus, to prayer shaped by palm trees, let us add the strength of wild oxen and suppleness from fine oils. We will be stronger for our weekday battles if we spend our Sabbaths in meaningful play, in cultivating freedom in relation to the earth, and in allowing God's Creation to nudge us into creativity.

Prayer Guide

How can you use Sundays for a balance between praying and playing? On which side do you tend to err? Does your job prevent you from doing either? How can you let Creation nudge you into creativity? What are the enemies you face between Sundays among whom you need to be like a wild ox anointed with oil? Use these reflections to end your prayer for Saturday night.

Have a great Sunday (tomorrow?)

Chapter 6

Psalm 127:
Turning Houses into Homes

1 *Unless the* LORD *builds the house, its builders labor in vain. Unless the* LORD *watches over the city, the watchmen stand guard in vain. 2 In vain you rise early and stay up late, toiling for food to eat – for he grants sleep to those he loves. 3 Sons are a heritage from the* LORD, *children a reward from him. 4 Like arrows in the hands of a warrior are sons born in one's youth. 5 Blessed is the man whose quiver is full of them. They will not be put to shame when they contend with their enemies in the gate.*

A Critical Mandate

Church buildings always interest me, not as buildings per se, but as expressions of the underlying philosophy of ministry of those who built them. So when I am fortunate enough to have the pastor (or other knowledgeable leader) of the church take me on a guided tour of the facilities, I ask a lot of questions about how the architectural details relate to what the church leaders are attempting to accomplish in the lives of their people. As the conversation and tour proceed, I find myself making silent comparisons between that particular church and the one I minister in. Predictably, the comparisons are sometimes favourable and sometimes challenging, but on one point, I always come away thankful – even amazed at what God has blessed us with in our church. We have a library of over ten thousand books, catalogued and administered with precision and smoothness. Even in churches that are much larger than ours, the library almost always pales into near insignificance when compared with ours. But lest you readers think I'm on an unseemly ego trip, let me hasten to get to the point of all this: What has made our library what it is? Certainly not my skill or vision, indeed not that of any pastoral staff, present or past. It is because two laypeople, a husband-and-wife team, have devoted thirty-six continuous years to this ministry. They are, in my experience, the most powerful illustration of one of Friedrich Nietzsche's surprising observations (surprising because one wouldn't expect it from the father of nihilism – a philosophy of meaninglessness – and the "death of God" movement). In a rare moment of spiritual clarity and insight, he wrote, "The essential thing in heaven and on earth is ... that there should be a long obedience in the same direction; there thereby results, and has always resulted in the long run, something which has made life worth living."[1] And it is precisely this "long obedience in the same direction" that the prevailing spirit of the age does little to encourage and much to discourage. That's why it is important to both thank God for, and publicly honour, people like these librarians, who have demonstrated dedication to one ministry for nearly three decades.

If there is any one God-given task where such perseverance over decades is critical, it is the challenge of passing on our faith to the next generation. When Moses preached his farewell message to his beloved Israel on the banks of the Jordan, he made this charge central to his entire exhortation (Deuteronomy 6). Their success in a land of prosperity would depend on the successful transmission of their faith to their children. Much of the rest of Scripture seems to be a tragic record of their unbelievable failure to carry out this mandate. According to the Book of Judges, Israel prospered under Joshua and the elders of his generation. But after they died, a whole generation grew up that did not know the Lord or what He had done for them. The result? Four hundred years of total anarchy. When God graciously restored the fortunes of His people through Samuel's courageous leadership, we are startled to find that this great man nevertheless failed where it mattered most: in his home. That is all the more remarkable, considering that Samuel grew up in Eli's household, where he had ample opportunity to see the devastation caused to the priesthood by Eli's miserable failure to parent his own sons properly. If anyone had an incentive to succeed, it should have been Samuel. But he failed. Later, when Israel reached its zenith under David's leadership, this devoted man, who had a heart for God and who wrote many of the Psalms, also failed in his home. His sons played such havoc with his kingdom that it never recovered.

In contrast, the closing words of the Old Testament contain Malachi's prophecy that the forerunner of the Messiah will turn the hearts of the fathers to the children, a theme that is picked up almost without a hiccup when the prophetic silence is broken four hundred years later. Certainly there are covenantal dimensions to this prophecy that embrace more than transmitting the faith to the next generation, but not less. This biblical data taken as a whole emphasize not only the critical importance of passing on our faith to our children, but also the difficulties we will encounter in doing this. Hence the need for perseverance over decades.

Here, too (perhaps I should say, here, especially), the prevailing mood today is likely to discourage us from wholeheartedly accepting this assignment. In fact, secular society does its best to disparage and downgrade parenting as a valuable calling. Certainly, we need help from each other, but above all, we need God's help in prayer that roots eternal, faith-building perspectives from God's Word deep in our hearts. We find such help in Psalm 127. It is part of a group of fifteen Psalms (120–134) known as the Songs of Ascent. They were sung by Hebrew pilgrims as they made their way to the temple in Jerusalem to participate in the three great worship festivals: the Feasts of Passover, Pentecost, and Tabernacles.

Because of the elevation of Jerusalem, most of this journey involved a climb – hence their title. Now, these pilgrimages were not only marked by excitement and anticipation at what lay ahead, but also (as we have observed earlier) fraught with danger: the terrain was rough, robbers waylaid defenceless travellers on the road, and wild beasts attacked. So the Hebrew pilgrims sang these songs of ascent to quiet their anxious fears, to reinforce their dependence upon their Lord, and to persevere on the journey in spite of the dangers.

Parents: our journey with our children, especially young children, bears a striking resemblance to that of these Hebrew pilgrims. We share a measure of anticipation and excitement at what our children are going to be like when they reach maturity, but the way is often marked with all kinds of pitfalls and potential dangers. We thrill with wonder and we quake before fearful prospects. We, like the Hebrew pilgrims, need a song to sing on this journey, and Psalm 127 is the quintessential candidate. It will quiet our anxious fears, reinforce our dependence upon God, and keep us persevering at the task of transmitting our faith in Christ to the next generation.

Gifts of God

Since we are using this Psalm to guide us in our prayers and since flexibility and freedom are the essence of true prayer, let's begin, not at the beginning, but at verse 3: "*Sons are a heritage from the* LORD, *children a reward from him.*" This was unquestionably the dominant perspective in the entire Old Testament. Immediately after creating Adam and Eve, God commanded them to multiply and populate the earth. The subsequent record of sacred history is filled with the stories of barren couples longing for children. We see it in the stories of Sarah, Rebecca, Rachel, Leah, and Hannah – to name just a few of them. And it wasn't only God's chosen people who felt this way about children; it was a universal perspective. In Old Testament times, the heathen nations also considered the barrenness of their womenfolk to be a punishment from God. For example, when God struck the household of Abimelech with infertility, they regarded that as a punishment from God. Nothing changes in the New Testament. Elizabeth and Zachariah's joy at the birth of a child in their old age is but one of many illustrations. Now, certainly, in many of these cases, the desire for children was mixed up with all kinds of ulterior motives. Leah and Rachel's shameless bartering for their spineless husband Jacob is perhaps the outstanding example of this. But on one thing they were all agreed: children were a gift of God and a reward from Him.

This attitude still prevails in many Eastern societies. I think of my native country, India, where I grew up. A question about parenting there puzzled me for a long time: many, if not most, parents do not follow what we would consider critically important biblical and psychological principles in parenting, especially when disciplining children for misbehaviour. As a result, it is not uncommon to see "bratty" youngsters. Yet by the time these same kids are in their late teens or early twenties, they are almost always on excellent terms with their parents and treat them with great respect and care.

I have been able to come up with only one plausible explanation for this paradox. One of the things I remember very vividly about my own childhood is that children were part and parcel of everything that happened in life. Babysitting was almost unknown in my time. Children went with their parents to movies, to weddings, to dinners – everywhere. It was just assumed that they were an integral part of the whole family. One message came through to us children very clearly: we were, for the most part, wanted, loved, welcomed, and not considered a hindrance. Sadly, in my own country, this is changing with the process of secularization. And as for totally secularized North America, listen to this quotation from a recent book, *Sex and Destiny*, by Germaine Greer. "Historically," she says, "human societies have been pro children, but modern society is unique in that it is profoundly hostile to children. We in the West do not refrain from childbirth because we are concerned about the population, or because we feel we cannot afford children. We do so because we don't like children any more."[2] This is not the railing of a wild-eyed religious "fundamentalist"; it is a secular humanist's acknowledgement of the dominant reason behind the exhortations and policies of people and organizations that clamour for abortion on demand, that would like teenagers to be able to terminate pregnancies without parental consent – they don't like children.

"Not so with Christian parents," you might respond. Hopefully not. Why, then, belabour the thrust of verse 3 that children are a gift – in fact, a reward – from God? To keep it that way – that's the main reason. To be forewarned, as the old saying goes, is to be forearmed. The attitudes of the world around us and the spirit of the age have a way of steadily and subtly creeping into our way of life without our even being aware of them. I think, for example, of the increasing tendency, even among Christian couples, to keep on postponing having children, maybe indefinitely. We don't quite share Germaine Greer's attitude, but we are not in any great hurry either.

About a year before I was married, my roommate, a fine Christian man, went to the altar. I knew him well enough to know that he wasn't really planning to have children for quite a while, but within six months of their marriage, he announced the good news that they were soon going to be parents. Again, I knew them well enough to ask, "How come the change in plans?" I have never forgotten his answer. He shared with me some advice that had been given to him by an older believer, who had been his mentor for many years. This man had said to him, "If your wife ever desires to have children, don't stand in the way. That desire comes from God." Well, six months into their marriage, that's exactly what happened.

I was married about a year later and our initial plans were to not have any children for at least a couple of years, so we could get adjusted to each other and give the marriage the attention it would need and deserve. Need I say more? Exactly six months into our marriage, my wife experienced that same desire. I immediately remembered what my friend had told me and agreed. I have no regrets. The daughter who was born not too long afterwards has been, and continues to be, a source of legitimate pride and joy to us, as has our son, who arrived three years later. Many other couples with whom I have shared this principle and who have dared to take God at His Word can add their confirming testimonies to mine.

But what if we can't afford them? One day, while I was working in my study at the church, I overheard one of our elders, a godly man whose spirituality I have seen develop in the furnace of affliction and whose integrity I deeply respect, make a comment in the hall. I don't know to this day who he was speaking to, but I heard what he said: "Brother, if I had waited till I felt I could afford to have a child, I wouldn't have one today." He has several. Now don't get me wrong. I'm not saying there's no need, or place, for responsible family planning (though some Christians would). I have seen what the lack of that can do to devastate countries like my own, whose every attempt to improve the economic lot of their people is stymied by the problem of an uncontrolled population explosion. What I am asking us to guard against, though, is the avoidance of children because they are perceived to be, either directly or indirectly, an interference with our careers and our lifestyles. This is a flat contradiction of the scriptural declaration, *"Children are a gift from God and a reward from Him."*

Prayer Guide

Parents, take a few moments to examine your present attitude to each child entrusted to your care. Be honest, write it down, and evaluate it against the unequivocal declaration of Psalm 127:3. Do you see your children as gifts of God, as rewards from Him? Yield your present thoughts to Him and ask the Spirit to renew your mind regarding your children, so you will see them according to His Word.

- Jot down a few ways in which your children have been a gift and a reward. Take time to thank God for these gifts and rewards. Then read Deuteronomy 6. Recommit yourself to fulfilling this critical mandate to pass on your faith to your children.

- Then take a few moments to pray for one or more of the Children's / Youth Ministries in your church – that those involved will see the young people in their care as gifts of God and accept the mandate of Deuteronomy 6. (Your own children's teachers may be a logical place to start.) Those of you who are not or are not yet parents, remember that the mandate of Deuteronomy 6 was addressed to the community. You can pray along the lines indicated above for any children to whom you have a natural emotional link (nephews, nieces, the kids you may be teaching).

- Conclude this phase by praying for the school system your kids are in, that the teachers may see the children entrusted to them in this light. Pray for God to destroy the prevailing anti-children attitude in society and to prevent its intrusion into the Church.

- Finally, for those of you who have chosen not to have children, take a few moments to examine your motives before God. Ask the Holy Spirit to either confirm right motives or transform selfish motives based on seeing children as a hindrance.

Polished Arrows

In verses 4 and 5, the psalmist expands on specific ways in which our children are gifts from God. *"Like arrows in the hands of a warrior are sons born in one's youth. Blessed is the man whose quiver is full of them. They will not be put to shame when they contend with their enemies in the gate."* He paints an intriguing picture of a man with a bow in his hand, with the bowstring drawn taut, aimed at some threatening enemy. What catches the observer's attention immediately is that it's not an arrow in the bow; it's a son or a daughter ready to be launched into enemy territory. This is a recurring metaphor in Scripture. Isaiah 49 puts the following words in the mouth of the suffering servant of Israel (prophetically referring to the Messiah, Jesus Christ): *"Listen to me, you islands; hear this, you distant nations: Before I was born the LORD called me; from my birth he has made mention of my name. He made my mouth like a sharpened sword, in the shadow of his hand he hid me; he made me into a polished arrow and concealed me in his quiver. He said to me, 'You are my servant, Israel, in whom I will display my splendor'"* (vv. 1–2). Then again in Zechariah 9:13, God says, this time of ordinary Israelites, *"I will bend Judah as I bend my bow and fill it with Ephraim. I will rouse your sons, O Zion, against your sons, O Greece."*

The basic image is the same, but the details are modified. Judah is the bow and Ephraim the arrow. And they are aimed at Greece. Psalm 127 takes this image and extends it beyond a special individual, Messiah, and beyond chosen soldiers in Judah, applying it to every child who is a blessing from God to His people. What's more, the Psalm also makes it clear that while it is God who polishes the arrow, fits it into a bow, and bends it, the primary human instrument He uses for this work is parents. Now why are children born in one's youth especially suited to be arrows? Why is "the earlier, the better" a good thing when it comes to having children? It's because we have that much longer to polish them while we as parents are still young enough to have all the skills and energy needed to do a thorough job. Then, when we (and they) both grow older, we *"will not be put to shame when they contend with their enemies in the gate"* (Psalm 127:5). In the psalmist's time, the city gates referred to the place where business and legal transactions took place. In other words, these sons and daughters, born when the parents were young and polished by them (according to the blueprint of Deuteronomy 6) become the protectors of their parents in their golden years, making sure, for instance, that they don't get "fleeced" by unscrupulous legal professionals and businesspersons – in a word, ensuring justice in their time of need.

Now some people, for whatever reason, either cannot have children or have had to wait. Are they cut off from the blessing of God? Without taking away from the real advantages portrayed in the Psalm, two observations are pertinent. We must remember that in the Old Testament, biological growth was one of the key means of building the family of God on earth. Separation from the nations was the watchword for Israel. Neither is true in the New Testament. The primary family is not the biological family but the family of God, whom God commanded to take care of one another – especially widows (and, I presume, widowers). Also, barrenness is no longer a curse. Spiritual children are an equally wonderful heritage. And when all is said and done, merely having biological children is no guarantee of old-age security. Only God is worthy of that trust. In fact, even the Old Testament hints at this, in Isaiah 56:3b–5: "*And let not any eunuch complain, 'I am only a dry tree.' For this is what the* Lord *says: 'To the eunuchs who keep my Sabbaths, who choose what pleases me and hold fast to my covenant – to them I will give within my temple and its walls a memorial and a name better than sons and daughters; I will give them an everlasting name that will not be cut off.*"

Let's update this picture as it might apply to the twenty-first century. Where do we aim the arrows that our children represent, once we have polished them? Instead of the city gates, read the "real world." Take, for example, the halls of higher learning in the secular schools and universities of our day. How many times have we heard of children raised in good, orthodox, traditional Christian homes that "come a cropper," so to speak, in these hostile venues? That's one "city-gate" experience for which we need to polish our children as arrows. Then, instead of shielding them from "those academics" in a bout of paranoia, we can shoot them straight into the secular classrooms to battle with those who will attempt to teach them what is contrary to the Word of God, knowing that they will stand at the gate and not be ashamed.

Then I think of *the world of work*, be it so called "white-collar" or "blue-collar." At a leadership conference I was privileged to attend many years ago, I still recall Howard Hendricks, a longtime professor at Dallas Theological Seminary and a well-known, much travelled, and respected Christian leader, telling us that there was a tremendous opportunity in the real world (read "city gates") for Christians to make an impact, but that in his travels, he was becoming aware of a major crisis of Christian leadership: only a very few people were available to lead. That's the challenge we as parents can rise to. Our homes are the places where we can sharpen and polish our arrows and shoot them out into vocational leadership.

For one final (but by no means exhaustive) example of the city gates, I think of *the whole missionary enterprise*. In Psalm 110 God promises to extend the kingdom of His Son, Jesus, through a whole host of young, holy, willing, fresh troops. These are the ones about whom it is said in Isaiah 52:7: *"How beautiful on the mountains are the feet of those who bring good news, who proclaim peace, who bring good tidings, who proclaim salvation, who say to Zion, 'Your God reigns!'"* (applied in Romans 10:15 to those who proclaim Christ to those who have never heard). That's another direction in which we can polish our children and shoot them as arrows: right into the heart of Satan's territory, so the kingdom of Jesus Christ can be extended among those who have yet to hear the Gospel.

Precisely where we point our particular sons and daughters depends, of course, on their God-given spiritual gifts, skills, and inclinations. And who is positioned to know these things better than we, their parents, by maintaining a continual dialogue with our children, by watching them at work and in relationships (in short, by following the prescription of Deuteronomy 6:4–8)! In the process, we become aware of the rough edges that need to be polished. Then, when the time comes, we can put them in our bow, pull back, and let go.

Prayer Guide

Take a few moments to list the specific gifts, talents, and inclinations of your children's hearts. In light of these, what "city gates" do you feel God is equipping them for? Where might you aim them as arrows to do maximum damage to Satan's strategies? Where do the arrows still need polishing? Use your responses to shape your prayers as you dedicate your children afresh to fight at the "city gates" and as you pray for the wisdom you need to polish them. Pray also that their hearts might be responsive to your polishing.

Vanity, Vanity – All Is Vanity

By now the task must seem rather formidable, perhaps increasingly so as we grapple with it in the detail suggested in the Prayer Guide. But this perspective – which sees our children as gifts and rewards from God, as arrows to be polished and shot into enemy territory, and as requiring an unflinching commitment to the hard task of polishing – is only half the story. The other half has not yet been told. Here's how the psalmist tells it in verses 1 and 2 of Psalm 127: "*Unless the* LORD *builds the house, its builders labor in* **vain***. Unless the* LORD *watches over the city, the watchmen stand guard in* **vain***.* **In vain** *you rise early and stay up late, toiling for food to eat – for he grants sleep to those he loves.*" We may have heard verse 1 at the beginning of, and often during, a building program in a church, and then again at the dedication of the completed building. But it seems totally out of place in a Psalm dealing with the welcoming and training of children. Not so to the original readers, because scholars tell us that the Hebrew words for "son" and "house" come from the same root. They would have seen the connection immediately. (That's why we so often see a play on the word "house" in the Scriptures. In 2 Samuel 7, we read that David wanted to build a "house" for God, meaning a physical temple. The Lord replied in essence, "No, you won't build a house for me until I have first built a 'house' for you." When God said "house," however, He meant the succession of David's sons who would form a dynasty.)

Having established the linguistic connection between verse 1 and the major theme of the Psalm, what's the point? Three times in these first two verses we find the phrase "in vain." Here, as elsewhere in the Scriptures, the word "vanity" does not mean pride; instead, it refers to something that is futile, unproductive, not accomplishing its intended purpose. Specifically, the psalmist says that three things are futile: there is no point building a house if God isn't behind the building; there is no point guarding a city (which is but a collection of houses) unless God is going to guard it; and you are not going to change that by burning the candle at both ends – rising up early and staying up late.

My father spent the last few years of his life with us in our home. During that time, I had occasion to take him to the hospital for doctor's appointments. Once, while in the waiting room, I overheard a conversation between a toddler and his mother, both of whom had just emerged from the doctor's inner sanctum. As she bundled him up, the mother told her child that she was going to drop him off somewhere. The child didn't seem to like the idea and wanted to know why Mummy couldn't stay with him. "I have to go to work," she said. "Why do you have to go to work?" the child asked. That's when my ears perked up. I know only too well that there are many legitimate answers one could give to such a question. I didn't want to miss hers. This is what she said: "So I can gets lots of money to buy you lots of toys." "Then can I have a Care Bear, Mummy?" were the last words I heard of that conversation. Burning the candle at both ends can enable us to build houses, to fill them with all kinds of gadgets and toys, and to install elaborate security systems to guard against burglary. *But none of this will ever make the house into a home.* People build houses and cities; God alone can build homes.

It has been that way from the very beginning. In Chapter 4 we encountered the exploits of Nimrod, the godless "warrior"-descendant of Cain. When he gathered together all the humans on earth in yet another act of rebellion against God, what strategy did he employ? A building project, the Tower of Babel. But that, too, was undertaken in vain, because God grounded the whole show mid-stream by confusing the languages of the people so no one could understand each other. Even more significant is what God did in reply. He didn't start a building of his own. He called out a man who was beyond the age when men normally became fathers, who was married to a woman who had not been able to conceive any children and said in effect, "I am going to build a dynasty, a succession of sons and daughters and fuse them into a nation through whom all the nations of the world are going to be blessed." Nimrod built a building, a city; God built a home.

Jacques Ellul, the renowned sociologist, captured the modern-day "Nimrod" spirit succinctly when he wrote: "The first great fact which emerges from our civilization is that, today, everything has become 'means.' There is no longer an 'end'; we do not know whither we are going. We have forgotten our collective ends, though we possess great means: we set huge machines in motion in order to arrive nowhere."[3] Ironically, I first read these words not too long before the space shuttle *Challenger* exploded seventy-three seconds after take-off, killing all seven astronauts aboard and setting the space mission back several months and billions of dollars.

Is the psalmist against hard work, then? Not at all. Verses 1 and 2 are not an excuse for laziness. They are a severe warning against work for work's sake – work that sacrifices relationships and runs rough-shod over people, particularly our children. Such work can build impressive edifices and achieve much in the eyes of the world, but according to the Scriptures, it is in vain. The psalmist amplifies his caution in verse 2: "*In vain you rise early and stay up late.*" The phrase translated "stay up late" literally means, "who delays sitting down." It refers to somebody who works relentlessly without taking time to rest. Not surprisingly, the biblical concept of "rest" doesn't mean sitting around "twid-dling our thumbs," wasting precious hours amusing ourselves. Biblical "rest" and empty amusement are worlds apart. It was American pastor and author Gordon MacDonald[4] who first pointed out to me that the word "amusement" comes from the Latin word "muse," which means "to think," and the Latin prefix "a," which means "not." So amusement literally means "unthinking activity." That's one reason why we live in a society where we have more leisure than ever before and more amusement parks than we can visit in a lifetime – yet we are a frazzled, tired people.

In sharp contrast to this state of affairs, the biblical concept of "rest" is to pause (the word Sabbath literally means "stop") in order to reflect on our work, who we have done it for, how we have treated the people with whom we have worked, and where we are headed with our work in the coming days and weeks. This kind of rest reinvests our work with meaning. Without it, our work, no matter what it is, will ultimately be destined for vanity or uselessness. That's the general principle. And in keeping with this line of thinking, before we draw out more specific applications of verses 1 and 2 to the issue of polishing our precious arrows, it's time for a pause.

Prayer Guide

- Parents, take a few moments to evaluate your work. How does it measure up against the psalmist's caution? Are all your efforts going into building houses and filling them with things and guarding them, or are you gradually transforming your houses into homes? Where both parents are working and you have children at home, ask yourself why. If you had been the mother (or father, for that matter) in the doctor's office, what answer would you have given your toddler? "So I can make lots of money to buy you toys" or ... ?

- Do you ever rest in the biblical sense or are you, in an adaptation of Neil Postman's memorable phrase, merely "amusing yourselves to death," mainly before the "almighty TV"? Be as honest as you can. Submit your answers to the Holy Spirit's scrutiny. Ask Him to guide you in identifying any necessary changes in your work, leisure, and home arrangements. Ask Him for grace and courage to make those changes. If the Spirit affirms the wisdom of your present situation, thank Him for His grace and provision.

- Then think of a single parent with whom you may have natural ties (in your church or your neighbourhood, etc.). They do not have the flexibility that two-parent families have in this matter. Pray for them as you have for yourself and for your children, using the various elements of the Prayer Guide. Remember that transmitting the faith to the next generation is doubly hard for them. Since most single parents are usually mothers, pray that God will truly be a husband to them and a father to their children.

Sleep Well

Let's look now at the latter part of verse 2 once again: "In vain you rise early and stay up late, toiling for food to eat – *for he grants sleep to those he loves.*" Happy the man or woman who can work hard and sleep well at night. That's a rare combination, indeed. Some people sleep only too well but don't work. Other people work hard but can't sleep properly at night. The combination of hard work and sleep is a gift that comes from God to people who have realized that after they have done all they can, especially in this "polishing arrows business," it is up to the Lord to do the rest. He must build the house; He must guard the city.

Sure, we need books, seminars, sermons, and adult education classes on effective parenting, but we cannot put our ultimate trust in these things. God is the Master Builder, and we have to look to Him to "deliver the goods" after we have done our work. Now our dependence on God must be more than just lip-service to a nice doctrinal affirmation or a recitation of Psalm 127 by rote memory. Our dependence upon God (as parents) needs to be expressed in regular, sustained intercession for our children. If we really believe that unless the Lord builds the house and watches over a city all our efforts will be in vain, then prayer for our children will be the most tangible expression of this conviction. And it has to be more than just a "God bless them, look after them, be with them in a very real way [you remember that one, don't you?] and make them turn out all right" type of prayer. Rather, our prayer has to be geared specifically to the ways in which we are attempting to polish our children into sharp arrows. I can only suggest five broad aspects of such intercessory prayer that are general enough to be widespread in their application. They have come from several years of my own experience in polishing the two arrows God has blessed us with.

1. First of all, we can pray for their genuine conversion. Don't rest content because they "accepted Jesus" – a phrase which is almost impossible to find in the Bible – a long time ago at some meeting somewhere. I do not by any means intend to denigrate the possibility of real conversions in this manner, but I am encouraging you to pray for the day when your God will become their God. Remember Jacob at Bethel (Genesis 28)? After a long period of preparation, there came a day when his father's God, the God of Abraham, the God of Isaac, the God of Sarah, the God of Rebecca, became his

God. Remember Timothy? The faith of two generations of mothers was instilled in him. Think of people like that and pray for a genuine conversion – when your God will become their God.

2. Secondly, we can pray for God to build two qualities into their lives: *courage and loyalty*. Loyalty to ourselves as parents and to God. We can pray, as the Book of Proverbs says, *"that the teaching of their father and their mother will truly become a garland to grace their head and a chain to adorn their neck"* (Proverbs 1:9). Then we can pray for courage that they will be able to stand up in the city gates (in the high schools, in the universities, in their eventual places of business), and speak, even though they may be the only person who believes and thinks in a certain way while everyone around them is affirming something different. As the Book of Acts makes clear, that kind of boldness can come only from the Holy Spirit; hence the need to pray for it.

3. Thirdly, we can pray that God will make them *"mighty in their spirit."* I think of a captivating verse in the Book of Ezekiel, where God said to the prophet, *"I will make your forehead like the hardest stone, harder than flint"* (Ezekiel 3:9). What a beautiful image to shape our prayers – that God will make their spiritual foreheads so hard that every weapon of the devil will just shatter in pieces at their feet as soon as it touches them. And what brings this kind of hardness? It is the Word of God. So pray that the Word of God they hear from you at home, from their faithful teachers in Sunday School classes, and from their own reading of the Scriptures, will continue the hardening process.

4. Fourthly, and this is critical, we can (nay, we must) pray for the women and men who will one day become *our children's spouses*. I cannot think of any one thing that will do more to either help or hinder our children from becoming the polished arrows that they were intended to be than their future spouses. I have seen both positive and negative examples of this. I would even dare to go one step further. It may sound silly to you, but I would encourage you to at least think about it. Pray for the *parents* of your children's future spouses, that they may be building into their sons and daughters precisely those qualities that you know your son or daughter is going to need, so that the two of them

109

together can become flaming arrows for God and can themselves raise up a new generation of arrows for God. I can't
think of a greater challenge to commit ourselves to.

5. Finally, let's not forget to *pray with our children*. As we pray
not only *for* them, but also *with* them, we communicate the
fact that ultimately we do not trust in ourselves, but in God.
They learn by watching and hearing us pray that "Unless
God builds the house, unless God builds the home, we all
labour in vain."

Prayer Guide

Use the five categories of prayer suggestions I have outlined
above to pray right now for your children. Feel free to expand and
modify the list as dictated by your specific situation. Once again,
those of you who do not have children of your own, pray along
these lines for children you know.

I Have a Dream ...

You all know the phrase and the man who immortalized it, Martin Luther King, Jr. But while the phrase is his, the possibility of
dreaming God's dreams is for all of us – and I have a dream when
it comes to this matter of polishing "arrows." In the twenty-one-
plus years I have been in so-called "full-time ministry," I have
come to realize (through my reading, observations, and conversations with many, many pastors) that one of the hardest, most
heartbreaking, and most thankless ministries is that of a youth
pastor. What if every Christian parent in every church began to
see their children as gifts from God, as rewards from Him, as
arrows to be polished – and then gave themselves to the task of
polishing as one of life's highest priorities? What a heritage we
could leave to the youth pastors of the next decade. Instead of
having to spend all their time trying to get kids to just clean up
their lives and solve interpersonal problems in their homes, all
the while wringing their hands to come up with yet another ex-
citing "games night," they would have a quiver full of arrows

with whom they could invade all the high schools in their neighbourhood. Sure, school authorities can shut the door to Christian
ministries, but how will they stop fiery strong arrows flying
around all over school? Of course, it's going to be hard work.
Polishing is not a matter of weeks or months, but years. We need
to think in terms of a twenty-year project. If we do, one day we
will see our children at the city gates and we won't be ashamed.
Instead our cups will be overflowing with joy and gratitude to
God.

A recent biography of Karl Barth, the famous German theologian, apparently includes a photograph that shows him climbing
a mountain in Switzerland, flanked by his two sons, Marcus and
Kristoff. This photograph was taken in 1941, just after their
younger brother, Matthias, had died as a result of a climbing accident. The two remaining sons were upholding their father in
his hour of great grief, defending him against the enemies of his
soul. Barth was proud of his sons, of whom he said, "My grownup
sons are my best comrades which is not a gift bestowed on every
father." When both these sons became teachers of theology –
Marcus in the United States and Kristoff in Indonesia – Barth in
Europe used to comfort himself in his old age with the thought
that "the sun now constantly finds at least one of our family awake
and at work in the service of the most beautiful of all sciences
[theology]."[5]

I trust that God will give each of us such a grand blessing in
the years that are ahead, if we persevere. And to help us do that,
He has given us a travel song, Psalm 127, to reinvest our twenty-
year assignment with meaning, to calm our anxious fears, and to
keep us journeying on that long road until we stand before Him
in Zion, our children around us.

Chapter 7

Psalm 72:
Mixing Politics and
Religion

1 Endow the king with your justice, O God, the royal son with your righteousness. 2 He will judge your people in righteousness, your afflicted ones with justice. 3 The mountains will bring prosperity to the people, the hills the fruit of righteousness. 4 He will defend the afflicted among the people and save the children of the needy; he will crush the oppressor. 5 He will endure as long as the sun, as long as the moon, through all generations. 6 He will be like rain falling on a mown field, like showers watering the earth. 7 In his days the righteous will flourish; prosperity will abound till the moon is no more. 8 He will rule from sea to sea and from the River to the ends of the earth. 9 The desert tribes will bow before him and his enemies will lick the dust. 10 The kings of Tarshish and of distant shores will bring tribute to him; the kings of Sheba and Seba will present him gifts.
11 All kings will bow down to him and all nations will serve him. 12 For he will deliver the needy who cry out, the afflicted who have no one to help. 13 He will take pity on the weak and the needy and save the needy from death. 14 He will rescue them from oppression and violence, for precious is their blood in his sight. 15 Long may he live! May gold from Sheba be given him. May people ever pray for him and bless him all day long. 16 Let grain abound throughout the land; on the tops of the hills may it sway. Let its fruit flourish like Lebanon; let

it thrive like the grass of the field. 17 May his name endure forever;
may it continue as long as the sun. All nations will be blessed
through him, and they will call him blessed. 18 Praise be to the LORD
God, the God of Israel, who alone does marvelous deeds. 19 Praise be
to his glorious name forever; may the whole earth be filled with his
glory. Amen and Amen.

What Is an Idiot, Anyway?

In August 1987, Pam Shriver of the United States won the Canadian Open Tennis Championship at York University, in Toronto.
In the final, she defeated Chris Evert Lloyd – something she had
not been able to do in eighteen previous meetings throughout
her career. The day after her momentous victory, one of the city
newspapers ran a substantial article on the match, along with a
detailed interview with Ms. Shriver on her political views and
involvement. At one point in the interview, she reportedly observed that she was frustrated by the fact that few of her female
colleagues on the tennis circuit exercised their right to vote. In
response to this inaction, she almost always pointed out to these
colleagues that if they got a government they did not like, they
had yielded all rights to complain. Ancient Greeks would have
heartily agreed with Pam. They called such people *"idiotes"* – too
close for comfort to the familiar English "idiot."

    This interesting bit of information does not at first sight seem
at all relevant to Bible times, when there was little or no democracy. Instead, we read of kings and princes succeeding each other,
sometimes by virtue of dynastic succession and at other times by
force. As for God's people, Rome ruled an extensive kingdom
and Caesar was a demi-god. Elections, and hence voting, were
simply not an issue. But there was another activity prescribed by
God for His people, pertaining to their responsibility to their
human rulers. In the New Testament this is spelled out explicitly
by the Apostle Paul in 1 Timothy 2:1–2: *"I urge, then, first of all,*
that requests, prayers, intercession and thanksgiving be made for eve-
ryone – for kings and all those in authority … ." Paul uses four different words to describe such prayers, so that it is impossible to
miss their importance. In the Old Testament, the exhortation is
implicit in Israel's worship: many of the Psalms were prayers for

their king. So while they couldn't vote, a refusal to pray for those in political authority over them would also qualify them for the epithet "*idiotes*."

That's when it hits home, for even fewer of us pray regularly for our leaders than those who do not vote. I can think of several reasons for what is in fact this blatant disobedience with regard to an inescapable command. The first is *apathy*. Some of us don't pray, period. Others pray but mostly for "me and mine." Theirs is an "I'm all right, Jack! So what's there to worry?" mentality. A second reason is *unbelief*. What difference will it make anyway? goes the thinking here. The polls tell us we're heading downhill rapidly. Besides, that's just a fulfillment of prophecy, isn't it? The Bible tells us that the end times will be marked by godlessness and unbridled evil and that it's bound to get worse before He returns. A third reason is a feeling that *involvement in politics is unspiritual*. After all, our job is to focus on the Gospel and pray for those involved in its propagation. That's more than enough to fill up the available space on our prayer lists, if we have one. If we somehow conquer these three, the fourth one gets us: "*What do I say?* I mean, after praying for their salvation and for Christians to be elected to influential positions, what else is there to say?"

There may be other reasons for our "idiotic" behaviour, but I suspect that the four I have mentioned apply to most of us. Much could be written in rebuttal of the first three, but eventually they must yield to the clear, unequivocal biblical command to pray. So let's key in on the last obstacle – how and what to pray for our political masters. This time it's Psalm 72 that comes to our rescue, helping us to strike the delicate balance between silence and babbling and to bring delight into the discipline of praying for our leaders. The title suggests that it is either a prayer by Solomon, or for him, and it divides naturally into three parts. We begin with the national dimension.

The National Dimension

The opening line of Psalm 72 is "*Endow the king with your justice, O God, the royal son with your righteousness.*" Eastern peoples in those days usually prayed that their gods would make their kings powerful. In sharp contrast, the psalmist prays that God would grant his king justice and righteousness. That is a desperate need for our leaders today. Here in North America, *justice* has been displaced by a subtle yet deadly distortion termed *fairness*. I am indebted to Bill Gothard for an excellent monograph[1] elaborating the distinction between biblical justice and human fairness. Some people might have wished Gothard had not used "fairness" in opposition to the term "justice" (meaning biblical justice). The dictionary defines "fair" as "just, unbiased," so "fair" may not have been the best choice of term. With that caveat, here is a representative extract from Gothard's insights into godly vs. secular justice ("fairness"):

- *Justice* is based on the universal unchangeable principles of God's Word. For example God alone is the giver of life. Therefore no individual has the right to destroy it on his or her own whim. *Fairness* is based on the variable customs of a society and the changing will of the majority. e.g. Fairness laws now give mothers the right to decide whether or not they want their unborn children to live.

- *Justice* establishes God's view of what is essential for a nation to be successful. e.g. God places great value on the life and worth of an individual. He requires punishment for anyone who murders another person. *Fairness* establishes man's view of what is essential for a nation to be successful. e.g. Fairness laws make it legal to kill millions of unborn children, our national heritage; but they bring swift, harsh fines and imprisonment for killing an endangered species such as our national bird, the eagle. [Gothard's examples are for the U.S. In Canada, the equivalent would be the uproar over the clubbing of baby seals to death for their fur while free-standing abortion clinics are legalized. Both are violations of God's Creation, and both are therefore unjust. Gothard goes on to note that "fairness laws will often overreact to parents who spank their children, while neglecting drug pushers and pornographers who violate the morality of those same children." Another example of this sort of misplaced zeal and overreaction crossed my desk a few years ago. I read about a Florida prison inmate who had gone out on a day pass and had managed to smuggle some beer back into jail. He earned an additional sentence of fifteen years – more than if he had been caught breaking out of jail. That's what happens when justice is distorted by a merely human-centred sense of fairness.]

- *Justice* is impartial. It is objective and non-emotional. e.g. the impartiality of justice is expressed by the blindfold on the statue of Justice. God warns that we shouldn't show favoritism to either the rich or the poor. *Fairness* is partial. It is subjective and based on arbitrary emotional considerations. e.g. In trying to enforce traffic laws fairly, a California policeman testified, "I have found that when I attempt to be fair, I inevitably cite those who should have been warned and warn those who should've been cited."

- *Justice* emphasizes personal responsibility. *Fairness* emphasizes personal rights.

That's why the psalmist first prays for justice and links it with righteousness; for while godly justice has to do with what is righteous, fairness has to do with rights. Righteousness in the Scriptures is one dimension of God's central attribute of holiness. It refers to His absolute moral perfection. Justice, in turn, is the form that righteousness takes when it finds expression both in God's relationship to humans and in what He prescribes as being appropriate in our relationships with one another.

North American society is plagued with a preoccupation with rights, which translates to a government that is busy enacting one bill after another, based on protecting someone's or some group's rights. Several years ago, when the Communist government in Vietnam began an ethnic-cleansing purge in their country and created the phenomenon that came to be known as the "boat people," a boatload of 174 refugees who landed on Canadian shores. When authorities confiscated knives from some of them, they immediately began to clamour for their rights. They had been in North America for barely a few hours, and they had already been bitten by the fairness and rights bug. But don't refugees and other disenfranchised people have rights? The psalmist certainly thinks so. Notice how his prayer develops in verses 2 and 4, "*He will judge your people in righteousness, your afflicted ones with justice. He will defend the afflicted among the people and save the children of the needy; he will crush the oppressor.*" Whereas our instinctive idea of justice is expressed in phrases like "one person, one vote" and "everyone must receive their due," the biblical concept is intimately linked with concern for the needy, especially in the law courts, where the poor can be exploited by the rich while unscrupulous judges look away.

In allowing this link to shape his prayers, the psalmist was reflecting a major theme of the biblical prophets as they warned Israel's kings and rulers. Here's a sobering example from Jeremiah

22:3–16: "'*Hear the word of the* LORD, *O king of Judah … Do what is* **just and right.** *Rescue from the hand of his oppressor the one who has been robbed … Woe to him who builds his palace by* **unrighteousness,** *his upper rooms by* **injustice,** *making his countrymen work for nothing, not paying them for their labor … Does it make you a king to have more and more cedar? Did not your father have food and drink? He did what was* **right and just,** *so all went well with him. He defended the cause of the poor and needy, and so all went well. Is that not what it means to know me?' declares the* LORD."

Now what will happen if the king is endowed with this kind of justice and righteousness? The consequences for the nation are spelled out in verse 3: "*The mountains will bring prosperity to the people, the hills the fruit of righteousness.*" According to this verse, prosperity involves more than wealth. It is the word "*shalom,*" which is usually translated as "peace." It literally means "wholeness" – with every part properly related to the others, forming a harmonious whole. Such wholeness is related to righteousness. Applied to a nation, it means that when justice and righteousness mark a ruler, the various parts of a nation are properly related to one another and there is wholeness, integrity, and peace—in a word, "*shalom.*" This implies that when there is no justice and righteousness in a ruler, there is no wholeness in the nation. It inevitably begins to disintegrate on the inside, a threat that no "Star Wars" system can guard against: hence the scriptural declaration that righteousness exalts a nation, while sin is a disgrace to its people.

Even in a democracy, where the moral tone is set by all people, this tone is greatly influenced by those at the "top." In Israel, the king played an even more important role in leading his people to greater or less moral strength. And as for the king himself, consider what justice and righteousness do for him. In verse 5, the psalmist tells us, "*He will endure as long as the sun, as long as the moon, through all generations.*" A just and righteous king will endure. This is not a prediction of immortality for an individual king: it is an assurance that his dynasty will continue even as God promised to David in His Covenant with him in 2 Samuel 7. And each of these dynastic kings – if they are righteous – "*will be like rain falling on a mown field, like showers watering the earth*" (v. 6). Rain on a mown field ensures that future growth will be lush and green. A king marked by justice and righteousness will be like rain that causes a crop of righteousness and prosperity (wholeness) to spring up throughout the nation that he rules.

How does a king bring about justice and righteousness in practical terms? In some cases, it will be *through the salvation of the individual*. (Note that 1 Timothy 2, which contains the command to pray for leaders, goes on to point out that Christ died as a ransom for all sorts of people – including those in authority.) This emphasis has been made, among other things, to dispel the crippling power of unbelief that will stunt our prayers more effectively than anything else. God can save anyone – even kings and powerful politicians. (Remember, for instance, what God has done in and through the life of a man like Charles Colson, former "hatchet-man" in the Nixon administration, involved up to his neck in the Watergate scandal, who converted to Christ as a result of that débâcle.) Even if particular leaders do not come to faith in Christ, God can awaken in them *a sense of the Judæo-Christian ethic* that lies latent and buried deep in the consciousness of many leaders who have strayed from it in their conscious, adult lives. Such awakening often comes through a great tragedy. One personal experience with the lack of justice and righteousness can be enough to shatter twenty years of carefully cultivated political ideology. For example, if a prisoner convicted of rape and assault gets out on good behaviour and ends up attacking a person dear to the ruler, I suspect his views on criminal rehabilitation might change drastically.

At other times, an awareness of justice and righteousness may dawn upon leaders by virtue of *the magnitude of their office*. Two outstanding examples of this in history (one past and one recent) are Thomas à Becket in England in the times of Henry II and Archbishop Oscar Romero of El Salvador in the late twentieth century. Both were appointed to high religious offices to serve the nefarious schemes of their political masters, but the plans backfired in both cases, when they took their callings seriously.

Another powerful tool through which God can influence leaders is that of allowing them to experience true love. The famous Swiss Christian doctor Paul Tournier points out that a remarkable number of world political leaders over the past few centuries have been orphans, which suggests that behind their great drive and hunger for power lies a deep need to be loved.

Christians who are already involved in politics form another prime channel through which God sends justice and righteousness. Christians in politics need to be not only loving but also courageous. In his book *A Reasonable Faith*, Tony Campolo points out a significant distinction between power and authority, which should set Christian politicians apart from non-Christians. A powerful person makes other people do what he or she wants them to do, regardless of whether they want it or not; one with authority, on the other hand, awakens within others the desire to follow in his or her footsteps. Jesus, Mother Theresa, and Martin Luther King, Jr., provide Campolo with three remarkable illustrations of authority, as opposed to raw power.[2] However difficult it is, Christians in politics must refuse to grasp for power, reaching, instead, for authority that comes from moral purity and serving their unbelieving colleagues sacrificially. In this way, they may well become channels through which this deep-seated desire for love will be met, and the hearts of non-believers may be opened to the love of justice and righteousness.

By now, it must be obvious that the writer of Psalm 72 is making sure we never have to run out of meaningful words when praying for our leaders. It gives us a framework within which to place specific issues of the day and helps us as we pray for specific rulers.

Prayer Guide

Choose a specific ruler or group of rulers (at the municipal, provincial, state, or national level). If there are natural ties to the ruler (or the geographical region for which the ruler is responsible), it will make your prayers that much more heartfelt.

1. Pray that God will endow our rulers with justice and righteousness through their *salvation*.

2. For those not saved, pray that they will see *the connection between their justice and righteousness* and the value of their work, that they don't have to depend on giving political handouts to their supporters, that they do not need to pander to interest groups; that true prosperity is related to wholeness through righteousness. We may need to be daring in this phase of our praying. (Remember the possible role of tragedy. Certainly we can't play God in their lives, but we can ask God to be God and ordain whatever He deems necessary to awaken them to act with justice and righteousness.)

3. Pray that some of them *might be suddenly overwhelmed by the nobility of their office* like Romero and Becket.

4. Pray that our rulers *may experience genuine love* through Christians in politics. Pray that these Christians will reach for authority, not power, and then pray that they will have open doors to the homes and lives of their non-Christian colleagues. Then, finally, pray that they will be courageous to share their faith, model righteousness, speak out for justice, and serve in love.

5. Pray that our rulers might have *compassion for the poor and needy*. Pray for the enactment of legislation that will ensure justice for the poor and the rich alike and for judges to be courageous and compassionate enough not to be influenced by those who have the wealth and the power to pervert justice. Notice the emphasis in verse 4 on *"the children of the needy."* How often are children the ones most affected by the lack of justice and righteousness in our law courts and halls of legislation? How often do they grow up to become tomorrow's delinquents? Pray for rulers to have the wisdom to enact legislation and direct public spending such that it will help break the cycle of poverty and set the children of the needy free.

The International Dimension

In addition to ruling Israel, her king had another important function. He was to represent Jehovah to His people and to the surrounding pagan nations. Solomon, at least in the early stages of his rule, exemplified this aspect of the Israelite monarchy better than any other king. As his fame and the splendour of his achievements spread to other nations, their kings and queens came to visit him: *"King Solomon was greater in riches and wisdom than all the other kings of the earth. The whole world sought audience with Solomon to hear the wisdom God had put in his heart"* (1 Kings 10:23–24). The result was that they went away with a clearer picture of the blessedness of a nation whose God was Jehovah. This comes through most clearly in the tribute paid by the Queen of Sheba after she had spent some time visiting Solomon: *"She said to the king, 'The report I heard in my own country about your achievements and your wisdom is true. But I did not believe these things until I came and saw with my own eyes. Indeed, not even half was told me; in wisdom and wealth you have far exceeded the report I heard. How happy your men must be! How happy your officials, who continually stand before you and hear your wisdom! Praise be to the LORD your God, who has delighted in you and placed you on the throne of Israel. Because of the LORD's eternal love for Israel, he has made you king, to maintain* **justice and righteousness'"** (1 Kings 10:6–9). (Notice the reference to justice and righteousness, the subject of the first part of the psalmist's prayer).

That is why, in verses 8–11, we find the psalmist praying for a continuation of the king's global fame: "*He will rule from sea to sea and from the River to the ends of the earth. The desert tribes will bow before him and his enemies will lick the dust. The kings of Tarshish and of distant shores will bring tribute to him; the kings of Sheba and Seba will present him gifts. All kings will bow down to him and all nations will serve him.*" And why will the kings of the nations honour Israel's monarch? The psalmist tells us in verses 12–14: "*For he will deliver the needy who cry out, the afflicted who have no one to help. He will take pity on the weak and the needy and save the needy from death. He will rescue them from oppression and violence, for precious is their blood in his sight.*" Israel's king pities the needy and works for the release of their oppression not only in his own country, but in other countries, too. That's why they will end up calling him blessed: "*All nations will be blessed through him, and they will call him blessed*" (v. 17b). Isn't that a perspective our leaders here in North America desperately need to recover? That the route to true blessedness and an international reputation is having compassion for the needy of the world.

Have you ever wondered why a Sovereign God has allowed the Western nations, and especially North America, to be so disproportionately wealthy that most of us don't even realize how incredible the gap is? We bathe and wash in water that is cleaner than the drinking water in many "developing" and "underdeveloped" nations. Why, when many other nations are battling double- and even triple-digit inflation, do we chug along year after year at well below 10 percent (and not much above that, even at our worst)? I am not an economist and will therefore offer no answers from that perspective. But I can make reasonably educated guesses from a theological point of view. At least part of the reason for their prosperity (if we look at centuries and not just years) is that in the past, the Western nations have been rooted in a Judaeo-Christian ethic and have therefore reaped the blessing of God materially as nations.

Psalm 72 suggests a second reason for our disproportionate wealth. We may have wealth as a nation so that we can be compassionate toward the needy and oppressed of the world and be in a position to put "teeth" to our compassion, so to speak. The executive branches of our governments need to grasp this, because they are the ones to whom power has been delegated to make economic decisions on an international scale. Consider a group like CIDA (Canadian International Development Agency), which authorizes the release of funds to developing countries, especially in an emergency, but also for long-term relief projects. In some cases, these are outright grants, and in other cases, they offer to match every dollar raised by non-governmental relief agencies like World Relief and World Vision according to a 1:1, a 3:1, or even a 10:1 ratio.

Then there are international agreements like those negotiated under the World Trade Organization, which deal with such things as how much duty we will charge on goods imported from other countries – usually in order to protect our own indigenous industries. Certainly a balance is needed between national considerations and global needs. However, greedily and selfishly slapping huge duties on goods manufactured in Third World countries to increase domestic profits even further usually jerks the rug out from under the economies of developing nations desperately trying to raise their people's profits to mere subsistence level. While I am not in a position to debate the economics of such issues (nor is it the purpose of this exposition to do so), certainly those who make such decisions in the Western world need a good dose of compassion for the needy. That is something we can pray for, along with the psalmist.

Prayer Guide

1. Pray that our leaders will:
   - see the real purpose of our superabundance,
   - become people of compassion who will develop an international conscience,
   - see the connection between such compassion and a worthy international reputation.
2. Pray for leaders of relief agencies (choose one with whom you may already be involved):

- for open doors to contact and speak with our political
  leaders and for wisdom and authority in such sessions,
- for their own efforts to be dominated by the perspective of
  Psalm 72 (i.e., a passion for justice and righteousness, and
  compassion for the poor and needy).

3. Pray for bureaucrats who make economic aid decisions (e.g.,
   CIDA officials) and pray that God will lead Christian men and
   women to key positions in such offices.

4. Finally, with such a perspective well established, we can freely
   and without any hint of embarrassment or greed, pray for
   continued abundance in our own land: *"Let grain abound
   throughout the land; on the tops of the hills may it sway. Let its
   fruit flourish like Lebanon; let it thrive like the grass of the
   field"* (Psalm 72:16).

Sounds good so far, but doesn't it all seem somewhat unrealistic? Faced with the flow of history as we know it today and with the magnitude and nature of both national and international problems, doesn't the psalmist's prayer seem wildly optimistic? That takes us to the grand climax of the psalmist's prayer.

The Divine Perspective

The same King Solomon who began by exemplifying the psalmist's ideals finished deplorably as far as justice and righteousness were concerned. His sons were so much worse that in their time, Solomon's kingdom split into two, Israel and Judah, both of which were eventually conquered. Assyria demolished Israel, and Babylon conquered Judah. According to the Old Testament prophets (Hosea and Jeremiah in particular), one of the main reasons in both cases was their total lack of compassion for the needy and for justice in the law courts. In both nations, the rich and influential actively oppressed the poor. So if any community would have had a reason to look with skepticism at a prayer like Psalm 72, it would be the community of Judah exiled in Babylon. They, of all people, should have discarded it as the pious, but totally unrealistic, wishes of a sentimental monarchist of a bygone era. Not so. The Psalm was preserved, handed down to succeeding generations, and used in Israel's worship. The reason? The original author of the Psalm did not know it, but even as he was composing this prayer for an earthly king, the Holy Spirit had taken hold of him and was widening its applicability to another king altogether. So what began as a prayer turned into prophecy, that this king *will rule* in justice and righteousness, that *He will deliver* the poor and needy, that *He will ... , He will ... .* Godly people in Israel slowly began to see this. Sure, most of their earthly kings had failed to measure up to the Psalm's lofty standard, but another king was coming – the promised son of David – who would fulfill the ideal perfectly.

We who live under the New Covenant know that they were right. King Jesus did come. And was He not endowed with a perfect sense of justice? Was this sense of justice not rooted in His flawless righteousness? Was anyone more compassionate toward the poor? Who else could be like rain on a freshly mown field? Did He not bring life – abundant life – to wasted bodies and souls? Is His Kingdom not enduring today as He, exalted by God the Father at the resurrection, waits for Him to make His enemies His footstool? Was not the secret of His sway over men due to the fact that their lives were precious to Him? Did not people marvel at His authority like no one else's? Has He not inspired incredible acts of loyalty and courage in human hearts for two thousand years? And will He not one day have worldwide dominion?

This legitimate interpretation of Psalm 72 as prophecy does not negate its primary function as a model prayer for our human leaders. Paul's exhortation to, first of all, pray for leaders and all those in authority is a New Testament command given after the resurrection and ascension of Christ. And it is precisely because of the perfect fulfillment of this Psalm in Christ and His present reign in justice and righteousness that we can resist the temptation to pessimism and keep praying along the lines I have indicated in the Prayer Guide.

Consider verses 18 and 19: "*Praise be to the LORD God, the God of Israel, who alone does marvelous deeds. Praise be to his glorious name forever; may the whole earth be filled with his glory. Amen and Amen.*" Verse 18 reminds us that only God can do marvellous deeds – among them the many wonderful deeds we have asked Him to perform in our prayers for our leaders. That's why the political teaching of this Psalm is set in the context of a prayer and is included in a worship manual for God's people. Verse 19 takes this one step further by underlining the ultimate purpose of peace through justice, righteousness, and compassion for the poor – that the whole earth may be filled with His glory.

We have ample evidence that sensitive and compassionate aid to the poor and oppressed in other nations is one of the most effective door openers for the proclamation of the Gospel. In the 1980s, World Relief Canada was involved in a long-term project of digging wells in a drought-stricken country in West Africa. A subsequent issue of World Relief's monthly magazine included a testimony by a native pastor after one of these wells was completed and fresh water was distributed to many people through the church in one area:

> It was truly a work of God. It was a good testimony for the church here in the village. We had prayed for God to provide water for all the village. All the non-Christians knew we were praying that way. Other groups have come along before and promised to help us with our need for water. They left and never came back. World Relief said they would help us and they did what they promised. And they did it in the name of Jesus. It was God's answer to our prayers. All of the village realizes that. The credibility of the church was at stake, and now the testimony of the church and of Christ here has been strengthened [Pastor Amahiru Saye].[3]

Nor is this an isolated incident. At the time of the drought in Mali, the political situation in the Philippines was extremely unstable. Reg Reimer, then director of World Relief, offered this analysis in yet another Word Relief bulletin.

> So while the city people just talk of politics, the real battle is being waged in the countryside. It's a battle over control of the poor. For whoever gets control of this major segment of the population, will eventually get control of the country. ... [The] long term future will ... be decided by who can win the hearts of the oppressed. Filipino Christians have no doubt about what their job is. They know they must reach out to the suffering in Jesus' name.[4]

Governing in justice, righteousness, and compassion for the needy here and in other countries truly accelerates the universal spread of God's glory. One final observation before we return to the Prayer Guide. In our exposition of Psalm 72 up to this point, we have not addressed verse 15 – especially the latter half: *"Long may he live! May gold from Sheba be given him. **May people ever pray for him and bless him all day long.**"* Interesting, isn't it, that prayer for the king includes a request that many will pray for him. Evidently, the psalmist recognized, as he was influenced by the Holy Spirit, that praying for leaders wouldn't win him any popularity contests. It will take nothing less than God's power at work in His people's hearts to convince them to take this responsibility seriously and stop being *"idiotes."* With that, we are ready for the final segment of our prayer, shaped by Psalm 72.

Prayer Guide

1. Take a few moments to *"**praise the Lord** who alone does marvelous deeds"* (v. 18). If the magnitude of the issues and problems you have been praying for has opened the door for pessimism to sneak in, it's time to look up. Sing hymns like "Jesus Shall Reign," "God of Our Fathers," "The Battle Hymn of the Republic," and "A Mighty Fortress Is Our God." Thank Him that He is indeed *"able to do immeasurably more than all we ask or imagine, according to his power that is at work within us"* (Ephesians 3:20).

2. Then choose a specific country where poverty, oppression, and natural disasters have rendered the plight of many truly pitiful. (If you are involved in supporting a specific relief effort, take out the organization's latest newsletter. It will help your prayers be that much more specific.) Then pray:

   • that the poor will be open to the demonstration of compassion through relief workers,

   • that God would raise up workers for the various relief organizations who are compassionate and who love justice and righteousness,

   • that God would intervene and destroy every effort by political rebels who oppose relief work, especially in Jesus' name. (The head of a Filipino relief organization a few years ago was found to be on the hit list of a guerrilla group with political aspirations.)

As we pray, there is no telling what God will accomplish. William Wilberforce was a great Christian philanthropist and vigorous opponent of the slave trade in England during the late eighteenth century. As he surveyed the terrible moral and spiritual climate of his day, he did not lose hope. And what was the reason for that hope? It lay in his conviction that his country was still graced by many who loved and obeyed Jesus' Gospel. He believed in the effectiveness of their prayers. Within a few years after he made a statement to that effect, the country he loved experienced one of the greatest revivals in modern times, bringing salvation to thousands and producing widespread social changes.[5] Let us conclude like the psalmist: Amen and Amen. So be it, Lord.

Chapter 8

Easter Music:
A Medley Based on
Psalms 2, 110, and 118

Psalm 2:1–7

1 *Why do the nations conspire and the peoples plot in vain?*
2 *The kings of the earth take their stand and the rulers gather together*
against the LORD *and against his Anointed One.* 3 *"Let us break their*
chains," they say, "and throw off their fetters." 4 *The One enthroned*
in heaven laughs; the LORD *scoffs at them.* 5 *Then he rebukes them in*
his anger and terrifies them in his wrath, saying,
6 *"I have installed my King on Zion, my holy hill."* 7 *I will proclaim*
the decree of the LORD: *He said to me, "You are my Son; today I have*
become your Father."

Psalm 110:1–3

1 *The* LORD *says to my Lord: "Sit at my right hand until I make*
your enemies a footstool for your feet." 2 *The* LORD *will extend*
your mighty scepter from Zion; you will rule in the midst of your
enemies. 3 *Your troops will be willing on your day of battle.*
Arrayed in holy majesty, from the womb of the dawn you will
receive the dew of your youth.

Psalm 2:8–12

8 *"Ask of me, and I will make the nations your inheritance, the ends of the earth your possession. 9 You will rule them with an iron scepter; you will dash them to pieces like pottery." 10 Therefore, you kings, be wise; be warned, you rulers of the earth. 11 Serve the L*ORD *with fear and rejoice with trembling. 12 Kiss the Son, lest he be angry and you be destroyed in your way, for his wrath can flare up in a moment. Blessed are all who take refuge in him.*

Psalm 110:4–7

4 *The L*ORD *has sworn and will not change his mind: "You are a priest forever, in the order of Melchizedek." 5 The L*ORD *is at your right hand; he will crush kings on the day of his wrath. 6 He will judge the nations, heaping up the dead and crushing the rulers of the whole earth. 7 He will drink from a brook beside the way; therefore he will lift up his head.*

Psalm 118:22–24

22 *The stone the builders rejected has become the capstone; 23 the L*ORD *has done this, and it is marvelous in our eyes. 24 This is the day the L*ORD *has made; let us rejoice and be glad in it.*

A First-Century "Hit Parade"

I don't remember who said it or where I read it, but I've never forgotten the words "Let me write the songs of a nation and I don't care who writes its laws." The author realized that music, combined with poetry, has a far greater influence on human behaviour than mere verbal, propositional truths or rules and regulations. Philosopher Allan Bloom expands on that thesis: "Music or poetry, which is what music becomes as reason emerges, always involves a delicate balance between passion and reason; and, even in its highest and most developed forms, that balance is always tipped, if ever so slightly, towards the passionate. Music, as everyone experiences, provides an unquestionable justification … for the activities it accompanies. The soldier who hears the marching band is enthralled and reassured, the religious man is exalted in his prayers by the sound of the organ in the church and the lover is carried away and his conscience stilled by the romantic guitar. Armed with music, man can damn rational doubt. Out of the music emerge the gods that suit it."[1] And if that is true of all music and poetry, imagine the energizing and motivating power of music whose lyrics also happen to cohere with what we believe verbally and propositionally. Therein lies the power of sacred lyrics set to music.

As with all music, we have favourites in the sacred realm, too. Some are year-round favourites; others are especially associated with the festive seasons of our faith, like Christmas and Easter. But what would happen if our selections had to be limited to the prayer book known as the Psalms? They are Hebrew poems, inspired by the Holy Spirit, which have been set to music and sung throughout the centuries in all kinds of Christian cultures. Which ones would make our "Top Ten" list? I suspect Psalm 23 would be Number 1, and with good reason. Those wonderful words, which affirm the presence of the Lord with us at all times, have brought incredible solace and comfort to people in sickness and especially when nearing death. But if we look at the New Testament to identify the favourite Psalms of the early church, we will be in for a real surprise. When I surveyed the footnotes in my New Testament, I discovered that only 38 out of 150 Psalms are quoted, of which a mere 10 are quoted more than once. Yet 3 of these 10, taken together, are quoted over 25 times. What were these three Psalms? Why were they such favourites of the early church? And why should we bother with such questions anyway? After all, tastes in music and poetry are extremely subjective. Nevertheless, first-century believers obviously preferred some Psalms much more than others. What is so distinctive about their choices?

Let me address the last question first. New Testament times were incredibly difficult for the early church. As Eugene Peterson has written: "Massive engines of persecution and scorn were arrayed against them. They had neither weapons nor votes. They had little money and no prestige. Why didn't they have mental breakdowns? Why didn't they cut and simply run? They prayed."[2] And the songs (prayers set to music) that they repeatedly turned to were Psalms 2, 110, and 118. Today, here in North America, we perhaps do not face massive engines of persecution; but scorn is another matter altogether.

During the Clinton years, for instance, a Focus on the Family newsletter pointed out that when Christians called Capitol Hill to object to President Clinton's goal of lifting the "homosexual ban" in the armed forces, one newspaper called these Christians "poor, uneducated and easy to command." Focus on the Family also referred to a political cartoon of the same year that showed fundamentalist Christian rats dragging a Republican elephant into a mission with a "Jesus Saves" sign above the door. In both cases, Christians were being depicted in ways that would likely have generated public outcry if they'd been used to characterize another minority or religious group.[3]

The massive weapons of scorn are indeed arrayed against us just as certainly as they were trained on our New Testament counterparts. What can sustain us as we face this kind of opposition? Not mere adherence to theological propositions, even though they may be accurate and necessary. We also need some battle songs: poetry and music that will capture our imaginations and catapult us into the middle of the fray, to fight with courage and perseverance. It is therefore imperative for us to understand those three battle songs that enabled the early Christians – faced with those massive weapons of persecution and scorn – to keep living obediently and victoriously.

For starters, Psalm 23 wasn't one of them. It isn't quoted even once in the entire New Testament. That was a revelation to me when I first realized it. The three at the top of their list of favourites were Psalm 2, Psalm 110, and Psalm 118. And to help us understand their significance for the early church and their relevance to us, I have rearranged them in a medley, as musicians often do with songs. Our medley begins with the opening verses of Psalm 2: "*Why do the nations conspire and the peoples plot in vain? The kings of the earth take their stand and the rulers gather together against the* LORD *and against his Anointed One. 'Let us break their chains,' they say, 'and throw off their fetters.'*"

The Opposition

Notice, first of all, the vivid picture of the opposition. They are raging: they are an *angry* group. They are plotting: they are a *strategic* group. They gather together: they are a *united* group. They take their stand: they are a *determined* group. They have kings on their side: they are a *powerful* group. Finally, they include the nations and the peoples: they are a *numerous* group. Taken together, this is a graphic portrayal of a formidable opposition: an angry, determined, united, strategic, powerful, and numerous group.

Our opposition today can be similarly characterized. Consider, for example, all those places in the world where Christians are being persecuted explicitly for their loyalty to Jesus Christ as the only and supreme Lord. Moreover, the oppressor's worldview (often, but not necessarily, their religion) provides transcendental justification for such persecution. Such activity is exactly what was happening in Psalm 2: attacking God's people because they stood for radical submission and loyalty to God's order. Such persecution is currently happening in my own country of origin (India), as well as in various Middle and Far Eastern countries. Sudan and China are terrifying examples. These six adjectives from Psalm 2 describe the persecutors to the proverbial "T": angry, united, strategic, determined, powerful, and numerous. These words also characterize some of the *militant*, and I emphasize militant, gay and abortion rights activists who are motivated in their convictions and lifestyle choices by a deliberate rejection of God's Word and are, in fact, ready to express hostility toward God, His Word, and the followers of the Lord Jesus Christ. (I am not at all speaking of many individuals who struggle with their homosexual orientations and others who may have actually had abortions in the past. They are most certainly not the enemies of Psalm 2.) What happens whenever a judge at any level in the judiciary system denies one of their requests? What do they always say? "We'll be back." They are absolutely determined. As for strategy, once President Clinton declared his intention to remove remaining roadblocks to gays serving in the armed forces, the *Washington Times* reported that a coalition of gay rights groups had prepared a broadened agenda of new policies to impose on the armed forces when the military ban is actually lifted. This thirteen-point plan would require the Pentagon to conduct programs for all heterosexual military personnel to ensure their acceptance of gays and lesbians.[4]

Who are the activists raging against? According to Psalm 2, they are raging against the Lord and His Anointed One. The reason for their rage? *"Let us break their chains, let us throw off their fetters."* They rage against Jesus Christ and His chosen representatives because they, together, represent the law of God; and groups like those described above find the law of God oppressive, like a chain that shackles them. Hence their one desire, "Let's throw off these chains." Nothing has changed in millennia.

Laughter

So how do we respond when we have numerous powerful, angry, united, strategic, and determined groups arrayed against us? Psalm 2 continues: *"The One enthroned in heaven laughs; the LORD scoffs at them."* We look up from earth to heaven, and to our surprise, even shock, we hear laughter. Now laughter is something that comes from a changed perspective. The punch line of a joke is exactly that: an unexpected juxtaposition of two divergent streams of thought or events. It also happens in life.

I remember an incident when my wife and her sister were teenagers, fresh immigrants to Canada. They were returning home by bus after an evening at college. It was late at night, and there were three people left on the bus, the two of them and one rather suspicious-looking individual, also evidently an immigrant. When they got up to ring the bell to stop the bus, he got up too. When they discovered it was the wrong stop and sat down again, so did he. When they did get to the right stop and disembarked, the man followed suit. By now, they were getting really nervous, so they quickened their steps. They could hear his steps pick up speed as well. At this point, they panicked and started running. So did he, and by now it was clear that he was running after them. They managed to reach their house a few scant steps ahead of him. Hearts pounding, they slammed the door shut and breathed a prayer of thanks. The next day, they happened to lock themselves out of their home and needed to make a phone call, so they knocked on their neighbour's door. Who should answer but their nocturnal pursuer! Apparently, that night on the bus, he had forgotten where he lived, but he had recognized my wife and her sister as his neighbours. Naturally, he did not want to lose sight of them. Hence, his seemingly alarming pursuit. The girls, faces flushed with embarrassment, forgot their original mission and returned home post haste. Today they laugh about the story, and so does everyone who hears it. How can the circumstances that once made hearts pound now call forth laughter? The radically different reaction comes as a result of a changed perspective.

That's the precise transition we find between verse 3 and verse 4 in Psalm 2. Down here on earth, massive engines of scorn are arrayed against us. But up there in heaven there is a radically different perspective: God laughs. And why does He laugh? Let's get His perspective. He looks down on the angry, strategic, determined, united, numerous, and powerful opponents of His law and His people and *"rebukes them in his anger and terrifies them in his wrath, saying, 'I have installed my King on Zion.'"* You have your kings and rulers – that's fine – but I have my own King who is installed on Zion, and that King says, *"I will proclaim the decree of the LORD concerning me."* What is that decree? *"You are my Son; today I have become your Father."*

While this promise was immediately applicable to King David (see 2 Samuel 7 for the details), the early church interpreted this decree as a prophecy that was fulfilled on resurrection morning, when God wiped out the ignominy of the crucifixion by giving His final verdict on who Jesus Christ really was. He raised Jesus up to His right hand and crowned Him King of kings and Lord of lords. Therefore God laughs. And the laughter says in effect, "It doesn't matter how massive, how impressive, how united, how strategic, how determined, how powerful you are, I have a King, and He reigns today; because of that, all your opposition is doomed in advance to be in vain."

Two small words, six letters in all, but what a difference they make: *"in vain." "Why do the nations conspire and the peoples plot in vain?"* The very verses that describe the opposition contain the kernel of the answer. All opposition against God and His Anointed servants is guaranteed to be in vain, because Jesus Christ has risen from the dead. So the first thing we need to do when we feel these massive engines of scorn and persecution arrayed against us is to look up into the heavens and listen to the laughter of Him who says, "I have installed my King on Zion. He is my Son and I am His Father." In practice, we don't hear an actual laugh. But

we do break through to a changed perspective by focusing on
God's absolute sovereignty against all opposition and Christ's
present reign as ascended king.

Prayer Guide

1. Take a few moments to list a specific individual(s) or group(s)
   whose opposition might be characterized by one of these six
   adjectives: determined, strategic, angry, united, powerful, or
   numerous. Remember that this opposition must be because of
   your commitment to Jesus Christ and His laws. It might be a
   personal opponent, one that the Church of Jesus Christ faces, or
   one that a missionary friend may be facing in his or her field of
   labour. Jot down what the enemies' key strategies might be to
   achieve their ends and the defeat of Jesus' people. Spread out
   that list before Almighty God and ask the Holy Spirit to guide
   you in an appropriate prayer response as you work your way
   through the rest of the chapter.

2. Take time to listen to God's laughter.

   • Read Isaiah 44:24–46:13. Don't analyze the passage; try
     instead to catch the mood – the irresistible decree of the
     Sovereign Jehovah and the futility of mere mortal attempts
     to resist His will for His people.

   • Sing one or two of your favourite ascension hymns that
     portray Christ seated on His throne now. "Christ Arose,"
     "Rejoice, the Lord Is King," and "See the Conqueror Mounts
     in Triumph" are three that I find most effective in making
     God's laughter audible. As the various images, poetically
     juxtaposed, stir your heart, pause to respond in praise and
     gratitude. The last hymn in particular (sung to the tune of
     "Joyful, Joyful, We Adore Thee") conjures up powerful
     imagery indeed.

> See the Conqueror mounts in triumph,
>   See the King in royal state
> Riding on the clouds His chariot
>   To His heavenly palace gate;
> Hark! The choirs of angel voices
>   Joyful alleluias sing,
> And the portals high are lifted
>   To receive their heavenly King.

Who is this that comes in glory,
    With the trump of jubilee?
Lord of battles, God of armies,
    He has gained the victory;
He who on the cross did suffer,
    He who from the grave arose,
He has vanquished sin and Satan,
    He by death has spoiled His foes.

Now our heavenly Aaron enters,
    With His blood within the veil;
Joshua now is come to Canaan,
    And the kings before Him quail;
Now He plants the tribes of Israel
    In their promised resting place;
Now our great Elijah offers
    Double portion of His grace.

He has raised our human nature
    On the clouds to God's right hand;
There we sit in heavenly places,
    There with Him in glory stand.
Jesus reigns, adored by angels;
    Man with God is on the throne;
Mighty Lord, in Thine ascension
    We by faith behold our own.[5]

Longsuffering

Now someone might object, "Well, if God is sovereign, if Christ reigns now, why doesn't He once in a while show us His power? Why do the opposition forces seem to be winning all the time? Victory after victory in their case and defeat after defeat in our case stifles whatever laughter I do hear in the heavens. In fact, it is Satan who seems to be laughing at us, and his laugh is all too audible." A pertinent question indeed. Hence the need for the second Psalm on their "hit parade," Psalm 110. It begins this way: *"The LORD says to my Lord: 'Sit at my right hand until I make your enemies a footstool for your feet.'"*

    The affirmation that Jesus is sitting at God's right hand doesn't mean that there are two chairs up there somewhere in heaven with Jesus sitting in a chair on the right-hand side of God the

Father. It is a metaphor we use regularly. When we say, "So-and-so is his or her right-hand man," it simply means that if you want to get to the "boss," there is no point trying to contact him or her directly: you have to go through the right-hand man. If that person doesn't give you the okay, you won't be able to get through. In other words, the boss's only contact with the outside world is through the person at his or her right hand. That's the way it is with Jesus Christ and God. God relates to everything outside of Him through His right-hand man, Jesus Christ. This is an indication of His exalted position, which He assumed at His ascension. So the starting point of Psalm 110 underlines the truth of Psalm 2 – that God has established Jesus as king. That is foundational, and repetition served to drive the point home to the souls of the New Testament worshipping community. Psalm 110 then proceeds to build on this foundation.

The fact that Jesus reigns in heaven today doesn't necessarily mean that the reign has been universally applied and translated into reality in this world. If the key phrase in Psalm 2 was "*in vain*," an important word here is "*until*": "*Sit at my right hand until I make your enemies a footstool.*" Sometimes, maybe often, we interpret God's apparent inactivity as either lack of concern or lack of power. Neither is right, for God is not only Sovereign, He is also longsuffering. Our God waits in patience, grace, and mercy, even demonstrating these qualities to those who are raging against Him. Then they might realize that their rebellion is in vain, that all their strategies are futile, that they can repent and eventually bow down to Him. What if they do not? That's where the "until" kicks in. There is coming a day when all of Christ's enemies will become His footstool – a day called "The day of His wrath." Verses 5 and 6 describe that day: "*The LORD is at your right hand; he will crush kings on the day of his wrath. He will judge the nations, heaping up the dead and crushing the rulers of the whole earth.*" There is coming a day when the longsuffering of God will reach its limit. On that day, His patience will run out, the "day of grace" will be over, and His holy wrath will be revealed against all ungodliness and unrighteousness. Just as the strain energy that is currently building up in the San Andreas Fault in California will one day be released explosively, perhaps plunging a considerable chunk of California into the Pacific, the day of His wrath is coming. And the encouraging truth is that God's victory does not depend on us. Psalm 110:1 begins like this: "*The LORD says to my Lord,*" indicating that the promise of conquest is one that God the Father has made to the resurrected and ascended Lord Jesus Christ, His Son. That means we can't mess it up; we can't "blow it" in any way. The eventual reign of Jesus Christ is as certain as God's promise to His Son, guaranteed by the resurrection and ascension. Not only did the early Christians use Psalm 2 to hear the laughter of God; they also sang Psalm 110 to be infected with confidence in the longsuffering of God and the certainty of Christ's eventual conquest.

Labourers for the Vineyard

Once this certainty of Christ's conquest begins to grip us, we are galvanized into action. Psalm 110 continues, in verses 2 and 3: "*The LORD will extend your mighty scepter from Zion; you will rule in the midst of your enemies. Your troops will be willing on your day of battle. Arrayed in holy majesty, from the womb of the dawn you will receive the dew of your youth.*" We rise from prayer and go to battle. We are not involved in the certainty of Christ's eventual visible conquest of His enemies (that is a promise made by the Father to the Son), but we are involved in the translation and progressive realization of Christ's present heavenly reign down here upon earth. We, His followers, become part of His battle troops – and in this particular army, there are no conscripts or draft dodgers. The Psalm says, "*Your troops will be willing on your day of battle. Your young men will come to you like the dew.*" What a fresh image! The scholars tell us that the precise interpretation of the Hebrew in this verse is indefinite, but the praying imagination can easily relish the image. The rising of the early morning sun sometimes reveals ground covered with dew – fresh, extensive, and pervasive – and this image, says God to His beloved Son, is like His armies. "Faced with an opposition that is angry, strategic, determined, united, powerful and numerous, you, my Son, won't have to go running after draft dodgers, you won't have to twist any arms. Your troops will come to you, numerous, fresh, and willing." What's the secret? Verse 3 tells us: "*Arrayed in holy majesty, you will receive them.*"

Three factors conspire to produce this willing, plentiful response to the call to arms against a formidable foe. Christians are realists. They do not pretend that everything is nice, that "by faith everything is okay." No! They take a good hard look at the massive engines of persecution and scorn arrayed against them. They acknowledge that the opposition is angry, united, strategic, determined, numerous, and powerful. Then they look up and hear the *laughter* of God, which puts these opponents in a new perspective; they look up and hear *the certainty of God's promise to Christ*, which gives birth to a holy optimism; they look up and see the majesty of Christ and they say, "It's worth it. With such a glorious Captain at our head, we'll come and fight." That's the way God extends Christ's mighty sceptre from Zion so He can rule in the midst of His enemies (v. 3). It is the laughter of God, the certainty of Christ's eventual conquest, and the majesty of the Conqueror that enlists willing, holy, and obedient troops for battle.

Unusual Weapons

Next question? How do these troops fight? Do they take on the strategy of the opposition? Do they resort to gossip, slander, angry slogans, and abusive epithets shouted across picket lines? Do they even perpetrate violence, as in the lamentable case of an anti-abortionist who shot an abortionist-doctor dead? Are these the strategies that King Jesus' troops should follow on the battlefield? No! Our Captain sets the example. We fight as He did. Let's move back to Psalm 2: *"Ask of me,"* says God to the King He has installed in Zion, *"ask of me and I will make the nations your inheritance."* And then He speaks, *"Therefore you kings, be wise: be warned, you rulers of the earth. Serve the LORD with fear and rejoice with trembling."* Here the anointed King is represented as *praying and asking His Father* to give Him the nations as His inheritance. In light of the teaching of the New Testament, especially the Epistle to the Hebrews, we see this as the intercessory ministry of Jesus Christ. Then, having asked His Father, He addresses the kings who are rebelling against Him. This is the ministry of the *proclamation of the Living Word*, which Jesus also confirms by His ongoing intercessory ministry for His soldiers. These are the two very things that God's troops are intended to use in battle in order to extend the sceptre of the King: *prayer* and *proclamation*. They pray to God because of His Word, which portrays Christ as interceding for the nations. Then they proclaim that Word to the nations.

To dispel any concern that this is merely one man's fanciful interpretation of how Psalm 2 guides our battle strategy, read Acts 4:23–31. After Peter and John's arrest and examination by the Sanhedrin, they were warned by the rulers and authorities of that day (the very same groups of people mentioned in Psalm 2) not to preach in Jesus' name, under threat of severe persecution. What did Paul and John do then? They went to the church and told them about the rulers' decision. And what did the gathered church do? Did they call a temporary halt to all proceedings while they devised a new strategy? No! They worshipped and prayed, and in their prayer, they began with an affirmation of the Sovereignty of God in creation and revelation. And which particular part of God's revelation did they turn to? Psalm 2 – our battle song. No doubt they reminded themselves of the very truths we have been learning so far. They looked up into heaven and heard the laughter of God, which reminded them that their former rebellion against God's chosen servant King David had been in vain.

Then they called to mind how kings, other rulers, Gentiles, and Israel (the same four groups identified in Psalm 2) had recently rebelled against Jesus, the true Son of David, and how that rebellion had also proved to be in vain. This assured them that the current threat by the Sanhedrin would also be in vain. Then they asked God for specifics. They moved from praise to intercession: "Lord, you promised Christ the nation as His inheritance. We are now asking you for the nations." They asked God for boldness to preach the Word, which if you recall, was the second arm of the strategy spelled out in Psalm 2: *pray* on the basis of God's Word and then *proclaim* that Word. Then they asked God to confirm that preaching with signs, wonders, and miracles.

Having prayed, they proclaimed the Word. That's how they fought the Sanhedrin: with praise and intercessory prayer, which filled them with boldness to continue preaching and healing. In other words, bolstered by praise and prayer, they continued to do exactly the things that had got them into trouble with the Sanhedrin in the first place. The result? Acts records that great power and great grace was upon them, and hundreds of people responded. Thus God extends the sceptre of Christ in the midst of His enemies then and now.

Prayer Guide

1. Look up to heaven again and dwell on His longsuffering. Pray for the individuals and groups on your list who are opposing the rule of God. Pray that God might have mercy on them and that His goodness will truly lead them to repentance. Then yield your pessimism and weariness in the battle to Him and ask for a holy optimism; ask Him to build up your faith regarding His Second Coming and eventual conquest. Do this for yourself and others involved in the battle that you listed earlier (your church, your missionary colleagues). Passages like 2 Thessalonians 1:5–11 and hymns affirming His Second Coming can be of great help at this stage in your prayers.

2. Celebrate the unique way in which Christ recruits His followers. Sing or meditate on the following verses of a battle hymn of the Church. Notice especially the action of God in the high-lighted phrases.

> Who is on the Lord's side?
>> Who will serve the King?
> Who will be His helpers,
>> Other lives to bring?
> Who will leave the world's side?
>> Who will face the foe?
> Who is on the Lord's side?
>> Who for Him will go?
> *By Thy call of mercy,*
>> *By Thy grace divine,*
> We are on the Lord's side;
>> Saviour, we are Thine.
>
> Jesus, Thou hast bought us,
>> Not with gold or gem,
> But with Thine own life blood,
>> For Thy diadem.
> With Thy blessing filling
>> Each who comes to Thee,
> *Thou hast made us willing,*
>> *Thou hast made us free.*
> *By Thy grand redemption,*
>> *By Thy grace divine,*
> We are on the Lord's side;
>> Saviour, we are Thine.

Fierce may be the conflict,
  Strong may be the foe,
But the King's own army
  None can overthrow.
Round His standard ranging
  Victory is secure;
For His truth unchanging
  Makes the triumph sure.
Joyfully enlisting
  By Thy grace divine,
We are on the Lord's side;
  Saviour, we are Thine.[6]

3. Pray that His mercy, His grace, His liberating blessing, His grand
   redemption, and His unchanging truth will raise up many joyful
   labourers for His kingdom, especially to reach those billions
   who have never heard of Christ. Choose a particular missionary
   organization to which you have natural ties (e.g., Wycliffe Bible
   Translators, Arab World Ministries, etc.) and focus your prayers
   on it. If you know of any individuals who are presently considering God's call to serve in difficult arenas of ministry (especially cross-cultural ones), either here "at home" or "overseas,"
   pray for their recruitment by grace and their perseverance in
   obeying "the call." Remember that this is the only strategy that
   the Lord Jesus gave for recruiting labourers for the harvest
   fields: *"Pray that the Lord of the harvest would send forth
   labourers."*

4. Pray for the specific missionary or worker you listed – that he or
   she *will hear the laughter of God* and know that their opponents fight in vain; that they will *hear God's promise* to Christ
   and be convinced of the eventual *conquest of Christ* and hence
   persevere with the longsuffering of God; and that they will *see
   the majesty of Christ* and thus count any hardship worthwhile
   for the promotion of such a glory.

5. Read the prayer of Acts 4:23–31 as a model for intercessory
   prayer. Pray for yourself, your church, your missionary friend,
   and all Christians that we will use God's strategy to fight; that
   we will abandon the enemy's strategies of force and subterfuge
   and instead learn to pray and proclaim His Word. Use your
   knowledge of the specifics of the situations you are praying for
   to flesh out these skeletal suggestions. Ask for courage and
   open doors to proclaim God's Word to the opponents in
   question.

An Objection

At about this time in the exercise of praying through these battle songs, some might be saying, "Well this is 'fine and dandy' if you are healthy and strong, but what about me today? The tragedies of life are 'doing a number' on me. I'm sick. I'm struggling. My family is falling apart. I am only now discovering the terrible past I had and its present effect on me. I am struggling with the injustices that have been committed against me. And now you want to take Psalm 23 away from me and substitute these battle songs. I don't have time for all of these Psalms. How can I be expected to fight in such a state? And didn't the early Christians have to deal with life problems like mine? How did they get comfort?" Well, those are good questions, but the favourite Psalms of the early church are equal to the challenge.

Let's go back to Psalm 110: "*The LORD has sworn and will not change his mind. You are a priest forever in the order of Melchizedek.*" Jesus Christ reigns now, not only as a King, but also as a merciful and faithful High Priest. As long as there have been worshippers in the world, priests have been needed. People have realized, regardless of their religion, that in attempting to worship their particular deity, however they conceive it to be, they did not have the right of individual approach to their god. They needed a mediator. Hence the priesthood. Priests also served a second important function. They regulated the daily life of worshippers to ensure the blessing of their deity on the worshipping community and to avert Divine wrath. So people would ask priests to define auspicious moments, to come and bless their houses, and to give them advice on any number of issues, among other things.

In many cultures, much of this priestly work of blessing and teaching had a secretive, mysterious air as far as the average man or woman was concerned. In Hinduism, for example, priests often chanted their pronouncements in Sanskrit, a language not known by the masses. In the Christian church, worship was conducted in Latin for many centuries, which, again, was obscure to most, if not all, of the worshipping community. Finally, and perhaps most important of all, these priests were human, and hence sinners. The same, of course, is true of present-day priests as well. Almost every day, newspapers catalogue the sins of yet another ecclesiastical leader. The very ones that we count on to mediate between us and God are marked with the same sins and weaknesses as we are. They do not, after all, have an "inside track" on

God. They need a mediator themselves. And that's where Jesus Christ's High Priesthood is unique.

In Jesus, God became human, and as a human being, He identified with all the trials and temptations of humanity, yet emerged victorious. Therefore, right now, we have at the right hand of God, the Father, not only a victorious King, but also a compassionate, sympathetic High Priest, who can represent us to God faithfully and completely because He senses our weaknesses. Yet at the same time, because He is a victorious High Priest, He does more than just plead with the Father for us. His prayers are powerful on our behalf, and they secure for us not only forgiveness of our sins and freedom from guilt that weighs us down, but also the power to take us through our pain and our suffering from injustice and to do for us what Psalm 23 by itself may not do.

So, wounded child of God, by all means acknowledge your problems and your pain. He knows, He cares, He will listen and faithfully represent you before the Father. Only remember that this Priest is also a King who is in the business of raising up warriors and troops. He is a Chief Surgeon, not of a civilian hospital, but of a military unit. The larger context of Psalm 110:4 never let the early church forget that. So when they were faced with the ravages of pain and injustice, they did not merely ask for a priest to come into their midst and heal them so life could go more smoothly. They also sang the battle songs which crowned Jesus both Priest and King.

Faced with massive engines of opposition and scorn, they looked to the heavens through these songs, which did three things for them: it made the laughter of God audible, it made Christ's eventual reign over His enemies believable, and it made the majesty of Christ visible. With this heavenly perspective firmly established, early Christians were able to take the sword of God (His Word), ask Him for the salvation of the nations as Christ's promised inheritance, and then preach the Word of God to friends and enemies, daring to trust God to affirm their preaching with signs, wonders, and miracles. Thus, they extended the sceptre of their King in the midst of His, and their, enemies.

Prayer Guide

1. Pause to reflect on any pain that has so far kept you from meaningful involvement in the battle, either in intercession for the nations or in proclamation of the Gospel to the nations, whether they be next door or across the ocean. How have you prayed about this problem in the past? Have you come to Him as the High Priest who can sympathize and fully enter into your pain? (Read Hebrews 4:14–5:6 and 7:11–28, both of which quote Psalm 2 and Psalm 110.)

2. Take time now to talk to this wonderful High Priest, who has an eternal, powerful, and effective priesthood, not plagued by the shortcomings of human priests. And as you ask Him for healing, remember that He is also King and the Chief Surgeon of a military, not a civilian, hospital. Pray for healing, but with the final purpose of becoming part of His army, which will fight His battle in His ways (through prayer and proclamation). Pray for Steps 1 to 5 from the previous Prayer Guide to become a regular part of your life with God. Pray along the same lines for other wounded soldiers that you know, close to home and "on the field."

A Redesigned Building

As we have already noted, the radical changes in perspective brought about by Psalms 2 and 110 were anchored in the reality of the resurrection and ascension of Christ. Without that, these new viewpoints would have been mere wishful thinking. The people of the early church never stopped reminding each other of this connection – which brings us to the third Psalm of their "Top Three" list, Psalm 118. The portion of this Psalm most often quoted in the New Testament is verses 22–24: *"The stone the builders rejected has become the capstone; the LORD has done this, and it is marvelous in our eyes. This is the day the LORD has made; let us rejoice and be glad in it."*

I am indebted to Leonard Griffith for the following inspiring comment on these verses: "The picture is that of a great building – a university, a cathedral, a library, a court of justice – rising from its foundations. The contractor inspects a load of quarried stones which has just been delivered. Some stones he approves, a few he rejects. Later in the day the architect arrives on the scene to survey the growing structure and sees a small heap of discarded stones piled on the edge of the site. One stone catches his attention and he examines it closely. He has never seen anything so flawless. Calling the contractor, he asks, 'Why have you rejected this one?' The builder replies, 'It doesn't fit in with the others.' 'Then the others must be chiselled to fit in with this one,' says the architect. So the stone which the builders rejected is polished, inscribed and set in the place of honor; it becomes the headstone of the corner."[7]

That's exactly what happened on resurrection morning. Those in Israel charged with building God's Kingdom on earth had looked at Jesus Christ and discarded Him, counting Him worthy of death as a common blasphemer. They mocked Him, they flogged Him, they crucified Him, and said, "We don't want Him. We will construct our building without Him." Three days later, the Architect of the universe showed up, looked at His flawless Son, and asked the builders, "Why haven't you used this Stone?" "It doesn't fit our idea of the kingdom, Lord," they said. His response: "Then I'm going to redesign the universe because everything is going to be built around Him as Cornerstone." And from that day on, He has been redesigning the universe to fit it around Jesus Christ. No wonder Psalm 118 was a "winner" with the early church.

This Psalm needs to be on our list of favourites, as well, because we, too, can forget. A famous Greek author of antiquity, Xenophon, records a moment when the Greek armies were facing the Persians in their attempt to conquer Persia. The armies were arrayed in long lines, facing each other. As soon as the battle began, the Greeks struck at the heart of the Persian lines and drove so deep into the centre of the line that the battle was, for all practical purposes, won right then and there. But precisely because the battle lines were so long, the Greek soldiers farther away from the centre of the line didn't see this strategic advance by their team at the centre. So when the battle got rough in their immediate zone, they turned around and ran. Thus, a battle already won was eventually lost.[8]

We are in exactly the same kind of situation. We are lined up against massive engines of scorn and, maybe, persecution. Jesus Christ, on that first Easter morning, struck a decisive blow deep at the centre of enemy lines, penetrating to the heart of the opposition. Therefore, our battle has already been won. Unlike other battles that are fought in order to be won, this battle has been won in order to be fought. But we will keep fighting only if we do not lose sight of the decisive victory already accomplished at the centre. To ensure that this does not happen, we need to learn these three favourite Psalms of the early church – battle songs that will make the laughter of God audible, the eventual conquest of Christ's enemies believable, and the majesty of God visible. Then we, too, will enlist as holy, willing, and obedient troops and fight until the day His enemies become His footstool.

Prayer Guide

End your time of prayer by celebrating the resurrection and ascension. Read Psalm 118 in its entirety as your thank offering to the Risen Christ. Sing one or more hymns about the resurrection.

Chapter 9

Psalm 51:
Recovering from
a King-Sized Failure

1 Have mercy on me, O God, according to your unfailing love;
according to your great compassion blot out my transgressions.
2 Wash away all my iniquity and cleanse me from my sin. 3 For I
know my transgressions, and my sin is always before me. 4 Against
you, you only, have I sinned and done what is evil in your sight, so
that you are proved right when you speak and justified when you
judge. 5 Surely I was sinful at birth, sinful from the time my mother
conceived me. 6 Surely you desire truth in the inner parts; you teach
me wisdom in the inmost place. 7 Cleanse me with hyssop, and I will
be clean; wash me, and I will be whiter than snow. 8 Let me hear joy
and gladness; let the bones you have crushed rejoice. 9 Hide your face
from my sins and blot out all my iniquity. 10 Create in me a pure
heart, O God, and renew a steadfast spirit within me. 11 Do not cast
me from your presence or take your Holy Spirit from me. 12 Restore
to me the joy of your salvation and grant me a willing spirit, to
sustain me. 13 Then I will teach transgressors your ways, and sinners
will turn back to you. 14 Save me from bloodguilt, O God, the God
who saves me, and my tongue will sing of your righteousness.
15 O LORD, open my lips, and my mouth will declare your praise.
16 You do not delight in sacrifice, or I would bring it; you do not take

pleasure in burnt offerings. 17 *The sacrifices of God are a broken*
spirit; a broken and contrite heart, O God, you will not despise.
18 *In your good pleasure make Zion prosper; build up the walls of*
Jerusalem. 19 *Then there will be righteous sacrifices, whole burnt*
offerings to delight you; then bulls will be offered on your altar.

A Cigar behind Our Back

Norman Vincent Peale is said to have told this story about a scrape
he got into as a child. One day, he found a cigar, slipped into an
alley, and lit it up. Unfortunately, while it was still smoking away,
he saw his father coming. So he slipped the cigar behind his back
and tried to act as if nothing was unusual. Hoping to distract his
father from the item at hand, Norman pointed to a billboard ad-
vertising a circus and asked eagerly if he could go. "Son," his
father replied quietly but firmly, "never make a petition while at
the same time trying to hide a smoldering disobedience."[1]

His advice was thoroughly biblical. When Israel's armies, under Joshua, had suffered a humiliating defeat by the much smaller
armies of Ai in Canaan, Joshua prostrated himself before God
asking, "*Ah, Sovereign LORD, why did you ever bring this people across*
the Jordan to deliver us into the hands of the Amorites to destroy us ...
O LORD, what can I say, now that Israel has been routed by its enemies
... What then will you do for your own great name?" (Joshua 7:7–9).
God's answer to this prayer was totally unexpected. In effect He
said, "Stand up! What are you doing down on your face? Israel
has sinned. Go deal with the sin first. Until then, don't bother
praying for insight into your predicament" (Joshua 7:10–11).

Centuries later, we find the people of Judah complaining to
the prophet Isaiah that God has been ignoring their prayers, thoroughly scriptural though they have been. The people have prayed
for God to draw near to them, they have asked Him for just decisions in their law courts, and they have fasted. God's response
through Isaiah is the same as His blunt advice to Joshua: "*Shout*
it aloud, do not hold back. Raise your voice like a trumpet. Declare to
my people their rebellion and to the house of Jacob their sins" (Isaiah
58:1). So whether our prayers are a request to go to the circus, a
cry for insight into a military defeat, or a longing for God's intimate and powerful presence, they will be to no avail if there is a
smoldering disobedience behind our backs as we pray. Sin must

be confessed and dealt with. Otherwise, all our prayers en route to Zion and for her welfare, our glad expectations of the celebration in Zion, our Saturday night prayers for a powerful Sabbath encounter, our cries for our children, for our national leaders, and for Christ's reign among the nations will fall on deaf ears. The only response we can expect is: "What are you doing on your face? Stand up. Get rid of the cigar. Then we'll talk."

And the same Psalms that helped engrave the highways to Zion on our hearts, and kept us moving toward it, also teach us how to confess our sin. (Recall Psalm 19 in Chapter 1, in which the author celebrates the wonderful ability of the multifaceted law of the Lord to reveal disorder in his inner being and then to re-order it.) A superficial survey of the Psalms would suggest that "breast beating" ought not to have a predominant place in our prayers to God. The bulk of Israel's prayers seem to focus on other matters: about 50 Psalms deal with individual laments, where the author is complaining about his predicament to God. Many of the remaining 100 are shot through with expressions of jubilant praise and thanksgiving. Only 7 out of 150 deal explicitly with confession – the so-called "penitential Psalms." Yet, even though there are only 7, they are sprinkled throughout the Psalter – 6, 32, 38, 51, 102, 130, and 143 – so that, in any sequential reading of the Psalms (the customary practice for most of Church history), one cannot go too long without encountering a penitential Psalm. They teach us that confession is much more than saying, "I'm sorry" after the fashion of children who say "sorry" to each other after a fight. They are not in the least bit sorry; they wouldn't apologize if it were left up to them, and their reluctance is written all over their faces even as they mouth the words. All too often, we approach our confession to God in a similar frame of mind. But true biblical confession is a far more profound and exhaustive process, involving three indispensable elements: cleansing, renewal, and restoration.

If there is one penitential Psalm that, more than any other, fuses these three elements into a heartfelt prayer that satisfies God, it is David's familiar confession in Psalm 51. Most of us are familiar with the historical setting (the full story can be found in 2 Samuel 11). David had committed adultery with Bathsheba, the wife of Uriah, a senior-ranking military commander in his army. When David discovered she was pregnant, he arranged to have Uriah assigned to a high-risk area of the battlefield. After Uriah's death, David married Bathsheba.

Unaware of the magnitude of his sin, David was busy conducting the affairs of his court when Nathan, the prophet of God, walked in. After skillfully exposing the shocking nature of David's murderous deed through a creative parable that tricked the king into pronouncing his own just judgement, Nathan pointed his finger at David and uttered the judgement of God: "You are the man." David, to his credit, did what no other contemporary monarch, especially one so powerful and well loved as he, would have done. He immediately acknowledged his sin. As part of the judgement of God, the child conceived in sin was struck with a fatal illness. David pleaded for its life, neither eating nor sleeping for the six days that the child's life hung in the balance. Psalm 51 was, in all probability, a poetic outcome of this prolonged confession to God.

Digging Deep

The prayer's first element contains David's progressive awareness of the true nature of his sin: *"Have mercy on me, O God, according to your unfailing love; according to your great compassion blot out my **transgressions**. Wash away all my **iniquity** and cleanse me from my sin. For I know my transgressions, and my **sin** is always before me"* (vv. 1–3). David is conscious not only of the fact of his sin, but also of its depth and defilement. He calls it "transgression" – a word which denotes an act of rebellion against someone in authority – and asks God to blot it out, to wipe the slate clean. He acknowledges that he has rebelled against the authority of God and has a "criminal record." He wants it wiped clean.

David also refers to his act as "iniquity" – referring to something that is twisted and bent as opposed to something straight. It can also mean the deliberate choosing of a wrong path as opposed to wandering off the path unintentionally or due to haste, misinformation, or some other less premeditated factor. David asks God to wash away his iniquity. The word "wash" does not mean a quick rinse but a thorough scrubbing by stamping the soiled garment with one's feet. People in many Third World countries still wash clothes that way – by first soaking them in a primitive soap and then beating them with a wooden club or smashing them against a rock. That's how David wants to be cleansed of his sin. Why the need for such a drastic cleansing? I love to walk and have done so at various times of the day. During one such walk at night, I stepped on something squishy and slippery. My heart sank as the unwelcome but familiar odour that assaulted my nostrils immediately telegraphed the bad news. I moved to the nearest patch of sod-covered turf, rubbed my foot vigorously, walked home quickly, hobbled on one foot while I opened the door, took off the offending shoe, and, holding it at arm's length, hopped down the stairs to the laundry room. There was no way I was going to let that shoe touch any part of the house. I repeatedly flushed it in hot water, scrubbing it with soap in between flushings, until every trace of the odour had gone from it. That was how David regarded his deed. It was something that had defiled him, something from which he needed to be scrubbed clean.

Even with that, David is not yet finished. His third term for his act is "sin" – missing the mark, falling short of God's standard. One common response to sin is to narrow the gap by lowering the standard. That's what we do when we make excuses like, "It wasn't such a big deal. Don't be too hard on yourself." Instead, David asks to be cleansed. When anyone in Israel was suspected of being contaminated by leprosy, that person would be immediately ostracized from society until pronounced clean by a priest. David sees his deed not only as a blot on his record that needs to be wiped clean and as a stinking stain that must be scrubbed out of his system, but also as a leprous sore that makes him unfit for contact with God and others until he is pronounced clean by God Himself.

What's more, this deep consciousness of the depth and defilement of his sin is not a passing emotion. He cannot get it out of his mind, no matter which way he turns: *"For I know my transgressions, and my sin is always before me"* (v. 3). He tells us why in the first part of verse 4: *"Against you, you only, have I sinned and done what is evil in your sight ... ."* That's a remarkable assertion if we pause to think about it. It was Bathsheba he had violated. It was Uriah he had deliberately murdered. It was to their families that his actions had brought grief. Yet he dares to assert that it was against God only that he had sinned. Later on, he would discover the full consequences of his act on a human level. His sin would ravage the lives of his children with a consequent blow to his kingdom from which it never recovered. And Bathsheba's relatives would be, in many cases, the human agents of this débâcle. But for now, only one thought fills his mind and torments his conscience. He has sinned against a Holy God who blessed him beyond anything he could have asked (2 Samuel 7)! To put it bluntly, he realizes that God was in the royal bedroom with him and Bathsheba. His alarming cry in verse 4 – "*I have done what is evil in your sight*" – was literally true. From this awareness comes the acknowledgement in the last part of verse 4: "*so that you are proved right when you speak and justified when you judge.*" In his confession, David ends up justifying God, rather than attempting to justify himself, as is so often done in confessions. He realizes that this is his only hope – just as the only hope of lost travellers is to recognize that they are lost and to head back to the very point at which they left the main road for the detour. To persist in the detour is to go even further astray.

But it isn't over yet. David digs even deeper in verse 5: "*Surely I was sinful at birth, sinful from the time my mother conceived me.*" Here David goes beyond the fact of his sins (adultery and murder), beyond the depth and defilement of his sin to the root cause of his sin – his sin nature, the congenital condition of his heart that rendered him capable of any sin. A vivid illustration of this "original sin" as theologians term it, comes from an unexpected source – pigs! Most pigs we see in North America are relatively clean, but not so in my native country of India. I recall seeing a large black sow sleeping in the midst of a nauseating mixture of excrement and mud that had been churned into a mess by the monsoon rains. Even as I was wondering how any living creature could step into, let alone sleep in, such muck, I got my answer. To my horror, I saw six little piglets drinking mama's milk right in that slime pit. That's when I realized why the adult sow was so much at home in filth. She'd been born in it – just like her litter.

That's exactly what the psalmist was saying about himself. I did this horrible deed because I was born and bred in sin. It's at the core of my being. As if this wasn't devastating enough, he is simultaneously assaulted by another conviction: "*Surely you desire truth in the inner parts; you teach me wisdom in the inmost place*" (v. 6). The very place where David locates his problem, the sin nature at the centre of his heart, is precisely where God desires truth and wisdom. Hence David's renewed cry for cleansing. He repeats the earlier threefold cry in verses 7 and 9 – "*Cleanse me … wash me … blot out all my iniquity*" – and goes on to add a fourth petition in verse 8: "*Let me hear joy and gladness; let the bones you have crushed rejoice.*" All of us can easily recall times when we have offended someone and are truly sorry for it. What we long for next is to hear the person say to us, "It's okay." That's the idea behind the psalmist's plea to hear joy and gladness. "God, please blot … , cleanse … , wash … , and then please say it's all right between you and me." This, by the way, is the hallmark of "a man after God's own heart," a recurring biblical description of David. The thought of an unresolved issue between him and God was unbearable.

How often have we regarded our sins in this light – that they are ultimately sins against God and God alone and that He is absolutely right in calling us to the bar of judgement and pronouncing us guilty? Have we then persevered long enough in our self-examination to go beyond the fact of our sin to see its depth and defilement – as a rebellion against God's authority, a stinking stain, and a leprous sore? Have we stuck with it until we reached the next stage, the underlying cause of our sin – our sin nature, imparted to us at birth? Then, and only then, will we cry out like David, "Blot it out, wash me, pronounce me clean, say it's okay." Admittedly, David's shocking, scheming murder to cover up his adultery, not to mention his subsequent cavalier attitude toward it (administering the affairs of his kingdom in a "business-as-usual" manner), aren't exactly everyday fare in our lives. This might tempt us to object: "Listen, if we were guilty of his sins, why then, we would have no trouble recognizing the fact, depth, defilement, and root cause of our sin. But surely angry words, gossip, flipping through the occasional pornographic magazine, a few white lies at the Immigration and Customs booth, and so on, can't be put in the same category as adultery and murder."

It depends on how we look at it. If we think in terms of visible effects and consequences, probably not. But are these "lesser" sins antithetical to the infinite holiness of God? Have they been committed in His sight so that He is right in judging us guilty? Are they acts of rebellion that need to be cleared from our record? Are they stains that are a stench in God's nostrils and would be in ours if only we could see them in their true light? Do they render us unfit for communion with God and our fellow human beings? Above all, do they spring from the same spoiled fountain as David's more obviously heinous sins? The answer is a reverberating "Yes!" on all counts.

Perhaps the most dramatic illustration of the universal application of David's shattering discovery (at least in my reading) is the one recounted by Charles Colson in his book *Who Speaks for God?*[2] He describes an interview that Mike Wallace conducted with Yehiel Dinur, a concentration camp survivor who testified against Adolf Eichmann. A film clip from Eichmann's 1961 trial showed Dinur walking into the courtroom, stopping short, and seeing Eichmann for the first time since the Nazi had sent him to Auschwitz eighteen years earlier. Dinur began to sob uncontrollably, then fainted, collapsing in a heap on the floor as the presiding judicial officer pounded his gavel for order in the crowded courtroom. Had Dinur been overcome by hatred? fear? horrid memories? No, it was none of these. Rather, as Dinur explained to Wallace, all at once he realized that Eichmann was not the god-like army officer who had sent so many to their deaths. This Eichmann was an ordinary man. "I was afraid about myself," said Dinur, "… I saw that I am capable to do this. I am exactly like he." Wallace's subsequent summation of Dinur's terrible discovery – "Eichmann is in all of us" – is absolutely right on. Everyone of us is capable of committing not only David's sin, but also those of Eichmann, because we, too, were sinful at birth, sinful from the time our mothers conceived us. It is only our specific circumstances and what theologians call the common grace of God that have prevented us from actualizing this dreadful potential.

Prayer Guide

Consider your "besetting sin" – the one that trips you up most often, the one you honestly feel stands in stark contrast to the holiness of God.

- Have you ever "dug deep" in regard to this sin, going beyond its fact to see its depth and feel its defilement? Do so now, until you can say, like David, that God is absolutely right and just to judge you for it. Pray over it until you sense its contamination enough to want cleansing. Acknowledge that before Him; then ask Him to blot out the sin, scrub you, pronounce you clean, and say everything's okay!

- Does the doctrine of "original sin" (you are a "piglet" born in the muck to sinful parents) offend you? Can you agree that "Eichmann is in all of us" and therefore in you? What other (worse) sins would you be capable of committing if the conditions were "right"? Use these reflections to confess your root nature as sinful and in need of a radical transformation.

- If you honestly cannot see yourself and your "little sins" in this light, acknowledge that before God and ask for such a confrontation with His holiness that you will see what David saw. Read passages that describe the holiness of God flashing out against sin (1 Samuel 5:1–6:21; 2 Samuel 6:1–8; 1 Kings 2:23–24; Isaiah 6:1–5; and Acts 5:1–11) and ask the Holy Spirit to help you see yourself accurately before such perfect, infinite holiness.

Renewal

Having reached rock bottom in the exploration of his sinfulness, David is ready for the next step. From cleansing, he moves to re-creation. From justification in God's sight, to sanctification. He expresses his desires in verses 10–12: "*Create in me a pure heart, O God, and renew a steadfast spirit within me. Do not cast me from your presence or take your Holy Spirit from me. Restore to me the joy of your salvation and grant me a willing spirit, to sustain me.*" Notice the repeated emphasis on "spirit." David realizes that if the root cause of sin is an inner disposition that is twisted from birth, the solution must be rooted in the spirit, too. He begins by asking God to create a pure heart within him.

The Hebrew word translated "create" is used three times in Genesis 1: when God created matter and space (Genesis 1:1 – "*In the beginning God created the heavens and the earth*"); when He created the first living creatures (Genesis 1:21 – "*So God created the great creatures of the sea and every living and moving thing …*"); and finally, when He created man and woman (Genesis 1:27 – "*So God created man in his own image …*"). Each of these three stages represents the bringing into being of something radically new, which did not exist before (i.e., matter and space, life, and human beings). Genesis 1 also draws our attention to the work of the Holy Spirit in this creative process. (Genesis 1:2 – "*Now the earth was formless and empty, darkness was over the surface of the deep, and the Spirit of God was hovering over the waters.*") God spoke, the Spirit brooded, and as a result, shapeless matter was formed and empty space was filled with radical, ordered newness.

All of this provides the context for David's prayer. He realizes that nothing less than the creative power of God, which brought order out of chaos by the brooding of the Holy Spirit, would suffice to deal with the congenital crookedness of his heart.

Something brand new was needed. Sin wreaks havoc in our lives (both internally and in our relationships with others) that needs re-ordering. So prayer for renewal begins by asking God to bring order out of that chaos through the creative energies of the Holy Spirit. Then David prays for a steadfast spirit so that he can maintain the newly cleansed, purified, and re-ordered inner springs of his life.

At this point, he interjects a surprising request, that he might not be abandoned by God or lose the Holy Spirit. David is afraid. The double revelation of his innate sinfulness and the fact that God desires truth in the "inner parts" is almost too much for him. The longer he stays in God's presence, the loftier God's standards seem to become and the deeper his own sin. The gap between him and God is widening, not narrowing. How far will this process go? Will he be cast off forever, irretrievably? David knew that his predecessor, King Saul, had experienced the influence of the Holy Spirit on many occasions, yet the Spirit was decisively and permanently taken from him (1 Samuel 16:14 – "*Now the Spirit of the LORD had departed from Saul, and an evil spirit from the LORD tormented him*"). The Lord had also promised David that this would never happen to his descendants (2 Samuel 7:15 – "*But my love will never be taken away from him, as I took it away from Saul, whom I removed from before you*"). Nevertheless, David was full of fear.

We can never say we've really understood the true nature of sin unless we've experienced, to some extent, its potential to separate us from God. In my early years as a Christian, I repeatedly struggled with certain temptations. I would confess, claim forgiveness and restoration, and get moving until – down I went one more time. On one of these occasions, I happened to read 2 Peter 2:20–22: "*If they have escaped the corruption of the world by knowing our LORD and Savior Jesus Christ and are again entangled in it and overcome, they are worse off at the end than they were at the beginning. It would have been better for them not to have known the way of righteousness, than to have known it and then to turn their backs on the sacred command that was passed on to them. Of them the proverbs are true: 'A dog returns to its vomit' and 'A sow that is washed goes back to her wallowing in the mud.'*" That's the closest I came to feeling David's fear of being cast off irretrievably. Today, as I look back to those days, I thank God for that fear. Certainly, my eventual freedom from the sins that dogged me and the power of consistent holiness involved far more constructive and positive elements than stark fear, but it played a significant role. And every time I need to confess any sin as thoroughly as the Scriptures exhort us to, that element of fear is never totally absent. In fact, God has, for good reason, ordained it to be so.

Jonathan Edwards, the eighteenth-century theologian and pastor, has given us this penetrating insight into the issue: "Distant experiences, when darkened by present prevailing lust and corruption, will never keep alive gracious confidence and assurance. So when men are in such a frame [of mind] and have no sensible experience of the exercise of grace but, on the contrary, are very much under the prevalence of their lusts and an unchristian spirit, they should be doubting their state [before God]. It is desirable and best in every way that they should. For God has so constituted things in His dispensation towards his own people that when their love decays, fear should arise; when love rises, then fear should vanish and be driven away. No other principle will make men conscientious but one of these two, fear or love. Hence God has wisely ordained that these two opposite principles of love and fear should rise and fall like the two opposite scales of a balance … That's why, when love is asleep and fear arises, in vain is all the saint's self examination, and poring on past experience, in order to establish His peace and get assurance. For it is contrary to the nature of things as God has constituted them that he should have assurances such as these."[3] Elsewhere Edwards writes of God's ways of dealing with His sinning children: "In the first place, conscience has been awakened and they have been brought into distressing fears of the wrath of God. Thus they have become subjects of a new work of humiliation and have been led deeply to feel that they deserve His wrath, even while they have feared it, before God has delivered them from their apprehension and comforted them with a renewed sense of His favour."[4]

David concludes his prayer for renewal with a request for the restoration of joy and a willing spirit. He wanted to be clean and he wanted to be steadfast in maintaining that cleanliness – but not as a burdensome task, reluctantly and unwillingly discharged out of fear. Instead he wanted it to be a joyful pursuit, gladly undertaken. Joy is something Christians talk about a lot, yet have a hard time pinning down. It is often confused with happiness, a sense that all is well, a cheery countenance. This definition by Oswald Chambers offers a helpful corrective: "Joy is neither happiness nor brightness; … [anything] that exactly fulfills the purpose of its creation experiences joy."[5] That's "the joy of his salvation" that David wanted restored. Could it be that most of us experience so little joy because of our superficial understanding and handling of sin? And even when we become sufficiently aware of the defilement and depth of our sin to cry out, "Blot it out, wash me, Eichmann is in me, ... ," could it be that true joy comes only when we follow this with an insistence on radical renewal by the work of the Holy Spirit, expressed in a prayer like "Lord, may the renewing, recreating Spirit brood over the chaos of my sin and its sinful spring; create in me a clean heart, grant me a steadfast and a willing spirit and keep me close to You throughout the process – in short, conquer and rule over my inner space, O Lord"?

It's time for an objection. Granted that all sins, and not just heinous ones like adultery and murder, defile us before One who is infinitely holy. But perhaps David's agonizing soul searching was rooted in a lack of assurance of his salvation. After all, he wasn't the beneficiary of the wonderful promises we have of forgiveness in Jesus Christ as expressed in statements like this: *"If we confess our sins, he is faithful and just and will forgive us our sins and purify us from all unrighteousness"* (1 John 1:9). Does "confess" in this verse really mean something that is modelled after David's tortuous experience, which we have traced above? The answer lies in the often overlooked fact that no sooner had David confessed his sin than the prophet Nathan replied, *"The LORD has taken away your sin. You are not going to die."* David agonized before God even though he had been promised forgiveness. Advance assurances of forgiveness, as in 1 John 1:9, are not intended as encouragements to regard our sin lightly or to look upon confession as a routine ritual. One of the marks of the genuineness of our repentance and confession is that we have taken the time necessary to experience the conviction of sin's fact, depth, and defilement, as well as the fear of separation from a Holy God.

Prayer Guide

1. Have you ever known the fear of separation from God? Read the five warning passages in Hebrews (2:1–4; 3:7–19; 5:11–6:8; 10:26–31; 12:18–29). Note the progression from "drifting away" to "turning away" to "falling away" to "falling into" to "refusing to listen." Let the holy fear stimulated by these warnings shape your prayers for mercy and preservation from such a downward spiral.

2. Are you convinced that you need a radical renewal at the core of your being? If the Spirit were to brood over you to bring order to the chaos wrought by your sin(s), what would that mean, and what form would it take in your life? If He gave you a steadfast and willing spirit, what changes would you see in yourself? Pray that this is exactly what will happen through the Spirit's influence.

3. Re-read Oswald Chambers' definition of joy in the preceding section. What do you think God has made you for? Use your reflections to pour your own content into David's prayer, "*Restore to me the joy of my salvation.*" Confess your past superficiality in understanding and confessing your sins and in your prayers for cleansing.

Restoration

If we have indeed travelled this far with David in our confession, we are ready for the third and final element of confessional prayer – a desire for restoration to fruitful ministry. Note that this request comes at the end of David's prayer. So often we substitute religious activity and ministry for a radical dealing with our sin before God. We attempt to drown the voice of conscience with louder singing, putting in an appearance at prayer meetings, perhaps increasing our offerings. David acknowledges the sheer futility of all such compensating activities: "*You do not delight in sacrifice, or I would bring it; you do not take pleasure in burnt offerings. The sacrifices of God are a broken spirit; a broken and contrite heart, O God, you will not despise*" (vv. 16–17). Where sin is concerned, religious rituals, even those ordained by God Himself, are useless without brokenness of the kind we have been studying so far. The only route to a pure heart, a steadfast and willing spirit, and the abiding presence of the Holy Spirit is a broken spirit. Then and only then are we ready to ask for a restoration to useful ministry. At this stage, David's faith begins to ring loud and clear. The gap between him and God is no longer widening but narrowing. Listen to His bold declaration: *"Then I will teach transgressors your ways, and sinners will turn back to you"* (v. 13). "What audacity!" might be our reaction. "You, an adulterer and murderer, are going to teach sinners God's way! What do you know of His ways?" What's more, David is confident that, as a result of his teaching, others would be restored to God. This is the specific "way" of God that David would teach: the sort of confession that makes a "way" back to a Holy God for those who have sinned grievously. I am sure that even David had no idea of the scale on which this assertion would prove true. For three thousand years, this Psalm has given broken-hearted sinners words with which to approach a Holy God – and countless sermons have unlocked the treasures of David's agonizing prayer so that the hopeless have dared to hope for restoration to usefulness in the Kingdom of God. And is He not doing that even now for some of us as we work our way through this chapter and Prayer Guide?

David goes further in verse 14: *"Save me from bloodguilt, O God, the God who saves me, and my tongue will sing of your righteousness."* We might have expected him to say, "Save me and I will sing of your mercy." The connection between salvation and gratitude for God's mercy is logical, but why did David want to sing of God's righteousness? Therein lies the marvel – not that a merciful God forgives us but that an infinitely Holy God can do so and still remain righteous. Let's move back to the opening verse of David's prayer: *"Have mercy on me, O God, according to your unfailing love; according to your great compassion blot out my transgressions."* The cry for mercy is literally a request that God may be gracious to him. As for the phrase "unfailing love" (or "lovingkindness" in the King James Version), scholars tell us that it is a critically important, but not easily translated, phrase. Most of the time it means "love," but it seldom occurs in isolation. It is almost always associated with words like "unending," "unfailing," "kindness," "faithfulness," "covenant loyalty." A combination yields the following definition of "lovingkindness": the unending, unfailing love and kindness of God flowing out of His faithfulness to His Covenant Word and His loyalty to His chosen people. David appealed to that.

He also refers to God's great compassion. These three attributes – "mercy, unfailing love, and compassion" – aren't arbitrary selections by a David hoping to prevail on God with impressive religious language. Almost certainly, David is thinking about another significant moment in Israel's history when they, as a nation, had sinned greatly – when they so quickly forsook Jehovah who had delivered them from Egypt and instead built and worshipped a golden calf even as Moses was on Mount Sinai, receiving the Holy Law from God. It seemed the people were doomed to destruction, and God's initial words to Moses reinforce that impression: "*'I have seen these people,' the* LORD *said to Moses, 'and they are a stiff-necked people. Now leave me alone so that my anger may burn against them and that I may destroy them. Then I will make you into a great nation'*" (Exodus 32:9–10).

Moses' determined intercession averts disaster and leads to his final prayer for a demonstration of God's glory, a prayer that God answers in this way: "*'Then the* LORD *came down in the cloud and stood there with him and proclaimed his name, the* LORD. *And he passed in front of Moses, proclaiming, 'The* LORD, *the* LORD, *the* **compassionate** *and* **gracious** *God, slow to anger, abounding in* **love and faithfulness**'*" (Exodus 34:5–6). The glory of the Lord is demonstrated by His compassion, grace, patience, love, and faithfulness (to His Covenant). The opening words of David's prayer for forgiveness in Psalm 51, while different in detail, clearly echo these very characteristics that God revealed to Moses. As he starts his confession, David has somehow latched onto the fact that, even in the face of a sin so terrible as to threaten the very survival of a nation, the blazingly Holy God of Sinai can forgive his people and give them a fresh start. If that happened once to his people, maybe it could happen again. So David finds courage to pray.

Certainly, David couldn't have foreseen the death of Christ, which alone allows God to forgive without compromising His righteousness, but the Spirit enabled him to believe that a righteous God can forgive and still remain righteous. It is this marvellous fact that he promises to celebrate in song if his guilt is removed. David concludes his assertion of a restored ministry with this declaration: "*O* LORD, *open my lips, and my mouth will declare your praise*" (v. 15). A man who has so painfully plumbed the depths of his own sin and broken through to God's forgiveness cannot bear to be silent. He has lots to tell, and he wants to tell, but not unless God opens his lips. Then he will teach, he will sing, he will praise.

Biblical history tells us that David's holy optimism was fully justified. The child conceived in sin died, just as Nathan had prophesied. As soon as David heard that, he got up from his prolonged period of fasting and prayer, washed and anointed himself, changed his clothes, worshipped God, and went home to eat and console his wife, Bathsheba. God blessed their union with another son, Solomon, who would eventually build the temple and write the Proverbs. As for David, certainly he had to live with the bitter fruit of his sin in the wanton lives of his sons, but he himself was fully forgiven and went on to complete a glorious reign.

Prayer Guide

1. Where have you used religious activity as a compensation for sin? Acknowledge this as sinful and futile, confess it, and permanently renounce this as a means of silencing your conscience.

2. If the Spirit were to grant you a "broken and contrite" heart, how would it be different? Again, use your reflections to stimulate prayer for such a work of the Spirit.

3. Praise Him for His grace, compassion, and unfailing love (review the descriptions in the preceding section), which enable Him to forgive, cleanse, renew, and restore Israel, David, and you without compromising His Holiness. Since these attributes of God are most clearly displayed in the suffering, crucifixion, and death of Christ, read Mark 14:1–15:38 as fuel for your praise.

4. Which "sinner" can you turn back to God by teaching him/her God's ways, now that you have travelled that road yourself? Ask God to prepare that person's heart and show you the right time to do this.

All Together Now

So far, the focus has been on an individual confessing sin and praying for forgiveness, but the final two verses of the Psalm introduce a corporate dimension to confession: "*In your good pleasure make Zion prosper; build up the walls of Jerusalem. Then there will be righteous sacrifices, whole burnt offerings to delight you; then bulls will be offered on your altar."* There are two ways to interpret these verses. Perhaps David is extending his confidence of restoration to the nation as a whole. (After all, the prophet who exposed and denounced his sin had also foretold its terrible effects on David's family and hence on the nation). If so, David is asserting that, just as his personal sins had brought judgement on a nation, his deep, personal confession and repentance would similarly affect the nation for good.

The other, far more likely, interpretation considers these verses as a Holy Spirit–inspired addition by another godly Israelite during the exile in Babylon. In this case, repentant Israel in exile had adopted David's prayer of individual confession and applied it corporately to a nation whose temple and city walls had been destroyed. Through it, they confessed that they had been exiled because of their sin; they acknowledged the defilement of that sin, as well as the sin nature from which it sprung; and they cried for renewal and restoration, expressing confidence that God would take them back to their land to rebuild the city walls and the temple so that sacrifices could once again be offered to God. And because they would be accompanied by a broken spirit and a contrite heart, they would be acceptable. The sacrifices and burnt offerings He would not otherwise have delighted in (v. 16), now delight Him (v. 19).

Today we stand not only in need of a thorough confession of private, individual sin but also of corporate offences against God. It is noteworthy that many of the famous confessional prayers in Scripture are corporate confessions: Abraham pleading for Sodom (Genesis 18), Moses staving off Israel's imminent destruction in the wilderness (Exodus 32–34), Nehemiah mourning for four months over the broken walls and burned gates of Judah (Nehemiah 1), and Ezra over the intermarriage of the leaders in resettled Judah with heathen women (Ezra 9–10). In none of these cases were the intercessors themselves guilty of the sins they confessed. But their laments were as intense as David's in Psalm 51. What sins are candidates for corporate confession with the thoroughness and intensity that characterized David's confession? Adultery? Most churches aren't filled with it. Murder? Even less so. What, then, should we confess?

I suspect the answer would vary with each person; however, twenty-one years of Church ministry, domestic and international, have convinced me that *relational sins* should top the list. Both the Old and New Testaments are filled with exhortations to pursue and guard harmony in our relationships with all human beings, and especially within the fellowship of believers. Remember, at issue here is not whether we personally have fallen short in this area. The Church at large has failed. So we, on the Church's behalf, need to confess and repent of such sins as conflicts between believers and jealousy and covetousness at the leadership level. A close second would be *the lack of passion for the lost.* We lament the erosion of "orthodoxy," that many leading evangelicals no longer believe in the eternality of hell and never experience any emotional wrenching over the fact that 2.5 billion people have yet to hear the name of Christ. Does the advance of Islam trouble us only because "they" are our "enemies," who are conspiring to destabilize our country, or because it is preventing countless millions from hearing the Gospel of the glory of our beloved Lord Jesus? To round out this "Top Three" list, how about the wholesale *neglect of the biblical injunction to pursue justice for the poor,* especially the widows, the orphans, and the disenfranchised, close to home and abroad? (Recall that this latter sin, along with idolatry, was responsible for Israel and Judah's eventual exile.)

Prayer Guide

1. Read scriptural prayers as models of corporate confession (Ezra 9–10; Nehemiah 1; Daniel 9). All of these were prayed when Israel was in exile or shortly after their return to the land (the context for the last two verses of the Psalm).

2. Confess relational sins and neglect of the Great Commission and of the poor, close to home and throughout the world. Pray that the Holy Spirit would convict all believers so we will deal with these sins as thoroughly as we have (hopefully) with our private sins.

The Two-Edged Sword

David's journey inward, upward, and eventually forward began when Nathan the prophet of God walked in on an unsuspecting king, hooked him with a clever story, and laid the king's soul bare with a pointing finger and a thunderous voice, saying, "You are the man." Today we have no living prophets who can do likewise but we do have God's Living Word. I well remember a Saturday night in March 1977. Our children, aged four and one, were in bed, and my wife was out for the evening. I had settled down at the kitchen table to put the finishing touches to the Sunday School lesson I was scheduled to teach the next morning in church. It was a study of the warning in Hebrews 3 against hardening our hearts to God's Voice. As I pored over commentaries, making notes to share with the class, the following passage caught me totally off guard. It hit me "right between the eyes." "When we trust too much to the intellect in religion; when … [t]he mind is satisfied with beautiful thoughts and pleasant feelings, but the heart does not hear God; when we are secretly content with our religion, our sound doctrine and Christian life … ; when our life does not seek to keep pace with our knowledge and we have more pleasure in hearing and knowing than in obeying and doing, we utterly lose the meekness to which the promise is given and, amidst all the pleasing forms of godliness, the heart is too hard to discern the voice of the Spirit … Yes, it is an unspeakably solemn thought that, with a mind occupied with religious truth, and feelings stirred at times by the voice and words of men and a life apparently given to religious works, the heart may be closed to humble, direct intercourse with God, and a stranger to all the blessing the living Word can bring. *So, as the Holy Spirit says: 'Today, if you hear his voice, do not harden your hearts …'*" (Hebrews 3:7–8).[6]

I shut my commentaries and bowed speechless before God, reeling with conviction. Specifically, I was being confronted with my prayerlessness. Certainly I could, and did, pray eloquently in public. People would come up to me occasionally and comment on my facility in prayer and I would feel a warm glow suffuse through my soul; but that night, I saw it for the rubbish it was in God's holy eyes. My heart was being hardened, and all I could think of was Proverbs 29:1: "*A man who remains stiff-necked after many rebukes will suddenly be destroyed – without remedy.*" It was as if Nathan had walked in, pointed his finger at me, and said, "*You are the man.*"

The two-edged sword has lost none of its power to lay bare the intents and thoughts of our hearts. (That's why it's important to carefully read the Scripture passages included in the Prayer Guide.) Through them, and as you later encounter other Scripture in public preaching and in your private reading and study, the Word may well become the prophet's pointing finger and thundering assertion: "You are the man … you are the woman." When that happens, we cannot hide a smouldering cigar behind our backs and ask our Heavenly Father to take us to the circus. Hold that cigar out before Him, foul smell and all, and deal with it as David did.

Chapter 10

A Tornado in Alabama:
A Medley Based on
Psalms 22, 129, and 139

Psalm 129

*1 They have greatly oppressed me from my youth – let Israel say –
2 they have greatly oppressed me from my youth, but they have not
gained the victory over me. 3 Plowmen have plowed my back and made
their furrows long. 4 But the L*ORD *is righteous; he has cut me free from
the cords of the wicked. 5 May all who hate Zion be turned back in
shame. 6 May they be like grass on the roof, which withers before it can
grow; 7 with it the reaper cannot fill his hands, nor the one who gathers
fill his arms. 8 May those who pass by not say, "The blessing of the
L*ORD *be upon you; we bless you in the name of the L*ORD*."*

Psalm 22:1–10

*1 My God, my God, why have you forsaken me? Why are you so far
from saving me, so far from the words of my groaning? 2 O my God, I
cry out by day, but you do not answer, by night, and am not silent.
3 Yet you are enthroned as the Holy One; you are the praise of Israel.
4 In you our fathers put their trust; they trusted and you delivered
them. 5 They cried to you and were saved; in you they trusted and
were not disappointed. 6 But I am a worm and not a man, scorned by
men and despised by the people. 7 All who see me mock me; they hurl
insults, shaking their heads: 8 "He trusts in the L*ORD*; let the L*ORD

rescue him. Let him deliver him, since he delights in him." 9 Yet you
brought me out of the womb; you made me trust in you even at my
mother's breast. 10 From birth I was cast upon you; from my
mother's womb you have been my God.

Psalm 139:1–6

1 O LORD, you have searched me and you know me. 2 You know when
I sit and when I rise; you perceive my thoughts from afar. 3 You
discern my going out and my lying down; you are familiar with all
my ways. 4 Before a word is on my tongue you know it completely,
O LORD. 5 You hem me in – behind and before; you have laid your
hand upon me. 6 Such knowledge is too wonderful for me,
too lofty for me to attain.

7–12

7 Where can I go from your Spirit? Where can I flee from your
presence? 8 If I go up to the heavens, you are there; if I make my bed
in the depths, you are there. 9 If I rise on the wings of the dawn, if I
settle on the far side of the sea, 10 even there your hand will guide me,
your right hand will hold me fast. 11 If I say, "Surely the darkness
will hide me and the light become night around me," 12 even the
darkness will not be dark to you; the night will shine like the day,
for darkness is as light to you.

13–16

13 For you created my inmost being; you knit me together in my
mother's womb. 14 I praise you because I am fearfully and
wonderfully made; your works are wonderful, I know that full well.
15 My frame was not hidden from you when I was made in the secret
place. When I was woven together in the depths of the earth, 16 your
eyes saw my unformed body. All the days ordained for me were
written in your book before one of them came to be.

17

17 How precious to me are your thoughts, O God!
How vast is the sum of them!

Psalm 22:12–18

12 *Many bulls surround me; strong bulls of Bashan encircle me.*
13 *Roaring lions tearing their prey open their mouths wide against*
me. 14 I am poured out like water, and all my bones are out of joint.
My heart has turned to wax; it has melted away within me. 15 My
strength is dried up like a potsherd, and my tongue sticks to the roof
of my mouth; you lay me in the dust of death. 16 Dogs have
surrounded me; a band of evil men has encircled me, they have pierced
my hands and my feet. 17 I can count all my bones; people stare and
gloat over me. 18 They divide my garments among them and
cast lots for my clothing.

Psalm 22:22–31

22 *I will declare your name to my brothers; in the congregation I*
will praise you. 23 You who fear the LORD, *praise him! All you*
descendants of Jacob, honor him! Revere him, all you descendants of
Israel! 24 For he has not despised or disdained the suffering of the
afflicted one; he has not hidden his face from him but has listened to
his cry for help. 25 From you comes my praise in the great assembly;
before those who fear you will I fulfill my vows. 26 The poor will eat
and be satisfied; they who seek the LORD *will praise him – may your*
hearts live forever! 27 All the ends of the earth will remember and
turn to the LORD, *and all the families of the nations will bow down*
before him, 28 for dominion belongs to the LORD *and he rules over*
the nations. 29 All the rich of the earth will feast and worship; all
who go down to the dust will kneel before him – those who cannot
keep themselves alive. 30 Posterity will serve him; future
generations will be told about the Lord. 31 They will proclaim his
righteousness to a people yet unborn – for he has done it.

Once upon a Palm Sunday

At 11:30 a.m. on February 25, 1994, a group of 140 worshippers in northern Alabama were celebrating Palm Sunday, when, without warning, a tornado went right through the church. By the time I heard the news on CNN the next morning, 19 people had died. My instinctive reaction was a question, "Why, Lord? Why? After all, you were the God who spared Saint Paul's Cathedral from major destruction when London was bombed during the Second World War; besides, these people were in the very act of worshipping You at that moment." To borrow a phrase from Tevye in *Fiddler on the Roof*, I felt like saying to Him, "Would it have spoiled some vast infinite, eternal plan of yours if that tornado had been deflected fifteen feet one way or another?"

The temptation is very strong at times like these to conclude that God either doesn't care enough to intervene (though He could) or is not powerful enough to do so (though He wants to). It's all the more amazing, therefore, how many people resist that conclusion, for in that same newsclip, CNN reported on tornado damage in the town of Perkins, Georgia. When they interviewed a father who had lost his home, he said, through tears and with speech broken by inaudible sobs, "But there's got to be a reason. I know there's got to be a reason." Is that just a naïve optimism that insists on meaning in the face of inexplicable tragedy? How would such optimism work for the several questions various individuals had confronted me with less than twenty-four hours earlier? "Why did my mother have to be abused while she was young? Why did she have to marry a man who didn't think it was important to resolve such issues? Why did they have to fight all through my life? Why did I have to lose a parent in my teenage years? Why did church after church reject us when we reached out for help? Why, why, why? It is the most basic question of human existence.

The answers do not lie ultimately in what is known as Christian apologetics – the intellectual and philosophical analysis of the problem, which shows that suffering is not necessarily inconsistent with a God who is both sovereign and good. Nor do they lie in bare theological assertions that God is both good and powerful at the same time – at least not in the initial stages of such questioning. The force behind the question "Why" is not intellectual, philosophical, or theological; it is emotional, because of the pain that is involved.

So where do we start?

Praying in a Tornado

When I read the newspaper report of the tornado damage the next morning, I discovered that, among the many understandable initial reactions of the people inside that church, some members prayed. You might say, "That's not surprising; people pray in times of difficulty." But think about it for a minute. What is the point in praying for help to a God who has just sent a tornado through the church? If He could have prevented the disaster but didn't, or if He wanted to, but couldn't, what use is prayer? Yet instinctively those worshippers – at least some of them – knew that the only sane thing to do, when a tornado rips through your church in the middle of Palm Sunday, when intellectual gymnastics and mere theological assertions are powerless, is to get on your knees and pray. For it is only in worship that the truths that make sanity possible at such times descend from the head to the heart and begin to affect our lives.

Now we don't know what they prayed amidst the rubble of what had been a beloved sanctuary, but the question is significant. What kind of prayer allows truths to filter from our heads to our hearts when God has just destroyed our church while we were in the very act of celebrating our Lord's triumphal entry into Jerusalem? What do we say after we have said, "Why God? Why now? Why me?" Let's build our answer in stages as we look at yet another medley from God's prayer book. Our trio is composed of extracts from Psalm 129, Psalm 139, and Psalm 22.

Don't "Let Sleeping Dogs Lie"!

Psalm 129 begins with these words: "*They have greatly oppressed me from my youth – let Israel say – they have greatly oppressed me from my youth.*" Israel's youth, as a nation, referred to their captivity and bondage in Egypt. In this Psalm, the people of Israel reminded themselves of that bondage, and they did not minimize its horrors. Consider the figure of speech they used to describe their youth: "*Plowmen have plowed my back and made their furrows long.*" Imagine a farmer ploughing a field. He has his oxen yoked to the plough and he moves systematically back and forth. With each pass, the plough cuts deeper and the furrows become broader. Only in this case, the field is Israel, flat on its face; the ploughmen are the taskmasters of Egypt; and the cutting edge of the plough is the lash of the taskmaster. What an incredibly vivid image of the emotional scarring that some of us have endured because of repeated offences against us in our youth whether from sexual abuse, verbal put-downs, insults on the sports field or in the schoolroom, or the trauma of repeated broken relationships. The damage is as real as that caused by a tornado ripping a church apart – but it hurts more and for a lot longer.

The first step in building an answer to the "Why, God, why me?" questions that abound in such situations is to acknowledge the reality of the pain and the depth of the hurt. The opening lines of the Psalm repeat the phrase *"They have greatly oppressed me from my youth."* And Israel is exhorted to say it or, in our idiom, tell it like it is. But so often, precisely because of the depth of the furrows and the repetition of the pain, we have buried them under several protective layers. It is now much more comfortable to "let sleeping dogs lie" and keep them asleep by using a whole series of rationalizations: "They didn't really mean to hurt me"; "They were doing their best"; "Besides, I am an adult now; stiff upper lip, old chap, and get on with life." The longer we persist in such rationalizations, the harder it becomes to face the hurt. The command is "Let Israel say ... " – that is, acknowledge the pain.

Why? Why bother to dredge up painful memories? What will it accomplish? The psalmist tells us: *"But the LORD is righteous; he has cut me free from the cords of the wicked."* While the *"cords of the wicked"* may be a simple metaphor based on a literal binding of a human being with ropes, a far richer possibility is that the cut ropes are a metaphor for disabling the plough so it can no longer dig deeply into the earth. The result? The plough still goes back and forth over the field, but it doesn't cut anymore.[1] That's the "longed for" result that God is promising if we begin to deal with such situations the way He wants us to. He will come and "cut the cords of the ploughman" so the plough loses its ability to bite. He will heal us in such a way that the memories of our traumatic past will remain but will have permanently lost their power to hurt us. Then we will be able to say like Israel in Psalm 129, *"They have greatly oppressed me from my youth, **but they have not gained the victory over me ... The LORD is righteous**."*

Negative Emotions

The psalmist continues to amplify the process: "*May all who hate Zion be turned back in shame. May they be like grass on the housetops which withers before it can grow; with it the reaper cannot fill his hands, nor the one who gathers fill his arms. May those who pass by not say, 'The blessing of the LORD be upon you; we bless you in the name of the LORD'* (vv. 5–8)." Apparently Palestinian rooftops were flat. To get some relief from the debilitating heat, people would often put a thin layer of soil on the roof. When the early morning dew moistened this soil, little shoots of grass would spring up, only to be withered by the heat of the sun as the day progressed. The psalmist uses that as an image to curse those who had oppressed his people. He says, in effect, "May you wither like that grass on a housetop, which will never be harvested because it withers before it reaches maturity. May your life be as joyless as farmers who will never know the joyful blessing of greeting one another in an abundant time of harvest."[2]

Pretty strong stuff! But actually, this is mild compared to the vindictiveness and hatred expressed in some other Psalms (see Psalms 69 and 137), but it is strong enough to raise the question: What are emotions like anger, cursing, and vengeance doing in the Psalms? When we take the first step seriously and begin to deal with the pain of repeated hurt in our lives, we will inevitably begin to feel anger, which is often rooted in hurt. That precipitates a crisis because Christians aren't supposed to get angry. We are called to forgive and forget, aren't we? Well, if it is a simple matter of forgiving and forgetting, why did God inspire some of His poets to write these "imprecatory Psalms" – and those, too, for inclusion in their worship manual so that they, and succeeding generations of Israelites, would sing them regularly?

The answer has many dimensions, but the one that is most pertinent for our present purposes is this: sometimes the most holy thing to do is to get angry. By far the majority of the references to anger, wrath, and related words in the Scriptures (an approximate count suggests five hundred out of seven hundred), deals with God's anger. To be angry at that which angers God is not sin; it is holiness. To *not* be angry at such things is therefore unholiness and sin. The danger, the possibility of sin, lies in how we express that anger. The Psalms train us in the only healthy way to do this, at least in the initial stages: on our knees, in the presence of Almighty God who can take anything we might throw at Him.

Prayer Guide

1. Begin your prayer time by recalling and naming the "furrows that have been ploughed into your back," so to speak – those repeated exposures to verbal, physical, and social abuse, injustices, etc., and especially those caused by, although not limited to, significant people during the early, formative years of your life. For some of you, these memories and the hurt are fresh, ready at hand, and easily expressed. Not so for others. The pain has been so great that it has been effectively suppressed over many years of practised denial. If so, pray for the Holy Spirit's illumination and empowerment, that He will allow those memories to surface so you can articulate them. (A word of caution here. This is not an invitation to a useless, debilitating introspection to manufacture non-existent experiences, nor is it an attempt to shift responsibility for dealing with your hurt to someone else. It is a step of obedience to God's command, "*Let Israel say they have greatly oppressed me ... .*" Hence the need of explicit dependence on the Holy Spirit in an attitude of prayer.) For those fortunate enough to have no such "baggage," use this Prayer Guide to pray for someone who does. Then look for an opportunity to help them work their way through the issues described in this Prayer Guide.

2. As the Holy Spirit surfaces and intensifies the memories of traumatic experiences, be they in the distant or recent past, a host of "negative emotions" will almost certainly accompany them. Do not be surprised at the anger, guilt, shame, desire for revenge, etc., that will likely arise. Each person's experience is unique and results in a unique combination and intensity of these emotions. Do not attempt to analyze them at this stage. Feel them, acknowledge them, and express them to God in prayer. Fight the tendency to rationalize, to soften the pain, to make excuses for those who ploughed your back. Remember that where their actions have been sinful, as oppression always is, God feels the same holy anger; not to feel that anger is sin.

Worm Theology

But now the questions become a bit more difficult. Let's move to Psalm 22. We are most accustomed to hearing this Psalm referred to in the context of Jesus on the cross – and Jesus did cry out this Psalm in the worst of His agony. However, we forget that an Old Testament saint first wrote it to describe his own experience: *"My God, my God, why have you forsaken me? Why are you so far from saving me, so far from the words of my groaning? O my God, I cry out by day, but you do not answer, by night, and am not silent"* (vv. 1–2). This is the cry of a man who is forsaken by God. God won't act; God won't listen; God won't speak. That sets in motion a devastating chain of reasoning. Here's what the psalmist says, *"Yet you are enthroned as the Holy One; you are the praise of Israel. In you our fathers put their trust; they trusted and you delivered them. They cried to you and were saved; in you they trusted and were not disappointed"* (vv. 3–5).

These are not words of praise, but self-recrimination. The psalmist's reasoning goes something like this: "Well, I know that my forefathers, Abraham, Moses, David, and others before me trusted God and He answered them. I have prayed to the same God and He hasn't answered me. There are only two ways I can explain the difference: either God has changed or there is something wrong with me. Now my theology teaches me that God hasn't changed, since He cannot change; therefore it must be my fault." Verses 6–8 fit this scheme precisely. *"But I am a worm and not a man,"* says the writer, *"scorned by men and despised by the people. All who see me mock me; they hurl insults, shaking their heads: 'He trusts in the Lord; let the Lord rescue him. Let him deliver him, since he delights in him.'"*

When we dare to take the first step and begin to feel the pain that is within us because of repeated violations against our being, when we take the next step and begin to express the anger that is logically related to that hurt, a question begins to form in our mind: "Where was God when the ploughmen were scarring my back?" God-forsakenness begins to enter the picture for the first time and we reason in exactly the same ways. We say, "Lord, I always hear grand testimonies of how You answer other people's prayers. I pray and nothing happens to me; therefore either You have changed or something's wrong with me. Since I am taught that You don't change, it must be me. Those people must be right after all, who say, 'You have some hidden, unconfessed sin. That's why God isn't answering your prayers. You don't have enough faith; you aren't reading the Bible enough.' That's why God doesn't delight in me." (This is one reason why personal testimonies aren't very helpful for hurting people at this stage, because they only strengthen the logic of the preceding reasoning.) The devastating thing about repeated ploughing of our backs by emotional pain is that lies about who we are, our value, and our worth get lodged at the very core of our being, and we come to the conclusion that we cannot be very valuable in God's eyes.

Where to next? So far, we don't seem to be making much progress, do we? We faced the hurt, we expressed the anger, and now things are much worse than before. We feel God-forsaken and less worthy than anyone else. It would seem that way, but the turning point is not far off. Let's see where the psalmist's reasoning takes him. He continues in verse 9: "*Yet you brought me out of the womb; you made me trust in you even at my mother's breast. From birth I was cast upon you; from my mother's womb you have been my God.*" He looks back at his own history to see what traces of God's faithfulness he can recover and finds evidences that he cannot argue with: his birth and his redemption, neither of which he had anything to do with. God brought him forth from his mother's womb and God made him trust in God from that time on. So it is with us. Our creation and our redemption are two unassailable evidences of God's goodness to us. That's the turning point that gets the psalmist moving out of the pit of worm theology. For the amplification of this evidence, and to radically break the power of the lies about our worth lodged deep within, we need to move to the third Psalm in our medley, Psalm 139.

Weighty Thoughts

I know of no other single passage in Scripture that is so exquisitely formulated for this particular stage of our prayer for freedom from emotional pain. The psalmist begins, first of all, with a description of *the God who knows him:* "*O LORD, you have searched me and you know me. You know when I sit and when I rise* [his passive and active moments]; *you perceive my thoughts from afar. You discern my going out and my lying down; you are familiar with all my ways* [his conscious and subconscious, his motives and his methods]. *Before a word is on my tongue you know it completely, O LORD. You hem me in – behind and before; you have laid your hand upon me. Such knowledge is too wonderful for me, too lofty for me to attain*" (vv. 1–6). When we study something exhaustively, when we pour our whole energies into that study so we can master the subject, that's an inarguable indication of how valuable the subject of our study is to us. That's the psalmist's argument here. He says, "If God knows me that well, my active and my passive moments, my conscious and subconscious moments, my motives and my methods, what does that say about how He regards me? If He cares enough to know me completely, He must love and delight in me." Hence the conclusion – such knowledge is too wonderful for me. This deep-seated assurance of God's love for, and delight in, us is as much a part of conquering disordered inner space as are His dealings with us to thoroughly take away our sins (as in Psalm 51).

Then the writer moves on to *the God who is with him*. "*Where can I go from your Spirit? Where can I flee from your presence? If I go up to the heavens you are there; if I make my bed in the depths, you are there. If I rise on the wings of the dawn, if I settle on the far side of the sea, even there your hand will guide me, your right hand will hold me fast. If I say, 'Surely the darkness will hide me and the light become night around me,' even the darkness will not be dark to you; the night will shine like the day, for darkness is as light to you*" (vv. 7–12). We often misinterpret the point of this affirmation. We picture a God who is always spying on us to catch us in some wrongdoing, and nothing escapes Him because He can see what we do in the dark. Nothing could be further from the psalmist's thoughts. He is saying, "God is with me wherever I go; the blackest darkness can't cut me off from His watchful care over me; and besides, He's holding onto me; I'm not holding onto Him." There is a big difference between the two. If we are holding onto God and happen to lose our footing on slippery ground, we may let go of God, since our grip may not be strong enough to stand the sudden force of our feet being yanked out from under us. But if He is holding onto us and the same thing happens, our continued contact with Him does not depend on the strength of our grip but His – and He will never let go.

The psalmist's meditation on the God who knows him and the God who is with him sets the stage for the finale: "*For you created my inmost being; you knit me together in my mother's womb. I praise you because I am fearfully and wonderfully made; your works are wonderful, I know that full well. My frame was not hidden from you when I was made in the secret place. When I was woven together in the depths of the earth, your eyes saw my unformed body. All the days ordained for me were written in your book before one of them came to be*" (vv. 13–16).

Let me paraphrase this in twenty-first-century, North American industrial language so we feel the full force of the psalmist's magnificent assertion of *the God who made, and is making, him:*[3] "I am not rolling off the assembly line as one more of a million identical manufactured pieces. I am a 'one-off,' hand-finished, hand-polished, truly unique creation." The psalmist's phrase "knit together" is drawn from a word meaning "embroidered" and suggests the massive difference between embroidery and stitching on a machine. Automatic stitching machines can ram through hundreds of stitches in short order, but embroidery never goes quickly. The very word speaks of loving care and attention to detail. That's how we have been made.

The psalmist's conclusion comes in verse 17: "*How precious to me are your thoughts, O God! How vast is the sum of them!*" The word translated "precious" literally means "weighty" or "heavy." To catch the full import of this verse, we need to understand how Eastern people weigh things. They didn't have, and in many Third World countries people still don't have, electronic balances. Instead they used a manual device with two pans suspended at either end of a steel rod and a needle to indicate when the bar became horizontal. If you wanted to buy five pounds of vegetables, the vendor would put a five-pound weight in one pan and keep throwing vegetables into the other pan until the needle was vertical, showing that the rod was horizontal and that the vegetables therefore weighed five pounds.

Let's use this picture to paraphrase the psalmist's summary of God's thoughts concerning him (and us). It's as if God is saying, "Take one of those balances and put down on one pan every negative word that has ever been spoken about you and all the negative thoughts about yourself that you have had (*viz.*, I am a worm, I am not a man, etc.). Put them all in one pan. Then, in the other pan, put down what I think about you. Guess which side will go plummeting down in an awful hurry? What I think about you outweighs everything else that anybody else (including yourself) can think or has thought, about you." Can you imagine the value of an affirmation like that to someone who has had their back ploughed repeatedly? When lies about ourselves lodge deep inside us, one of the consequent problems is that we are no longer able to receive even honest compliments. Someone will say to us, "Wow, that's a beautiful dress." Our immediate response is, "You're only saying that because you're my mother, my husband, my friend. If you really knew what I was like, you wouldn't be impressed with this dress. You wouldn't like me at all; you wouldn't want to be with me either; you're only tolerating me right now." God's response to that person is: "I know you inside out, and you are mine; I know you inside out, and I am always with you. In fact, you can't get rid of me. I have felt this way about you since the day I made you and before you had even lived out one day of your life on earth." This is bedrock truth, the only truth that will allow us to eventually break the power of the lies that have taken root deep inside us, because of repeated scarrings in the past.

Prayer Guide

Review the psalmist's "worm theology" (the reasoning that leads to the conclusion that he is a worm, in whom God cannot delight).

- What lies about your own worth and esteem in God's sight have taken hold because of a similar reasoning? Name the specific feelings of self-hatred and disparagement, the circumstances and/or people that tend to confirm the conclusions of "worm theology." Acknowledge these feelings as lies that do not represent the truth about how God sees you. Throughout this process, keep asking for the Holy Spirit's help and illumination. "Worm theology" is not easy to unmask. It often hides under a veneer of self-confidence, brashness masquerading as boldness, feverish activity undertaken to prove, by achieving success, that one is not a worm, verbal "put-downs" of others and various other nefarious disguises. Be done with all such posturing. Acknowledge such "cover-ups" as sinful dependence on human strategies.

- Now replace the lies with the truth as you follow the psalmist in Psalm 22. Review your individual history and look for evidence of God's faithfulness to you, especially in (but not restricted to) your birth and your salvation. Thank Him for what He shows you. Remember that your very praying is because of His gift of salvation to you, and that was accomplished before you had lived out even one day of your life. Amplify your prayers using the threefold scheme of the psalmist in Psalm 139: the God who knows you, who is with you, and who has embroidered you as a "one-off" unique exhibit of His grace and glory. Recall that these thoughts of God about you outweigh every other competing thought about you (i.e., the lies you identified above). So read Psalm 139 aloud, taking time to rehearse every affirmation as applying, not just to some poet who lived millennia ago, but to you now.

_____

Why Didn't He Stop It!

Now, just when things are beginning to look up, when it seems we've been able to salvage what appeared to be an irredeemable situation, we are hit broadside with the biggest question of them all. It goes like this: "Just a minute. If I am fearfully and wonderfully made by God, if I am thoroughly known by God and if He is with me, if there is no place where I am invisible to Him, even in the depths of 'hell,' that must mean God was present right there when the ploughmen were cutting my back to ribbons, watching it all. He was there when I was insulted over and over again on the sports field in elementary school. He was there when all my schoolmates, and even my teachers, made fun of me because I was different. He was there when I was abused, verbally, physically, and emotionally. He was there when I was beaten up. If so, why didn't He do anything? I thought it was bad enough to have to deal with a God who had forsaken me; it's ten thousand times harder to handle a God who was there and did nothing." Unless we answer this question, all the steps we've gone through so far, no matter how well conceived, are rendered powerless to heal.

Interestingly, it is at this point that the bankruptcy of secular psychology becomes evident. It can exhort us to acknowledge the pain of past traumas in our life. It can legitimize negative emotions and encourage us to express them, especially anger. From there, it can point out the danger of "worm theology" (usually by dismissing "guilt" altogether as a pathological emotion) and encourage us instead to think positively by affirming our intrinsic worth as human beings. But that's all! Secular psychology cannot pour meaning into suffering – especially suffering inflicted on us by the actions of another so that we truly bear no responsibility for our pain. At this point, not only secular psychology but all religious systems are equally bankrupt – with one startling exception.

A God with "Eternal" Wounds

Let's return to Psalm 22 for the answer to this final "Why?" "Why, if God was with me, did He allow the oppression – especially in my youth, when I was helpless and innocent?" In our first look at Psalm 22, we dwelt on its significance in the mouth of a human poet; this time, we will consider its meaning as it was wrenched from the anguished soul of Jesus Christ on the cross. Sure, the Gospel accounts of our Lord's suffering only record Him uttering the opening line of this Psalm: *"My God, my God, why have you forsaken me?"* but in all likelihood, this was a culmination of His reflections on the entire Psalm, since it presents such a graphic picture of the agony and shame of a public crucifixion surrounded by a mocking crowd. Listen as Jesus continues to speak, *"Many bulls surround me, strong bulls of Bashan encircle me. Roaring lions tearing their prey open their mouths wide against me. I am poured out like water, and all my bones are out of joint. My heart has turned to water; it has melted away within me. My strength has dried up like a potsherd, and my tongue sticks to the roof of my mouth; you lay me in the dust of death. Dogs have surrounded me; a band of evil men has encircled me, they have pierced my hands and my feet. I can count all my bones; people stare and gloat over me. They divide my garments among them and cast lots for my clothing"* (vv. 12–18). And when you add to these pathetic pleas the almost certain fact that Jesus was hanging naked on the cross, you get some idea of the incredible humiliation and the public shame to which He was subjected.

Physical pain of indescribable intensity is nearly forgotten in the pain of the emotional taunting – Jesus' own promises thrown back in His face, people actually taking delight in another human's misery. And what shall we say of the pain caused by some who were not even concerned enough to mock? They merely ignored Him while gambling for His only earthly possession. Whatever else God may say, or not, about the pain that comes into our lives, He makes one thing very clear. He is not a distant or detached God "up there," dispensing pious theological platitudes. He came down here. He wasn't just there with us when we were being emotionally scarred, He was receiving it in His person at the same time. We don't have a God who just knows about our pain; we have a God who was, and is, hurt in our hurt. If it scarred our back, it scarred His first. He bleeds now. (This is no empty exercise of the imagination. The Bible tells us that the Lamb of

God was slain before the foundation of the world. His wounds are eternal in a sense that we "time-bound" creatures can never grasp; we can only worship Him and thank Him that it is indeed so.)

A Daring Affirmation

But even that isn't enough, for eventually Jesus died, leaving us with a sympathetic, but very dead, Saviour – and that is not adequate to dignify our suffering with meaning. The dignity comes only through the unexpected, sudden, unbelievable, amazing transformation in the second half of Psalm 22. The very one who was pathetically affirming his status as a mere worm before God now cries out in victory, "*I will declare your name to my brothers; in the congregation I will praise you. You who fear the LORD, praise him! All you descendants of Jacob, honor him! Revere him, all you descendants of Israel! For he has not despised or disdained the suffering of the afflicted one; he has not hidden his face from him but has listened to his cry for help. From you comes the theme of my praise in the great assembly; before those who fear you will I fulfill my vows. The poor will eat and be satisfied; they who seek the LORD will praise him – may your hearts live forever! All the ends of the earth will remember and turn to the LORD, and all the families of the nations will bow down before him, for dominion belongs to the LORD and he rules over the nations. All the rich of the earth will feast and worship; all who go down to the dust will kneel before him – those who cannot keep themselves alive. Posterity will serve him; future generations will be told about the LORD. They will proclaim his righteousness to a people yet unborn – for he has done it*" (vv. 22–31).

Right on the cross, there is an unbelievable transition from sorrow to faith, not *in spite of* the incredible suffering He is undergoing, but because of it. Jesus on the cross sees that His suffering will result in universal praise to God the Father, universal praise to Himself and that from generations as yet unborn. That's why He is able to pray, "Father, forgive them, for they don't know what they are doing. They don't know that in abusing me they are your instruments for the universal conquest of the nations by the Lord God Himself."

Good Friday tells us that we have a God who experientially identified with us in our pain, but it took Easter Sunday morning to assure us that meaning can be poured into apparently meaningless suffering by a God who uses that suffering for the redemption of humanity. And because we are united with Christ by faith in His death and resurrection, we can dare to believe that God can do the same with our suffering – make it a redemptive influence in this world, setting people free and bringing joy to our own hearts. And because Jesus broke through to this conviction while still on the cross, so can we, while still stinging from the meaningless oppression of our youth. That's why it is possible to sit in a church that has just been totally devastated by a tornado (not one that God merely sent, but one that He "rode" into the church), and realize that, as a consequence of that, nations will experience the redemptive influence of Christ's suffering.

Prayer Guide

1. Re-read Psalm 22:1–21. Reflect on the extent to which these words might describe your trauma, the ploughing of your back. Then recall that these words describe Jesus' suffering. Thank God that, even as the plough cut its furrows in your back, it lacerated His. He, too, was feeling the pain, mockery, and shame. Then sing, or reflect on, a passion hymn like "O Sacred Head, Now Wounded."[4]

2. Read the rest of Psalm 22, Christ's grand affirmation of the Sovereignty of God in transforming His suffering into a universally redemptive force. Ask the Holy Spirit to show you how this might happen with your trauma. Pray for its fulfillment.

It Is Finished

The last words of Psalm 22 are *"For he has done it."* Scholars tell us that this phrase is dynamically equivalent to Jesus' cry on the cross, *"It is finished."* Here all legitimate demands for justice against the sins of the ploughmen and oppressors have been finally and fully met. It is this dual conviction that God's justice has been fully satisfied in Jesus' suffering and death on the cross and that His Sovereignty can take our suffering and dignify it by making it a redemptive influence – and this allows us to pray, "Father, forgive them for they didn't know what they were doing. They hurt me, but you have transformed it into a redemptive factor in this world." That, and only that, is God's way of "forgiving and forgetting"; anything else is cheap forgiveness. Rick Buller, a member of our congregation, a dear friend and brother in the Lord, became a paraplegic in a hunting accident over twenty-five years ago. He knows in practice what I have tried to explain (inadequately) in the preceding pages. He once observed, "You cannot really forgive unless you first fully count the cost of the offence against you."

That's what these Psalms teach us to do. Remember that their primary purpose is not to teach us doctrine but to shape our prayers. The various steps I have outlined above are really not so much for the psychologist's couch as they are for our prayer closets, although they belong in both places. Each one of those steps is most efficiently and effectively implemented on our knees, often with the help of others. Hurt and pain, caused by repeated ploughing, is best unearthed in the presence of God. The anger that inevitably comes from that kind of hurt, a just and holy anger, finds its best, most healthy expression, when the Psalms are allowed to shape the resulting expression of our wrath. The identifying and replacing of lies about ourselves by the wonderful truths of Psalm 139 are best done and are internalized most effectively in prayer. As for the critical conviction that our legitimate demand for justice has been met on the cross and that out of our suffering can come a redemptive function in other people's lives and joy to us – I know of no place where that can happen, except in prayer.

In his Gospel (5:5–6), John tells us how Jesus came across a man at the pool of Bethesda who *"had been an invalid for thirty-eight years. When Jesus saw him lying there and learned that he had been in this condition for a long time, he asked him, 'Do you want to get well?'"* He's asking it again, now. What is your answer?

Prayer Guide

Pray by name, and as specifically as you can, for the mercy of God toward the ploughmen who furrowed your back. Remember that the issue here is that of your readiness to forgive. For your oppressors to actually experience that forgiveness, they need to repent and confess their sin. That is not your responsibility.

Chapter 11

Psalm 37:
When You're Hot
under the Collar

1 *Do not fret because of evil men or be envious of those who do wrong; 2 for like the grass they will soon wither, like green plants they will soon die away. 3 Trust in the* Lord *and do good; dwell in the land and enjoy safe pasture. 4 Delight yourself in the* Lord *and he will give you the desires of your heart. 5 Commit your way to the* Lord; *trust in him and he will do this: 6 He will make your righteousness shine like the dawn, the justice of your cause like the noonday sun. 7 Be still before the* Lord *and wait patiently for him; do not fret when men succeed in their ways, when they carry out their wicked schemes. 8 Refrain from anger and turn from wrath; do not fret – it leads only to evil. 9 For evil men will be cut off, but those who hope in the* Lord *will inherit the land. 10 A little while, and the wicked will be no more; though you look for them, they will not be found. 11 But the meek will inherit the land and enjoy great peace. 12 The wicked plot against the righteous and gnash their teeth at them; 13 but the Lord laughs at the wicked, for he knows their day is coming. 14 The wicked draw the sword and bend the bow to bring down the poor and needy, to slay those whose ways are upright. 15 But their swords will pierce their own hearts, and their bows will be broken. 16 Better the little that the righteous have than the wealth of many wicked; 17 for the power of the wicked will be broken, but*

the LORD upholds the righteous. 18 The days of the blameless are
known to the LORD, and their inheritance will endure forever.
19 In times of disaster they will not wither; in days of famine they
will enjoy plenty. 20 But the wicked will perish: The LORD's enemies
will be like the beauty of the fields, they will vanish – vanish like
smoke. 21 The wicked borrow and do not repay, but the righteous
give generously; 22 those the LORD blesses will inherit the land, but
those he curses will be cut off. 23 If the LORD delights in a man's
way, he makes his steps firm; 24 though he stumble, he will not fall,
for the LORD upholds him with his hand. 25 I was young and now I
am old, yet I have never seen the righteous forsaken or their children
begging for bread. 26 They are always generous and lend freely;
their children will be blessed. 27 Turn from evil and do good; then
you will dwell in the land forever. 28 For the LORD loves the just and
will not forsake his faithful ones. They will be protected forever, but
the offspring of the wicked will be cut off; 29 the righteous will
inherit the land and dwell in it forever. 30 The mouth of the
righteous man utters wisdom, and his tongue speaks what is just.
31 The law of his God is in his heart; his feet do not slip.
32 The wicked lie in wait for the righteous, seeking their very lives;
33 but the LORD will not leave them in their power or let them be
condemned when brought to trial. 34 Wait for the LORD and keep his
way. He will exalt you to inherit the land; when the wicked are cut
off, you will see it. 35 I have seen a wicked and ruthless man
flourishing like a green tree in its native soil, 36 but he soon passed
away and was no more; though I looked for him, he could not be
found. 37 Consider the blameless, observe the upright; there is a
future [Or "there will be posterity"] for the man of peace. 38 But all
sinners will be destroyed; the future [Or "posterity"] of the wicked
will be cut off. 39 The salvation of the righteous comes from the
LORD; he is their stronghold in time of trouble. 40 The LORD helps
them and delivers them; he delivers them from the wicked and saves
them, because they take refuge in him.

Wisdom from an Old Man

Every issue of *Leadership* magazine carries one article entitled "Leadership Forum" – a panel discussion among three or four Christian leaders on the main theme of that particular issue. One forum dealt with the issue of clergy malpractice – pastors being sued for counsel that the counselee felt was detrimental to their well-being. Toward the end of the forum, the panelists were asked this question: "How does the sovereignty of God affect the way you handle such cases?" I was struck by the response of one man, named Ericsson: "Psalm 37 says, *'Do not fret because of evil men or be envious of those who do wrong; for like the grass they will soon wither, like green plants they will soon die away. Trust in the* LORD *and do good'* "(vv. 1–3). In these situations, the key is how we respond to the attack. The principle of Psalm 37 is to dwell in the land and cultivate faithfulness. What concerns me … is the anger I see in the church that professes the sovereignty of God … Right now, the group seen as most militant is conservative Christians. … By getting rattled, we react the same way the world reacts. They see no difference."[1]

Whether conservative Christians were indeed the most militant group then (1985) or now is beside the point. What remains relevant is the intensely practical question, How do we keep from getting rattled? How do we practically distill the sovereignty of God into the multitude of "little" irritations and injustices that make us hot under the collar? God's answer, as Ericsson suggested, is found in Psalm 37.

A few general observations before we get to the details. Evidently, this Psalm was written by David when he was an old man (see verse 25: "*I was young and now I am old*"). His advice to us comes from several years of experience that have been interpreted in light of, and that have shed light on, God's Word. That's an unbeatable combination for dispensing practical wisdom. And David gives it to us in the form of an acrostic. The forty verses of this Psalm are divided into twenty-two groups, each beginning with one of the letters of the Hebrew alphabet. Thus the Psalm is a product of careful reflection and not an impassioned outburst of his heart, as some of the other Psalms are. He uses this acrostic device to give some structure to his musings on several related topics which are distributed throughout the whole Psalm, rather than being compartmentalized into distinct, separate blocks of continuous verses. Therefore our study will not proceed sequentially from verses 1 to 40. We'll proceed instead from theme to theme, considering the various verses that bear on each.

Before launching into this discussion, however, a few words should be said about the psalmist's references to "evil men" and "the wicked." The biblical Wisdom Literature often refers to the wicked in contrast to the godly. While this can, and often does, refer to a definite difference in the moral convictions and behaviours of the two groups, the Bible is not at all reticent about the severe moral deficiencies and often horrible sins of the "godly." The fundamental idea behind the word "wicked" is that of leaving God out of the picture, whereas the godly have Him in the picture as the all-important reality. So we can, in fact, have a very clean-living ungodly person and a godly person who may struggle a lot more with sins. What is at issue is not who is better than whom but who is willing to make God the central reality of their lives and who wants to be totally autonomous.

Don't Fret!

The one big issue that ties verses 1 to 40 together is found in the opening verse, *"Do not fret because of evil men or be envious of those who do wrong"* (v. 1). This exhortation is repeated in verses 7 and 8: *"Be still before the LORD and wait patiently for him; do not fret when men succeed in their ways, when they carry out their wicked schemes. Refrain from anger and turn from wrath; do not fret – it leads only to evil."* But what is fretting? When I was in my early teens, my "engineer" uncle introduced my cousin and me to a fretsaw. Unlike the more conventional saws I had seen carpenters use on planks of wood, the fretsaw had a metallic "U" frame that was about eighteen inches long. Between its ends was a fine-toothed blade, barely an eighth of an inch wide and about five inches long. It was used to cut intricate patterns in plywood sheets – not by making large sweeping cuts, but by rapid sawing with several short strokes. It wore down, or fretted away, rather than cut through, the plywood. In the process, the thin blade got so hot you couldn't touch it without getting burned. That's the idea behind the Hebrew command translated as "don't fret" in these verses. Don't get heated up.

As for the word "envious" in verse 1, it literally means "to glow." So the psalmist is giving us some practical wisdom on how to handle those situations when repeated subjection to certain events, or repeated rehearsal of certain issues and events in our minds, can raise the temperature and get us hot under the collar. Specifically, he has in mind fretting over wrongdoers. He amplifies this in verse 7 as fretting caused by the success of wrongdoers in their wicked schemes: rogues going free and honest people taking it on the chin, and other apparent or real injustices that so typically characterize life.

Verses 12, 14, and 32 give us some examples of the success of the wicked that he is facing: *"The wicked plot against the righteous and gnash their teeth at them"* (v. 12); *"The wicked draw the sword and bend the bow to bring down the poor and needy, to slay those whose ways are upright"* (v. 14); *"The wicked lie in wait for the righteous, seeking their very lives"* (v. 32). Another source of fretting is *the wealth, power, and influence* of the wicked: *"Better the little that the righteous have than the wealth of many wicked; for the power of the wicked will be broken, but the* LORD *upholds the righteous"* (vv. 16–17). The psalmist is also irritated by *the progressive nature of their prosperity*, which he describes in four different images. Theirs is the beauty of grass and green plants (v. 2), of fields (v. 20), and of a flourishing tree (v. 35). We can probably identify with every one of these sources of fretting.

Why, however, should the success, wealth, power, influence, and prosperity of the wicked cause the psalmist and us to fret? Because we know that, by bending the rules a bit, by being willing to compromise just a bit, we, too, could have more money, influence, and prosperity. Yet at the same time, we feel an inward compulsion to lead a "God-fearing" life. Driven by the logic and truth of our faith, we know we cannot compromise and bend the rules. So we continue to face the hardships of a Christian life while the wicked seem to go merrily on their way with all the appearance of success – and the more we think about this, the more we fret. Now if just thinking about this general situation can cause us to fret, imagine what can happen when the scheming of the ungodly comes close enough to affect us personally. That's when the fretsaw speeds up and the temperature under the collar rises several degrees, and rapidly at that. The psalmist's opening salvo is "Don't fret." Good! But we need more. "Just say No" doesn't work any better when it comes to fretting than it does with drugs.

He gives us more in verse 8: *"Refrain from anger and turn from wrath; do not fret – it leads only to evil."* Fretting leads to anger, wrath, and evil. How? The longer we fret, the hotter we get under the collar and the more likely we are to turn to thoughts of retaliation and to lie in wait for an opportunity to take revenge.

Perhaps God in His mercy will foil our attempts at retaliation. Perhaps life being what it is, the opportunity will never arise. Nonetheless, our frustration level increases and so does the likelihood of our doing something rash and foolish. "Stop fretting," the psalmist implies, "by realizing that it is the first loop in a downward spiral leading to evil." To this negative motivation, he then adds several positive incentives.

Two Popular Verses

Let's begin with perhaps the two most popular, most often memorized, and most quoted verses from this Psalm: "*Delight yourself in the* LORD *and he will give you the desires of your heart. Commit your way to the* LORD; *trust in him and he will do this*" (vv. 4–5). The usual understanding of these verses goes something like this: "If you really want something from the Lord deep in your heart, keep praying, keep committing it to Him, trust Him to give it to you, and eventually you will get it because He will bring it to pass." But if we take a closer look at these verses in the overall context of the Psalm, we will find that this popular, comforting interpretation quite misses the mark. The psalmist's emphasis is altogether different. Let's consider a few of the key phrases in these two verses.

- *Delighting in the Lord* refers to a very deliberate refocusing and redirection of our thoughts toward God. Injustices at the hands of the ungodly (or the godly for that matter) have a way of making us focus on them. Even if we make a Herculean attempt to forgive the person(s) involved, the injustice itself has a way of cropping up and intruding into our thoughts. Why did Peter ask the Lord whether he needed to forgive someone seven times? It's quite likely that he had forgiven that person six times already and that not for six different wrongs, but for six remembrances of the same wrong. Jesus' reply, that he would have to forgive the man seventy times seven, suggests that the same injustice might come back to haunt Peter many more times. "Each time the injustice intrudes into your consciousness," says the psalmist, "focus your attention on God in worship – that is, focus on one of His attributes." (This is where a practised habit of daily withdrawal into His presence for meditation and worship becomes such an ally. If we wait to worship Him until we get hot under the collar and the fretsaw starts buzzing, we will find it almost impossible.)

Add to this the writer's affirmation in verse 31: "*The law of his God is in his heart; his feet do not slip.*" The psalmist's delight in his Lord was inseparable from his delight in the Law of the Lord. Hence his declaration elsewhere in the Psalms: "*I will bow down toward your holy temple and will praise your name … for you have exalted above all things your name and your word*" (Psalm 138:2). (This underlines the value of a regular encounter and increasing familiarity with His Word. A sudden turning to the Word when the fretsaw starts buzzing is likely to prove as unfruitful as a sudden attempt to worship Him in the same circumstances.) So *delighting in the Lord* means a deliberate focusing of our thoughts on the Lord in worship and through His Word. As we do this, one of two things, and perhaps both, begin to happen.

- *Our desires begin to change.* The fretsaw is no longer moving, since we have stopped thinking about the injustices. As our Gentle Shepherd promises to lead us to quiet waters, places His healing hands on our foreheads, and begins to draw out the heat generated by the fretting, we begin to cool down. Wrong desires for retaliation are slowly replaced with desires consistent with His Word. That's why the link with verse 31 is so critical. If the law is in our hearts, the desires of our hearts will slowly gravitate toward those in harmony with that law. And once the desires of the heart are transformed, the mouth speaks appropriately, for these two are intimately related. Instead of rash, hot, retaliatory words come words of justice and wisdom: "*The mouth of the righteous man utters wisdom, and his tongue speaks what is just*" (v. 30).

I recall a marriage that was on the verge of breakdown after many years of turmoil. The wife was bitter and filled with hatred. Her only thought was for retaliation. My suggestion as to how they could start rebuilding their marriage was met with the immediate objection, "But I don't want things to change, for if it does and we start loving each other, how can I get back at him for what he has done to me all these years?" That's fretting. The wife's reaction after several weeks of learning to refocus on the Lord and His Word? She still had many negative feelings and was still unsure, but there was a new willingness to give the marriage a sincere try because she recognized the inevitable downward spiral that would be caused by fretting and planning for retaliation.

This is one way the Lord will give us the desires of our heart – by transforming them into harmony with His Law. God will also give us more of Himself if we delight in Him and His Word. It is not surprising, then, that the Lord Himself becomes the desire of our hearts. We want more of the same experiences of worship through His Word. And that is one desire He will always satisfy. We can have as much of Him as we want.

Delighting in the Lord when we are tempted to fret has one other aspect. Let's go back to verse 30 for a minute: "*The mouth of the righteous man utters wisdom, and his tongue speaks what is just.*" Not only is this a description of what happens to us when we delight in the Lord; it also suggests who we should be looking to for help when we are fretting. Our usual reaction is to search out and talk to those who will stimulate and encourage our desire for retaliation or, if that is not possible, those who would at least affirm our negative feelings and encourage us to stoke them and nurse our grudge because "We owe it to ourselves." The psalmist's words suggest it is far wiser to go to those whose hearts are full of the Word of God and who therefore speak wisdom. They can help us immensely in this matter of delighting ourselves in the Lord.

- As for verse 5 – "*Commit your way to the LORD; trust in him and he will do this*" – what exactly is the "way" here? In context, the most likely reference is to our deliberate decision to delight ourselves in the Lord and not to pursue the way of retaliation. What is the "this" He promises to do? Again, in context, it does not mean that God will carry out our plans *for* us. Instead, it refers to what follows, in verse 6: "*He will make your righteousness shine like the dawn, the justice of your cause like the noonday sun.*" Traditionally, the latter part of verse 6 is translated as "He will bring it to pass" (which may have led to the popular idea that God would fulfill our plans). However, this obscures the key link between verses 5 and 6. So verse 4 ("*Delight yourself in the LORD ... *") to verse 6 form a unity which, taken together, tells us that when we choose to delight in the Lord, He will not only transform the desires of our hearts; He will also vindicate us. Our character will be demonstrated in the kind of response we have chosen, and eventually, it will become clear to all that we were indeed in the right as far as the specific injustice against us was concerned. The contrast to the popular interpretation of verses 4 and 5 couldn't be more stark.

Now at first, this vindication may not be startling or dramatic. It may be only like the faint light of dawn. But eventually it will be as plain as the noonday sun, there for all to see and acknowledge. Verse 7 follows this interpretation naturally: *"Be still before the LORD and wait patiently for him … ."* In other words, wait! Don't plunge into ill-conceived, emotion-driven steps to retaliate or vindicate your own name and the justice of your cause. Wait for God to do it. That's where the *"trust also in him"* comes in. This waiting for His vindication, especially for the faint light of dawn to blossom into the full brightness of the noonday sun, calls for faith in His Word, since there is no time element in the promise of vindication.

Next question? What do we do while we wait for His Divine vindication?

- *"**Trust in the LORD and do good**; dwell in the land and enjoy safe pasture"* (v. 3). While we wait (as a demonstration of our trust in His timing for our evident vindication), we are to do good. Fretting not only begins the downward spiral toward evil, it also paralyzes our good acts. The energy spent in fretting and planning retaliation drains us. So after we have refocused and delighted in the Lord through His Word, the psalmist tells us to get back to doing good, perhaps even, or especially, toward the one who has caused us to fret.

This, by the way, is where the New Testament definition of "doing good" goes more deeply than any definition found in the Psalms. For Jesus tells us in Luke 6:27, *"But I tell you who hear me: Love your enemies, do good to those who hate you, bless those who curse you, pray for those who mistreat you."* Blessing and praying for those who have caused us to fret is part of the good we are encouraged to do while we wait. Paul builds on this in Romans 12:20, where he tells us that, by doing good to one who has done wrong to us, *"we … will heap burning coals on his head."* In other words, they will burn while we will cool. The "burning coals" have nothing to do with their judgement. Wishing for that is the very attitude

Jesus and Paul warn us against. Rather they refer to the remorse, shame, and possible softening of the enemy's heart by our totally unexpected response toward them – one that consists of the sequence (1) delight in the Lord, (2) commit your way, (3) trust your vindication to Him, and (4) do good. One possible, even likely, interpretation of "heaping burning coals on someone's head" in the biblical Wisdom Literature is as a metaphor for something that produces a radical change of heart.

Admittedly, doing good to the one who has caused us to fret is the most difficult step of all. I find, in my own experience, that I am usually able to delight, commit, and trust, and do other kinds of good while I wait, but doing good to the offender, that's always a struggle. However, the times I have been able to carry my obedience that far, I have discovered that the fretting stops almost instantaneously and there has often been a quick change in the other person's heart.

• The entire process I have described above (based on a contextual consideration of verses 4 to 6) is one that needs to be deliberately cultivated. Consider the second part of verse 3: *"Trust in the LORD and do good; dwell in the land and enjoy safe pasture."* At first sight, it seems totally out of place. What does the enjoyment of "safe pasture" have to do with the psalmist's carefully woven prescription for handling the temptation to fret over our injustices? Once again I am indebted to scholars of the original languages who have pointed out that other translations of this verse are just as plausible. The verb translated "to dwell" can also mean "to strive after" or "to tend." The phrase translated "safe pasture" can be translated as "faithfulness." So the psalmist could be saying, "Trust in the Lord and do good; strive after or cultivate [tend to] faithfulness." That would fit the context, for then the psalmist would be saying, "Delight, commit, trust, do good, and by the way, carefully cultivate this response sequence. Keep responding this way in every fretful situation until it becomes second nature."

Yet another way to translate this latter part of verse 3 could be: "Feed on His faithfulness." Depend on His strength to keep you on this admittedly difficult, though wise, course of action. This interpretation also fits the larger context of the Psalm and is consistent with what we find in verse 23: *"If the LORD delights in a man's way, he makes his steps firm."*

We begin by delighting, committing, trusting in Him, doing good, and progressively making this a habit. Now He is the one who delights in us and our way and makes our steps firm. He is the one who makes this response a habit in our lives. He does what we cannot do by ourselves.

Does that mean there will be no relapses on our part? Is this a formula guaranteeing immediate success? No! There will be failures along the way. Having begun with every good intention to follow the psalmist's approach to dealing with fretful situations, we might recant. We might go part way and then yield. We might succeed on two or three occasions and blow it on the fourth attempt. No matter. In verse 24 we read, *"Though he stumble, he will not fall, for the* LORD *upholds him with his hand."* We may be down, but never out. The Lord Himself will pick us up. And don't forget, these are the words of an experienced old man. A lifetime of mistakes and obedience have taught him these principles; we know he failed at times – including committing adultery and murder (see Chapter 9) – but equally certainly, the Lord must have picked him up repeatedly and sent him on the wise way again until he broke through to freedom from fretting and to doing good to those who caused him to fret.

But what if the external circumstances that tempt us to fret don't change quickly? Even when we change, others do not always change. Even when individuals (e.g., a spouse or a fellow worker) change, societal injustice continues unabated. That can be a continued source of fretting. What perspectives will help us continue to win the battle? Enter the psalmist's second major theme.

The Certain Judgement of the Wicked

The writer builds his case from several angles. The wicked are *transient: "But the wicked will perish: The* LORD'*s enemies will be like the beauty of the fields, they will vanish – vanish like smoke"* (v. 20). Their *destruction is total: " … he soon passed away and was no more; though I looked for him, he could not be found"* (v. 36). Even *their offspring are affected: " … but the offspring of the wicked will be cut off … But all sinners will be destroyed; the future of the wicked will be cut off"* (vv. 28, 38). The instruments they use to carry out their wicked schemes *will return to haunt them* like boomerangs: *"But their swords will pierce their own hearts, and their bows will be broken"* (v. 15).

Their *judgement is certain: "* ... *but the Lord laughs at the wicked, for he knows their day is coming"* (v. 13).

The certainty of their destruction lies not just in the fact that God will one day intervene to stop them in their tracks, but that, as far as God is concerned, judgement is already on its way, somewhat like the radiation from the Chernobyl nuclear plant disaster in the Ukraine. Countries like Poland and Sweden knew the deadly stuff was on its way, and certain to reach them, even though they were as yet free from any contamination. And they were helpless to do anything about it. Only global changes in the weather patterns on an unprecedented scale could have diverted the radiation. God's judgement is similarly inevitable, but for one thing. It can be diverted through true repentance and changed ways which reflect that repentance.

What's more, says the psalmist, this isn't just theory. I've lived long enough to know that it is true: *"I have seen a wicked and ruthless man flourishing like a green tree in its native soil, but he soon passed away and was no more; though I looked for him, he could not be found"* (vv. 35–36). He had to wait until the fourth stage of the wicked man's prosperity (grass, green plants, fields, flourishing tree) until he saw his destruction, but it came. And the psalmist assures us that we won't just have to take his word for it, though it is reliable. What he has seen, we will see: *"A little while, and the wicked will be no more; though **you** look for them, they will not be found ... Wait for the* LORD *and keep his way ... when the wicked are cut off, **you** will see it"* (vv. 10, 34).

Prayer Guide

1. Think of one or more successes of "the wicked" that currently make you "hot under the collar." Apply the psalmist's prescription to the situation in prayer. If the temptation to fret is irrelevant to you at this point, use this guide to intercede for someone who is struggling with a situation that is making them fret.

   • Acknowledge any anger, thoughts of retaliation, and actual acts of "evil" toward the offender that have resulted from fretting.

   • Delight, commit, trust in Him by refocusing your thoughts (from yourself to Him) through His Word. Until this becomes a habit, use the following example, based on Psalm 115, as a starting point.

2. Psalm 115 begins with a prayer of refocusing. *"Not to us, O Lord, not to us but to your name be the glory, because of your love and faithfulness"* (v. 1). Make that your opening affirmation. The Psalm goes on to describe several stark contrasts between idols and Jehovah. What the psalmist affirms negatively about idols (they cannot speak or see, etc.) is, by implication, a positive affirmation of Jehovah's attributes. Focus on the significance of each of these, think about what they mean for you, and then respond in thanksgiving, petition, or praise, as appropriate. Because God has a *mouth*, He can speak His Living Word to us, and that will counter the taunts of those who may be oppressing us (v. 5). Because He has *eyes*, He can see; He can look into our hearts and those of our oppressors to know who needs vindication (v. 5). He has *ears* and so can hear our cry for help and vindication when we are tempted to fret. The heavens are not like brass. He is not a distant, uninvolved God (v. 6). He has a *nose* and can smell; our worship rises as an acceptable offering to Him. Our present attempt to delight in Him does in fact delight Him. He takes pleasure in it and in us (v. 6). He has *hands* and so can feel. Like the hands of a skillful surgeon or an expert masseur, He can still the agitation caused by injustice and the clamour of our hearts for retaliation. He can clean and bandage the raw wounds of our enemies' taunts (v. 7). He has *feet* and can walk. Like our shepherd, He goes before us, paving the way through a fretful life strewn with injustices (v. 7). He has a *throat* so He can roar. He can, and will, judge the "wicked," no matter how much they are flourishing at present (v. 7). He is *able to transform* us even as we delight in Him (v. 8).

   Because of God's personal care for us, we, too, will speak lifegiving words to others, see the real nature of things, listen to others, smell the fragrance of God's Creation, feel the hurts of others, and heal and walk before others to guide them. Thus, we will transform those who walk with us. This is the blessing He will bless us with. No one will be able to curse us, for He can turn even their curses into a blessing (vv. 12–13).

3. Once you have *delighted* in Him in this way, it is so much easier to *commit* to this way of responding to Him, to affirm your *trust* in Him for eventual vindication, and to ask Him what *good* He would have you do (especially toward those who have misused you), and to pray for the grace to obey.

4. End this phase of your prayer by asking the Lord to *sustain* you in this process of "delighting, committing, and trusting" until it becomes a habit and to pick you up if you stumble and suffer a relapse.

In sharp contrast to the destiny of the wicked is the destiny of the righteous. If the wicked are transient and destined for total and certain destruction, what can the righteous look forward to? That takes us to the third theme of the psalmist's multistranded encouragement in the face of the temptation to fret.

The Promise of the Land

We find this promise strewn in various places throughout the Psalm: " ... *but those who hope in the* LORD *will inherit the land"* (v. 9); *"But the meek will inherit the land and enjoy great peace"* (v. 11); *"The days of the blameless are known to the* LORD, *and their inheritance will endure forever"* (v. 18); *"the righteous will inherit the land and dwell in it forever"* (v. 29); *"Wait for the* LORD *and keep his way. He will exalt you to inherit the land; when the wicked are cut off, you will see it"* (v. 34). What's more, the immediate context for each of these verses is the destiny of the wicked, which we have already considered. This is one of the essential techniques of the Wisdom Literature in the Bible: contrasting the eventual outcome of the two ways of living. Notice how the psalmist rings the changes in his description of the righteous. All of their characteristics – hopefulness, meekness, blamelessness – are to be interpreted in light of the main purpose of the Psalm. These qualities belong to those who follow the process of delighting, committing, trusting, and doing good while leaving retribution and vindication to the Lord. People who follow this path are the ones who will inherit the land – a promise that acts as a further incentive to continue the process of delighting and committing.

This brings us to an important question: What does the promise of inheriting the land mean? In the Old Testament, God's spiritual blessings upon a people were inseparably linked with His material blessings on them – health, an abundant harvest, protection from their enemies, and so on (although it is important to remember that even these promises were most often given collectively to the nation and not explicitly to individuals). In the New Covenant, inaugurated by the Lord Jesus Christ, we know that God's blessings are not automatically connected with material abundance, notwithstanding the silky-smooth delusions of the prosperity preachers who promise health, wealth, and happiness for all believers. Yet none other than the Lord Jesus quoted this promise of the land in His Beatitudes, *"Blessed are the meek, for they will inherit the earth"* (Matthew 5:5). So these promises are in some way pertinent to us as well. What, then, does it mean for us to inherit the land?

- Sometimes it works out literally. I recall reading in the Toronto newspapers about a wealthy old lady who, in her will, said, "To my family, I leave exactly what they gave me when I was alive – nothing!" She bequeathed a couple of million dollars to several faithful friends who used to visit her and take her for drives. The meek, rather than the aggressive, literally inherited material goods. Whether they were Christians or not is beside the point. Some biblical principles can be seen at work in the lives of unbelievers who happen to live according to His way. Theologians call this "common grace."

  Further proof of this literal fulfillment of the promise of land inheritance comes from this observation about the reaction of many lawyers to certain clients: "When greedy, self-serving survivors come to the lawyer of their relative's estate, demanding more than their share, my lawyer friends tell me that just the opposite takes place. Rather than work for those whose interest is in themselves, the lawyer would rather work for those whose affection was for their client. Rather than let the wrongdoer, the greedy one, grab the prize, lawyers will often respond in ways that support the meek. Such is not always the case. But as often as it does take place, it mirrors God's approach to justice."[2] Similarly, the "Leadership Forum" I referred to at the beginning of this chapter notes that churches that responded meekly to malpractice lawsuits ended up receiving judgements in their favour.

- A truly meek person who has persevered in the "delighting, committing, trusting, and doing good" process becomes a very teachable person. Such a person has also learned self-control. And a teachable, self-controlled person is one who is bound to learn rapidly and well, thus inheriting much spiritual wealth and character.

- Now true as these two interpretations of inheriting the land may be, I believe the fundamental New Testament interpretation lies elsewhere. When was the promise of the land first given, and to whom? It was part of the Abrahamic Covenant: "*The LORD had said to Abram, 'Leave your country, your people and your father's household and go to the land I will show you'"* (Genesis 12:1); *"The LORD appeared to Abram and said, 'To your offspring I will give this land'"* (Genesis 12:7). So the promise of the land is, at its root, a reference to the promised blessings attached to God's Covenants with His people.

Let's apply that principle to the New Covenant. What are its essential blessings? We don't have to guess. Hebrews 6:12, 17–20 tells us: *"We do not want you to become lazy, but to imitate those who through faith and patience inherit what has been promised ... Because God wanted to make the unchanging nature of his purpose very clear to the heirs of what was promised, he confirmed it with an oath. God did this so that, by two unchangeable things in which it is impossible for God to lie, we who have fled to take hold of the hope offered to us may be greatly encouraged. We have this hope as an anchor for the soul, firm and secure. It enters the inner sanctuary behind the curtain, where Jesus, who went before us, has entered on our behalf. He has become a high priest forever, in the order of Melchizedek."* The land promised to us under the New Covenant is the privilege of entrance into the Holy of Holies. Even when all of God's land promises to Israel had been fulfilled, there was one piece of real estate they dared not set foot on: the Holy of Holies. Only the High Priest could do that, but even he could enter only once a year, on the Day of Atonement and that very briefly. But because Jesus has gone ahead of us into the Holy of Holies as our forerunner, ordinary believers like us can follow Him there, trusting in His intercessory ministry on our behalf.

We can live in intimate relationship with the same Holy God whose proximity will destroy the wicked. Other sections of the New Testament make it clear that one of the privileges of this proximity to the throne, perhaps the greatest of all, is participation in the global purposes of God through the weapon of intercessory prayer. After all, that is what Jesus is doing in His ascended state, asking the Father for the nations as His inheritance (Psalm 2:8). He, the meek, thus inherits all the earth and we, in meekness, inherit the earth with Him.

Prayer Guide

1. If you know someone who is involved in a legitimate lawsuit and who is "being victimized by the system," pray that they will be meek, that they will find favour in the sight of the lawyers and judges involved in arguing the case and passing judgement. Even if you don't personally know anyone in this position, pray especially for widows and the fatherless who may be affected by the outcomes of such legal proceedings. Ask God to fulfill His promises regarding the meek on their behalf.

2. As you persevere in the "delighting, committing … " process, ask God to make you into a teachable and self-controlled person. Thank Him for the wealth of spiritual wisdom and character you will thus inherit.

3. Thank Him for the privilege of access into His Holy presence; that, right now, you are standing where no Old Testament saint ever stood; that the very Holiness that will judge and destroy the wicked will purify and transform you. Then thank Him for the privilege of intercessory prayer, through which you can share in His conquest of the nations. Take time to pray for a missionary and his or her efforts to "possess land for Christ." Use your knowledge of the specifics (e.g., their latest prayer letters) to make your prayers specific, too. As you pray, thank God that this is indeed "front-line" activity you are involved in; your prayers are really having an effect in a battle being waged in the heavenly realms for the souls of the men and women of the nations.

Question! If the dominant New Testament understanding of the land promise is spiritual, does it have nothing to say to us about material prosperity? How are the meek to relate to money and possessions? This is an important question because the success and wealth of the wicked was one possible source of our fretting. That's the psalmist's fourth and final theme.

A Perspective on Money

Let's begin with verse 16: *"Better the little that the righteous have than the wealth of many wicked."* According to the psalmist, righteousness with little money is far better than lots of money with wickedness. Long experience, both the psalmist's and ours, has repeatedly proven that money without righteousness is an unbelievably powerful curse, wreaking incredible havoc in human lives. On the contrary, anything in the hands of the righteous becomes a powerful weapon for good. Why?

• It is righteousness that breeds generosity and not mere possession of wealth: *"The wicked borrow and do not repay, but the righteous give generously"* (v. 21); *"They* [the righteous] *are always generous and lend freely"* (v. 26). This is true whether the generosity is expressed through giving away (v. 21) or through lending (v. 26). These insights are amply demonstrated by experience. I once had the pleasure of spending six days overseas with a missionary from our church. Only one person I met in that country gave me a gift to take back to Canada. Not that I wanted anything, but significantly, she was a single parent who had very little of this world's resources. As for Canada, government statistics repeatedly show that the higher a person's income bracket, the lower the amount they give to charity (not just in terms of percentage of income but in total amount given). Yet another statistic, unearthed by a former colleague of mine on staff at our church, showed that the per capita giving in larger churches was lower than in smaller churches. It seems that the more individuals or groups have, the less they give away.

Here is another interesting aside, which shows a connection between giving, or not giving, and fretting. Many years ago, a certain individual borrowed a significant sum of money from us, which he agreed to pay back in instalments. He conveniently forgot the last instalment of about five hundred dollars. The one sure way I was able to keep from fretting about this oversight, accidental or deliberate, was to continue giving to that individual whenever he was in need. You might object, "What about the future? Don't we risk jeopardizing it if we are "overgenerous" – and won't that become a source of fretting? The wicked seem to have their retirement and the education of their children all taken care of, but not us. Our continuing generosity is only going to make matters worse." The psalmist has an answer for that, too:

- "*I was young and now I am old, yet I have never seen the righteous forsaken or their children begging for bread*" (v. 25). "*In times of disaster they will not wither; in days of famine they will enjoy plenty*" (v. 19); "*They are always generous and lend freely; their children will be blessed*" (v. 26). The meek and generous are promised sufficiency in old age, in hard times, and for their children's needs – all because God knows the days of the blameless as well as the day of judgement that awaits the wicked: "*The days of the blameless are known to the LORD, and their inheritance will endure forever*" (v. 18).

Now these verses immediately raise a question that positively screams for attention. If the psalmist's words are true, what about Third World Christians, at least some of whom are living under the curse of debilitating poverty? I have no complete answer for this question. Let me give you two that are not of the "pat" variety and which help me.

In one of his books dealing with the subject of money and giving, Ron Hembree, former pastor of Kennedy Road Tabernacle in Brampton, Ontario, tells how he was so troubled by this very question after a visit to India that he stopped using verse 25 of Psalm 37 in his preaching. One day, Mark Buntane, a missionary in Calcutta (who was known as the male Mother Teresa because of his many magnificent ministries to the poor in that city), visited Hembree's church in Brampton. When asked how he reconciled Psalm 37:25 with his experiences in Calcutta, he replied that in his twenty-five years in Calcutta – a city full of desperately poor people – he had never known of one Christian who had starved or begged. "I have found some who had an awareness of Christianity, and maybe were raised in a church, who have suffered hunger," he said. "But I have never once in all my years discovered a faithful believer whose needs were not being met by our Lord. I can report that Scripture is still true."[3]

While that doesn't answer our question completely, it does suggest that there are many records of God's faithfulness to His Word that we aren't even aware of and that our willingness to trust Him may be an important factor in realizing His provision. The second answer that helps me is this: One way in which God will keep His promise to the "faithful poor" is through the generosity of those of us who do have enough. So struggle with the question by all means, but let's keep our eyes open to see His faithfulness and keep on being part of the answer as we give generously.

• The bottom line question is, not surprisingly, an issue of trust. To whom will we trust our financial future? Shortly before I completed my first study of this Psalm, *Newsweek* magazine ran a cover which read, "I'm sorry, America. Your insurance policy is cancelled." The cover story dealt with the insurance crisis in North America. Because of the ridiculously large settlements being awarded by judges to claimants, more and more insurance companies were closing down, others began refusing any coverage for whole classes of accidents, and doctors were facing skyrocketing premiums for malpractice insurance. The article also included predictions that government and private pension funds in North America would all be bankrupt by the year 2000. Before we are too quick (with the benefit of hindsight) to ridicule this "prophecy," we should remember that the events of 9/11; the recent wild gyrations of the stock market; the Enron, Anderson, and WorldCom disasters; and the escalating massacres of human beings in the Middle East all underline that economic and political predictions are always fraught with extreme uncertainty.

But there is one insurance policy that no economic or political disaster will be able to touch. Its terms are written in Psalm 37, and without it, every other policy we have, that we may be looking to for security, isn't worth the paper it's written on. Whose promises will we trust? The insurance companies of Middletown, North America, or Psalm 37?

Prayer Guide

1. Do you give and lend freely for God's causes or do you struggle? What sort of righteousness can free you in this regard? Ask Him to work exactly that transformation in you and to help you break away from the stranglehold of "things." Remember, He has eyes, hands, feet, ears, a nose, a mouth, and a throat. Refer to one or more of these attributes to lend fervency and faith to your prayers for righteousness. If God blesses you with material prosperity in the future (one possible way in which your meekness might lead to inheriting the land), resolve in advance to give more, not less. Commit that resolution to Him, recognizing the seriousness of the pledge. (Remember Ananias and Sapphira in Acts 5.)

2. Ask God to show you if, and how, you are trusting in anything or anyone else but Him for your future and that of your children. Acknowledge this as sin and confess it. Do you need to re-direct any money that you are hoarding in fear to His causes, especially to the poor? Again pray, confess, and resolve to obey. Take a few moments to pray for the poor, especially poor believers, that God will fulfill the affirmation of the psalmist. Pray for the efforts of one specific relief organization through which you are seeking to help the poor. Once again, their reports and newsletters will help you make your prayers specific.

Chapter 12

Psalm 90:
If Only I Had More Time

A Prayer of Moses, the Man of God

1 Lord, you have been our dwelling place throughout all generations.
2 Before the mountains were born or you brought forth the earth and
the world, from everlasting to everlasting you are God. 3 You turn
men back to dust, saying, "Return to dust, O sons of men." 4 For a
thousand years in your sight are like a day that has just gone by, or
like a watch in the night. 5 You sweep men away in the sleep of death;
they are like the new grass of the morning – 6 though in the morning
it springs up new, by evening it is dry and withered. 7 We are
consumed by your anger and terrified by your indignation.
8 You have set our iniquities before you, our secret sins in the light of
your presence. 9 All our days pass away under your wrath; we finish
our years with a moan. 10 The length of our days is seventy years – or
eighty, if we have the strength; yet their span is but trouble and
sorrow, for they quickly pass, and we fly away. 11 Who knows the
power of your anger? For your wrath is as great as the fear that is due
you. 12 Teach us to number our days aright, that we may gain a heart
of wisdom. 13 Relent, O LORD! How long will it be? Have compassion
on your servants. 14 Satisfy us in the morning with your unfailing
love, that we may sing for joy and be glad all our days. 15 Make us

glad for as many days as you have afflicted us, for as many years as
we have seen trouble. 16 May your deeds be shown to your servants,
your splendor to their children. 17 May the favor of the Lord our God
rest upon us; establish the work of our hands for us – yes, establish
the work of our hands.

Think It Through

When William Ewart Gladstone was Prime Minister of England,
a young man asked to speak with him about his life plans. He
started off by telling the Prime Minister that he wanted to study
law and be admitted to the Bar of England. "Yes, young man,"
said Gladstone, "and what then?" Next, the man answered, he
hoped to have a seat in the House of Lords before he retired. "Yes,
young man," said Gladstone again, "and what then?" The young
man supposed he'd die. "Yes, young man, and what then?"
Gladstone pressed on, relentlessly. "I never thought any further
than that," said the would-be lawyer. "Young man," said the Prime
Minister, "you are a fool. Go home and think life through."[1] I do
not know whether the young man followed Gladstone's advice,
but the Prime Minister was right. All the same, most of us need
help to "think life through" and God has provided that help in
Psalm 90. Scholars tell us that it is probably the oldest Psalm (so
it is the real "Psalm 1"). It was written by Moses, most probably
toward the end of Israel's wanderings in the wilderness en route
to Canaan from Egypt, when Moses was also nearing the end of
his life.

The Big Idea

"Lord, you have been our dwelling place throughout all generations.
Before the mountains were born or you brought forth the earth and the
world, from everlasting to everlasting you are God" (vv. 1–2). Generations of human beings come and go, but the same Lord has been
there throughout. He not only preceded humans; He also existed
before the mountains, the world, the universe. Current estimates
of the age of the universe run at about 15 billion years. Whether
scientists are right in their interpretation of astronomical data is
beside the point – because even if they are, the psalmist, who

knew nothing of quasars and black holes, says that God was there long before that. And if the thought of a God who has been "around," unchanging, for 15 billion years staggers our imagination, what will we do with the psalmist's leap beyond time to eternity: *"from everlasting to everlasting you are God."*

Time itself is part of God's Creation, so He is outside of time altogether. That is why His relation to time is unique. In verse 4 we read, *"For a thousand years in your sight are like a day that has just gone by, or like a watch in the night."* God has no past, present, or future. He experiences all of time as a huge "now," an infinite present. For God, every event in human history is presently happening. So, too, the history that is yet to unfold. He doesn't just know *that* it is going to happen, He experiences it *now*. But when His experience intersects ours, creatures of space and time, we are forced to speak as if He is subject to the limitations of time past, present, and future. So Moses writes this about our experience of Him: *"**You have been** our dwelling place throughout all generations."* But with respect to His own existence from everlasting to everlasting, *you are God.* (Note the change in tense from "have been" to "are," from past to present.) Such a concept of God is unique in all ancient literature, for all the pagan gods had beginnings in time.

In sharp contrast to this, humans are anything but eternal, and for the most part, only too aware that time is passing at an alarming rate: *"All our days pass away under your wrath; we finish our years with a moan. The length of our days is seventy years – or eighty, if we have the strength; yet their span is but trouble and sorrow, for they quickly pass, and we fly away"* (vv. 9–10). To get at least an appearance of control over rapidly passing time, humans have devised many ways of measuring that passing so they can keep track. Notice the many measures of time in the Psalm: generations, years, days; then the breakdown of a day into a "watch in the night" (a four-hour period) and morning and evening (a twelve-hour period). Today we have sophisticated measuring devices that allow us to break time down into even smaller fragments: milli, micro, nano, and pico seconds (a thousandth, millionth, billionth, and trillionth of a second). But all of this does nothing to change one alarming fact: time is flowing by at the same inalterable rate for all of us, and we are moving inexorably toward our individual appointments with death: *"You turn men back to dust, saying, 'Return to dust, O sons of men'"* (v. 3).

In our youth, life stretches ahead as an unending reality with lots of time to do all that we want, or intend, to do; but the closer we get to our appointments with death, the faster time seems to have gone by when we look back. Moses was an old man when he wrote, "*You sweep men away in the sleep of death; they are like the new grass of the morning – though in the morning it springs up new, by evening it is dry and withered … we finish our years with a moan. The length of our days is seventy years – or eighty, if we have the strength; yet their span is but trouble and sorrow, for they quickly pass, and we fly away*" (vv. 5–6; 9–10). Not only have the years flown by; they have been largely marked by trouble and hardship. An alternate translation of the phrase "*yet their span is*" reads, "*Even the best of them is.*" If so, Moses is saying that even the high points of our life, as we look back, are really "nothing much to write home about." They last for such a short time and so do we. At least if they lasted for a long time and so did we, there might be some value in them, but sadly, *both* are short lived.

Why is life like this, we might ask? The answer is found in verses 8 and 9: "*You have set our iniquities before you, our secret sins in the light of your presence. All our days pass away under your wrath … .*" Both our mortality and our troubled lives are due to our sins. Now we need to remember that the psalmist does not necessarily have a "forgiven" or a "fortunate" individual's life in mind. It is quite possible for any single person to have a charmed and relatively trouble-free life. But for humankind considered as a whole, Moses' analysis is inarguable. Human beings have sinned, and that sin has rendered them objects of God's wrath. Notice the many references to God's anger, indignation, and wrath in the Psalm: "*Who knows the power of your anger? For your wrath is as great as the fear that is due you*" (v. 11).

With that we have come to the end of Moses' analysis of life. To put it in everyday terms, God has been around for ever and a day, but we are going to be around for a very short time by comparison, and our lives are likely to be difficult, even at their high points. What response should such a sober reflection on the transitory nature of human life provoke? Abandon the life of faith and embrace agnosticism, if not atheism? Throw up our hands and resign ourselves to a life of pessimism and despair as we approach our deathbeds? "Neither," says Moses. Look at his response in verse 12: "*Teach us to number our days aright, that we may gain a heart of wisdom.*" This is the pivotal text of the Psalm, the heart of Moses' prayer as he "thinks life through," and it will be the primary focus of the rest of this chapter.

Two things are immediately apparent. If Moses' analysis of
life is correct, then the pursuit of wisdom is to become our primary goal in life, and to pursue wisdom, we have to (1) get a
handle on what biblical wisdom really is and (2) learn to think
properly about time (*number our days aright*).

Many of you are undoubtedly familiar with glossy magazines
and brochures put out by large financial institutions attempting
to persuade us to save money and invest with them. One graph
they are almost certain to include in their promotional material is
the one that illustrates how even a small amount of money set
aside regularly, and accumulating compound interest, can grow
over the years into a sizeable amount. Then comes the punch line
– delaying the start of such a savings program by even a few
years means a reduction of tens of thousands of dollars in the
final amount we collect.

Long before these financial institutions came into being, Moses had recognized the same principle – but he applied it to the
investment of time in gaining a heart of wisdom. His prayer, asking that God would teach him to number his days, is an acknowledgement that he cannot gain wisdom overnight. It is the result
of "compound interest" accumulating bit by bit over a long period of time. And procrastinating to put off the pursuit of wisdom is just as devastating in the long run as it is in the financial
realm. This is exactly the emphasis of the Apostle Paul in
Ephesians 5:15–16: "*Be very careful, then, how you live – not as unwise but as wise, making the most of every opportunity, because the
days are evil.*" Making the most of every opportunity means, literally, "buying back the time." The Greek language uses two different words for "time": *chronos* refers to quantity of time (i.e.,
hours, years, days, nanoseconds, and is featured much in this
Psalm), whereas *kairos* refers to quality of time, not quantity. For
example, when we ask, "How much *time* do I have to finish this
report?" that's *chronos*. But when a wife says to her husband,
"Honey, my labour pains are two minutes apart. This is no *time*
to be working on a report. Let's go to the hospital," that's *kairos*.
Paul uses *kairos* in Ephesians 5:16 to mean: *Seize the opportunity* to
resist evil and do good! This is what it means to be really wise in
days when evil is rampant.

As for the phrase "buy back," it is often translated "to redeem."
In biblical times, people bought and sold slaves. But every so often, someone would buy a slave outright, never to be put back
for sale on the open slave market. That's how we are to buy up

the *kairos* moments, according to Paul, if we are to live as wise people. So to be wise involves recognizing the right time to do certain things, the time when opportunity knocks, the time to take the plunge. In the spiritual realm, the price we pay or the wealth we gain is not in money but in chronological time – using *chronos* to make the most of *kairos* moments, so we don't lose them for ever. In light of Paul's New Testament exhortation, we could paraphrase Moses' prayer this way: "Lord, please help me to realize the value of not 'dilly dallying' in this matter of pursuing wisdom. Let me start my 'savings account' right away. Every day's delay means I stand to lose that much more at the end. And God, because time is such a precious commodity that I can't buy back at any price, help me to dole it out carefully, so that I am truly purchasing wisdom with it."

Prayer Guide

1. Have you ever thought seriously about the eternality of God and your own temporality? Reflect on the words of this familiar hymn based on Psalm 90. Praise the eternal God as you sing it. Let its poetry and images stimulate your imagination to further praise Him:

> O God, our help in ages past,
>   Our hope for years to come,
> Our shelter from the stormy blast,
>   And our eternal home!
>
> Under the shadow of Thy throne
>   Still may we dwell secure;
> Sufficient is Thine arm alone,
>   And our defense is sure.
>
> Before the hills in order stood,
>   Or earth received her frame,
> From everlasting Thou art God,
>   To endless years the same.
>
> A thousand ages, in Thy sight,
>   Are like an evening gone;
> Short as the watch that ends the night,
>   Before the rising sun.

O God, our help in ages past,
   Our hope for years to come,
Be Thou our guide while life shall last,
   And our eternal home.[2]

2. Have you usually recognized the *kairos* moments in your life
   that lead to wisdom? How long has your "wisdom savings
   account" been compounding? Have you wrenched yourself
   away from the temporally significant activities of *chronos* time,
   to invest in eternally significant ones – thus availing yourself of
   kairos moments in your life? Use your answers to these questions to write out your own amplification of Moses' prayer:
   "*Teach us to number our days aright, that we may gain a heart
   of wisdom.*" (Focus at this stage on your approach to "time"
   and its redemption. We'll get to the "wisdom" part in the next
   stage.) Then pray your prayer out loud a few times. As further
   insights come, incorporate them into your written prayer. Plan
   to use this prayer on a regular basis (e.g., at the end of each
   month). You may even want to memorize it.

Having established a biblical perspective on time as it relates
to wisdom, let's do the same for wisdom itself: What is it and
how do we acquire it? Then we will be more likely to recognize
the *kairos* opportunities when they come and we'll be ready to
buy them up.

What Is Wisdom?

The Scriptures make it clear that God is the source of all wisdom.
He alone is wise, and His wisdom is immeasurably deep, as described in Romans 11:33, "*Oh, the depth of the riches of the wisdom
and knowledge of God! How unsearchable his judgments, and his paths
beyond tracing out!*" and in Romans 16:27, " *… to the only wise God
be glory forever through Jesus Christ! Amen.*" And what is Divine
wisdom? A lucid definition given by Dr. A.W. Tozer is difficult to
improve upon: "Wisdom, among other things, is the ability to
devise perfect ends and to achieve those ends by the most perfect
means. … Wisdom sees everything in focus, each in proper relation to all, and is thus able to work towards predestined goals
with flawless perfection. All God's acts are done in perfect wisdom, first for His own glory, and then for the highest good for
the greatest number for the longest time … ."[3]

Now this wisdom of God finds its fullest manifestation in Jesus Christ. Isaiah, speaking of the Messiah who would come, tells us that "*The Spirit of the* LORD *will rest on him – the Spirit of wisdom and of understanding*" (11:2). And when He came, Jesus said, "*The Queen of the South ... came from the ends of the earth to listen to Solomon's wisdom, and now one greater than Solomon is here*" (Matthew 12:42). Surely His superlative does not refer with such force to the grandeur of Solomon's kingdom but to the infinite superiority of Jesus' wisdom compared to Solomon's. Paul completes this testimony to Jesus' wisdom when he writes that in Him "*are hidden all the treasures of wisdom and knowledge*" (Colossians 2:3). Lastly, God's wisdom is always associated with His power: "*Then Daniel praised the God of heaven and said: 'Praise be to the name of God for ever and ever; wisdom and power are his'*" (Daniel 2:19–20). As J.I. Packer points out in his observation on this matter, "wisdom without power would be pathetic ... power without wisdom would be merely frightening."[4]

Not only is God wise, but He also *imparts wisdom* to His children. Joseph, Solomon, and Daniel, three men most noted for wisdom in the Scriptures, all explicitly attributed their wisdom to God. These are Daniel's words: "'*He gives wisdom to the wise and knowledge to the discerning ... I thank and praise you, O God of my fathers: You have given me wisdom and power*'" (Daniel 2:21, 23). And lest we think that such words are intended only for the "elite," like the three named above, recall that the major theme of the first eight chapters of Proverbs is God's desire to impart wisdom to *all* His people. Chapter 8 personifies wisdom as a woman who has positioned herself at a major intersection in the city, crying out to a stream of indifferent passersby to seek wisdom: "*Does not wisdom call out? Does not understanding raise her voice? On the heights along the way, where the paths meet, she takes her stand; beside the gates leading into the city, at the entrances, she cries aloud: 'To you, O men, I call out; I raise my voice to all mankind. You who are simple, gain prudence; you who are foolish, gain understanding. Listen, for I have worthy things to say; I open my lips to speak what is right'*" (Proverbs 8:1–6).

The New Testament confirms this intention of God in Paul's exquisite chapter on wisdom: "*We do, however, speak a message of wisdom among the mature, but not the wisdom of this age or of the rulers of this age, who are coming to nothing. No, we speak of God's secret wisdom, a wisdom that has been hidden and that God destined for our glory before time began*" (1 Corinthians 2:6–7). Not content with expressing His desire to impart wisdom to us, *He exhorts us to seek for it: "Wisdom is supreme; therefore get wisdom. Though it cost all you have, get understanding"* (Proverbs 4:7). *"Choose my instruction instead of silver, knowledge rather than choice gold, for wisdom is more precious than rubies, and nothing you desire can compare with her"* (Proverbs 8:10–11). *"He who gets wisdom loves his own soul; he who cherishes understanding prospers"* (Proverbs 19:8).

"Wait a minute!" you might say. Given Dr. Tozer's definition, surely it's not possible for us to become wise in the same sense that God is wise. Right! That naturally raises a crucial question: "What form does God's wisdom take when He imparts it to us?" The most helpful answer (that I am aware of) comes from J.I. Packer in his chapter on wisdom in *Knowing God*.[5] Here it is, in my words. Imagine visiting a railway station and standing on a particular platform, watching the various trains pull in and out over a period of time. If we do this long enough, it will be possible to develop some idea of the larger plan that determines the movement of the trains "to" and "from" that particular platform. We could repeat the process at a second platform, combine our information, and sharpen our grasp of the big picture. If we then visited the central control station, we would see the entire system of platforms and tracks extending out a few miles in all directions from the station. The position of the various trains would be indicated by coloured lights. Now, we would see, at a glance, all the factors affecting the behaviour of a particular train with respect to a particular platform.

Some people think this is what happens when we get wisdom. We are increasingly able to see the large picture so we can figure out why things happen the way they do. Thus we acquire a better understanding of a specific event in our lives. So we embark on a pursuit of wisdom with gusto and feel as if we are doing fine until … something happens that we can't figure out, that won't fit the "system" we've devised. In fact, the longer we stay on the pilgrimage to Zion, the more such events we will encounter. The temptation is to draw one of two equally erroneous conclusions: (1) we aren't wise enough or (2) the pursuit of wisdom isn't all it's cracked up to be. It is to correct this false view of wisdom that God gave us a book like Ecclesiastes.

Packer states that the purpose of Ecclesiastes is to show us that the real basis of wisdom lies in acknowledging that many aspects of life are inexplicable and bear no evidence of being ordered by a rational, moral God.[6] Nor can we dismiss this as the pessimism of an honest observer of life under the Old Covenant which is, hence, no longer relevant to us. Paul echoes the same sentiment, but he finds in it a cause for praise: "*Oh, the depth of the riches of the wisdom and knowledge of God! How unsearchable his judgments, and his paths beyond tracing out! Who has known the mind of the* LORD? *Or who has been his counselor?*" (Romans 11:33–34). We can't possibly figure everything out. God's wisdom is too rich, too deep for that! That's the negative side of the wisdom God imparts to us.

On the positive side, wisdom involves turning our attention to something altogether different from figuring out life. Packer changes his analogy from watching trains at a station to that of driving an automobile. In driving, he writes, rather than figuring out why the road conditions are as they are, a wise driver would focus instead on responding to the actual situation, and, Packer continues, the "effect of divine wisdom is to enable … [us] to do … that in … every day life."[7] This is exactly what Paul affirms elsewhere: " … *be very careful, then, how you live – not as unwise but as wise, making the most of every opportunity, because the days are evil. Therefore do not be foolish, but understand what the Lord's will is*" (Ephesians 5:15–17).

Evil days will bring many perplexities to the fore. Wisdom, in the face of these perplexities, is not to figure them out but to live in obedience to God's will. To sum up: Biblical wisdom for God means perfect ends achieved by perfect means. For us, wisdom is believing that this is so, even when we can't figure things out, and instead, turning our attention to responding in obedience to the perplexing situations that face us. But in this task, we will meet opposition.

The Enemy

We have an enemy, Satan, who is also the source of a certain kind of wisdom. He, too, can impart his wisdom to human beings and he passionately desires to do so. Consider this description of Satan and the reason for his expulsion from the presence of God: "'*You were in Eden, the garden of God; every precious stone adorned you … Your settings and mountings were made of gold; on the day you were created they were prepared. You were anointed as a guardian cherub, for so I ordained you. You were on the holy mount of God; you walked among the fiery stones. You were blameless in your ways from the day you were created till wickedness was found in you. Through your wide-*

spread trade you were filled with violence, and you sinned. So I drove you in disgrace from the mount of God, and I expelled you, O guardian cherub, from among the fiery stones. Your heart became proud on account of your beauty, and you corrupted your wisdom because of your splendor. So I threw you to the earth'" (Ezekiel 28:13–17). This false, perverted wisdom he offered to humans as soon as God created the first two of them. Recall his strategy in tempting Eve and Adam: *"When the woman saw that the fruit of the tree was good for food and pleasing to the eye, and also desirable for gaining wisdom, she took some and ate it. She also gave some to her husband, who was with her, and he ate it"* (Genesis 3:6).

Eve rebelled against God because she couldn't figure out a reason for His commandment not to eat of the fruit of a certain tree. She accepted Satan's "figuring" instead and reached for the substitute wisdom. That fundamental temptation to become wise in our own eyes is still being paraded before us, although the forbidden fruit takes different forms and the setting may be a corporate boardroom rather than the Garden of Eden. The Scriptures abound with warnings against becoming wise in our own eyes: *"Do you see a man wise in his own eyes? There is more hope for a fool than for him"* (Proverbs 26:12); *"Although they claimed to be wise, they became fools"* (Romans 1:22); *"We do not dare to classify or compare ourselves with some who commend themselves. When they measure themselves by themselves and compare themselves with themselves, they are not wise"* (2 Corinthians 10:12).

A particularly subtle form of the forbidden fruit that constantly seduces us is the temptation to do God's work with Satan's wisdom. Moses is a classic example to which we've already alluded in an earlier chapter. He was well trained in Egypt's (i.e., Satan's) wisdom: *"Moses was educated in all the wisdom of the Egyptians and was powerful in speech and action"* (Acts 7:22). But when he tried to deliver his people Israel in ways consistent with this wisdom, he failed miserably. The New Testament generalizes this into a principle: God's ways are inaccessible to human wisdom. *"For since, in the wisdom of God, the world, through its wisdom, did not know him, God was pleased through the foolishness of what was preached to save those who believe"* (1 Corinthians 1:21). Not only is Satanic, self-sufficient wisdom incapable of understanding God's ways and doing His work, consider the legacy it leaves us: *"You have trusted in your wickedness and have said, 'No one sees me.' Your wisdom and knowledge mislead you when you say to yourself, 'I am, and there is none besides me'"* (Isaiah 47:10); *"I devoted myself to study and to explore by wisdom all that is done under heaven. What a heavy burden God has laid on men!"* (Ecclesiastes 1:13).

Finally, here, as in other cases, the New Testament puts the matter beyond doubt: *"But if you harbor bitter envy and selfish ambition in your hearts, do not boast about it or deny the truth. Such 'wisdom' does not come down from heaven but is earthly, unspiritual, of the devil"* (James 3:14–15). Satanic wisdom misleads us and eventually becomes a heavy burden as it ensnares us in bitter envy and driving ambition that never satisfies. And if we survive all these snares of Satanic wisdom, he plays the "ace up his sleeve," leading us to adopt a life of fruitless, crippling legalism, usually rooted in the pride of self-achievement in religious matters.

Look again at Paul's warning to the Colossians: *"Since you died with Christ to the basic principles of this world, why, as though you still belonged to it, do you submit to its rules: 'Do not handle! Do not taste! Do not touch!'? These are all destined to perish with use, because they are based on human commands and teachings. Such regulations indeed have an appearance of wisdom, with their self-imposed worship, their false humility and their harsh treatment of the body, but they lack any value in restraining sensual indulgence"* (2:20–23). And if he can't tempt us to pride, Satan will ensnare us with false humility. That's why wisdom in the Bible is so closely linked with true humility – the only sure way to avoid the Satanic substitute for God's wisdom. And where else can we go for a vivid illustration of such humility than to that one life in whom were hidden *"all the treasures of wisdom and knowledge,"* the incarnate Christ?

In 1 Corinthians 1:22–24, we read, *"Jews demand miraculous signs and Greeks look for wisdom, but we preach Christ crucified: a stumbling block to Jews and foolishness to Gentiles, but to those whom God has called, both Jews and Greeks, Christ the power of God and the wisdom of God."* Wisdom is supremely illustrated by the cross and the principle it represents: a life marked by a refusal to *clutch* (what it already has), *grasp* (for what it does not yet have), or *exploit* (every situation to its own advantage). Instead, those who live by this wisdom choose to serve others. And the legacy of this wisdom, in sharp contrast to the eventually enslaving consequences of Satan's substitute, is redemption, salvation, and resurrection life. The Corinthians were enamoured with the seemingly sophisticated wisdom of the Greeks. And later, the Second Century heresy of Gnosticism would be characterized by mysterious initiation rites into secret wisdom. In sharp contrast, Jesus Christ did something concrete about the human dilemma.

The eternal God, who is outside of time, invaded "time-bound" humanity to illustrate humility and submission to God's purposes as the essence of wisdom.

Prayer Guide

1. Re-read Dr. Tozer's definition of Divine Wisdom. Do you believe this? If not, ask the Spirit to reveal, teach, and persuade you of this attribute of God. Yield to Him those specific aspects of your life (or life in general) that make it difficult for you to believe in God's perfect wisdom. Then take a few moments to praise God that He is all wise. Use William Cowper's magnificent hymn "God Moves in a Mysterious Way" to help you.

   God moves in a mysterious way
      His wonders to perform;
   He plants His footsteps in the sea,
      And rides upon the storm.

   Ye fearful saints, fresh courage take;
      The clouds ye so much dread
   Are big with mercy, and shall break
      In blessings on your head.

   Judge not the Lord by feeble sense,
      But trust Him for His grace;
   Behind a frowning providence
      He hides a smiling face.

   His purposes will ripen fast,
      Unfolding every hour:
   The bud may have a bitter taste,
      But sweet will be the flower.

   Blind unbelief is sure to err,
      And scan His work in vain:
   God is His own interpreter,
      And He will make it plain.[8]

2. Does wisdom have the priority on our "wish list" that God's Word indicates it should? If not, confess this neglect to Him and ask for the awakening of such desire. In what life situations are you facing the temptation to "figure out" rather than focus on discerning a wise response? What "wise" short cuts and detours around obedience is Satan parading before you? (One key area

to examine is your relationships. This is the area God is most interested in, and which Satan dearly loves to sabotage. The call to live wisely by redeeming the *kairos* moments in Ephesians 5:15–17 is followed by a call to harmony in three key relationships: with our spouses, with our children, and with colleagues at work. It is preceded by a similar call to unity within the Church. Review Ephesians 4:1–16 and 5:21–6:4 to help you in self-examination.) Pray for wisdom and grace to obey in the areas the Spirit reveals to you.

Let's recap what we have learned so far. Given God's eternality and our temporality, a critically important response is to learn to number our days to gain a heart of wisdom. This requires a *kairos* mentality toward time, one that will cost us the investment of *chronos* time to become wise. We then learned what biblical wisdom is, as it applies to God and then to us. Finally, we considered the counterfeit wisdom that Satan is working overtime to ensnare us with. That sets the stage for the next question. Having understood Divine wisdom and having been warned of Satan's wisdom, how do we acquire God's wisdom?

A Surprising Answer

The usual response when we realize that time is hurrying by is to act, to do something – and we can bring that mentality to the pursuit of wisdom. So much so that we can easily forget that Psalm 90 is a prayer. Moses is asking God to teach him to number his days so he can gain a heart of wisdom. And while Moses does not explicitly extend this prayer to also ask God to grant him wisdom (once he has learned to number his days), that is clearly taught in the rest of Scripture. If God is "only wise" and He eagerly desires to impart wisdom to us, then we had better ask Him to do so.

Solomon asked for wisdom; Daniel prayed and asked his friends to pray for wisdom; Paul prayed for the Ephesians "*that the God of our Lord Jesus Christ, the glorious Father, may give you the Spirit of wisdom and revelation, so that you may know him better*" (Ephesians 1:17). He kept "*asking God to fill you with the knowledge of his will through all spiritual wisdom and understanding*" (Colossians 1:9). James says that if anyone lacks wisdom, they should ask God who gives it generously without looking for possible faults in us that will disqualify us from having this prayer answered (James 1:5). Recall also that the context of this promise in James is perseverance under suffering, a time when we are most likely to want to "figure things out" and hence are most vulnerable to yield to Satan's temptations to buy into his wisdom. Instead our greatest need is to break through to the conviction that God is wise and to focus instead on our response to our circumstances. That's the wisdom we need to ask God for.

This primacy of prayer as a means to wisdom is also implicit in the opening verses of the Psalm: "*Lord, you have been our dwelling place throughout all generations.*" This is a metaphor for intimate communion with God, similar to the psalmist's cry in Psalm 84 when the sparrow and the swallow resting in their nests made him long for the altar to become his natural habitat, his dwelling place. In Old Testament times, this truth about the proximity of God to His people was most vividly represented by the temple, especially the inner sanctum, where the presence of God was often visibly manifested in smoke and fire. With the coming of Jesus and the establishment of His priesthood, believers, individually and corporately, have become His dwelling place. As Jesus promised His disciples in the upper room, "*If anyone loves me, he will obey my teaching. My Father will love him, and we will come to him and make our home with him"* (John 14:23). If this is true, life's most urgent task then becomes to discover and experience God as our dwelling place (and to thank God for dwelling in us). That way, when this fleeting life of ours comes to its appointed end, there will be no change in our residential address.[9] It will still be God.

Conversely, if we have little or no desire to spend time regularly in God's presence (and so to dwell in Him), what reason do we have for believing that we will enjoy heaven? For the essence of heaven is that God will dwell among us and we shall see Him face to face and worship Him. Our salvation is not an insurance policy against the fires of hell but a preparation for eternal communion with God. Time spent with Him now is the best preparation for heaven. And whenever He beckons us to this encounter, that is a *kairos* moment that needs to be bought up by wrenching some *chronos* time from activities whose significance is short-lived.

And because prayer is genuine communion, God speaks and we can hear. Specifically, we can be sure that He will answer our prayer for wisdom. His customary way of imparting wisdom is through His Word. Psalm 19:7 tells us that *"the statutes of the LORD are trustworthy, making wise the simple,"* Paul exhorted the Colossians to *"let the word of Christ dwell in you richly as you teach and admonish one another with all wisdom"* (3:16) and he also reminded Timothy *"how from infancy you have known the Holy Scriptures, which are able to make you wise for salvation"* (2 Timothy 3:15). This is especially true when our prayers are being shaped by His Word.

We have come full circle, haven't we? The pilgrimage to Zion you embarked on was exactly that: believing that God speaks and that He wants you to harness the power of a sanctified imagination, you began to learn how to listen to Him by letting the Scriptures, and especially the Psalms, shape your prayers. Now, at the end of this pilgrimage, Psalm 90 tells us that's the way to gain a heart of wisdom – probably the key indicator of a conquered inner space, where God's order reigns by His Spirit. Gaining a heart of wisdom is our single most urgent task, given God's eternality and our pathetic temporality.

Prayer Guide

1. Look back on your prayer pilgrimage to Zion. How have you approached the Prayer Guides? Have you skipped them completely because you preferred to "learn" from the expositions? (To think we can learn spiritual truth apart from Divine illumination in prayer is another facet of Satanic wisdom.) If you did use them, did you take time to reflect on the words of the various hymns? Did you take time to read the various Scripture passages that were suggested? Did you examine yourself in light of the truths you acquired from the expositions of the Psalms? Did you pause to record insights in a journal where you could recover them (accumulating compound interest) or did you not have "enough time" for all this? If you have to answer "No" to the first four questions and "Yes" to the fifth, you have let your preoccupation with *chronos* rob you of seizing the *kairos* moments.

2. Confess your hurry as an act of "violence against time";[10] reword Moses' prayer in Psalm 90:13–15 to reflect the specifics of your procrastination to date. Then thank God that it's not yet too late to make a fresh start. Affirm your resolve to go back to the beginning of this book and re-read it, this time following the Prayer Guides leisurely and thoroughly. Thank Him that He will establish the work of your hands, especially in and through the next generation.

It's Too Late!

"All right. I'm convinced!" some of you may be saying. "But it's too late. I haven't numbered my days and it's too late to change." Consider how Moses continues in his prayer after the central petition of verse 12.

- *"Relent, O LORD! How long will it be? Have compassion on your servants"* (v. 13). You, too, can count on His compassion to forgive past failures – including wasted time.

- *"Satisfy us in the morning with your unfailing love, that we may sing for joy and be glad all our days"* (v. 14). You can count on His Covenant loyalty, for He has bound Himself to you through His Word.

- *"Make us glad for as many days as you have afflicted us, for as many years as we have seen trouble"* (v. 15). Surely this is one prayer that cannot be answered, especially for one who has wasted decades of time and passed up many *kairos* moments. "There aren't enough days left," you say, "Even if I lived to be 120 years old, no one could make me glad for as many days as I have been sad." Verse 15 is not meant to be understood quantitatively, but qualitatively. Precisely because He is the eternal God outside of time, God can touch whatever time remains in your earthly pilgrimage with the quality of eternity … if you really meant it when you prayed, "Teach me to number my days so I can gain a heart of wisdom."

- Finally, verses 16 and 17 form a fitting conclusion, a counterpoint to verse 1: *"May your deeds be shown to your servants, your splendor to their children. May the favor of the Lord our God rest upon us; establish the work of our hands for us – yes, establish the work of our hands."* In verse 1, the memory of generations past only served to remind Moses of the passing of time and the temporality of man. Here, at the end of this prayer, he sees each successive generation as spellbound witnesses to the splendour of God, revealed in His people, whom He has made truly wise. What's more, not only are they spectators, they are participants in the work of God. Sure, we are temporal, and our time on earth will pass, but the eternal God can, and will, establish our works, flowing out of wisdom, so they live on long after we have passed away.

No! It is definitely not too late. But there isn't a moment to waste either. Right now may be a *kairos* moment that you cannot dare to ignore.

Notes

Introduction

1 Calvin Miller, *Spirit, Word and Story* (Dallas: Word Publishing, 1989), p. 19.

2 Eugene H. Peterson, *Answering God: The Psalms as Tools for Prayer* (San Francisco: HarperSanFrancisco, 1991), p.132.

3 Ray Stedman, *Folk Psalms of Faith* (Glendale, CA: Regal Books, 1973).

4 Leonard Griffith, *Reactions to God: Man's Response to God's Activity in the Psalms* (London: Hodder and Stoughton, 1979), p. 7.

5 Stedman, *Folk Psalms of Faith*.

6 R.K. Johnston, *Psalms for God's People* (Ventura, CA: Regal Books, 1982), p.18.

7 John Piper, *Let the Nations Be Glad* (Grand Rapids, MI: Baker Books, 1993), p. 41.

8 Hans Urs von Balthasar, *Prayer* (San Francisco: Ignatius Press, 1986), p. 8.

9 Eugene H. Peterson, *Under the Unpredictable Plant: An Exploration in Vocational Holiness* (Grand Rapids, MI: Eerdmans, 1992), pp. 102–3.

10 *Hymns of the Christian Life* (Camp Hill, PA: Christian Publications Inc., 1978), no. 154.

11 Calvin Miller, *Spirit, Word and Story* (Dallas: Word Publishing, 1989), p. 3.

Chapter 1 – Who Speaks First?

1 Larry Christensen, *The Christian Family* (Minneapolis: Bethany Fellowship Inc., 1970), p. 141.

2 See Augustine of Hippo, *The Confessions of St. Augustine*, trans. Henry Chadwick (Oxford: Oxford University Press, 1998).

3 Hans Urs von Balthasar, *Prayer* (San Francisco: Ignatius Press, 1986), p. 18.

4 Eugene H. Peterson, *Working the Angles: The Shape of Pastoral Integrity* (Grand Rapids, MI: Eerdmans, 1987), pp. 63–67.

5 Eugene H. Peterson, *Answering God: The Psalms as Tools for Prayer* (San Francisco: HarperSanFrancisco, 1991), p. 60.

6 Eugene H. Peterson, *Reversed Thunder: The Revelation of John and the Praying Imagination* (San Francisco: Harper and Row, 1988), p. 13.

7 Eugene H. Peterson, *Under the Unpredictable Plant: An Exploration in Vocational Holiness* (Grand Rapids, MI: Eerdmans, 1992), p. 115.

8 Eugene H. Peterson, "Should We Pay More Attention to the Lord's Day?" *Tough Questions Christians Ask*, ed. David Neff (Wheaton, IL: Victor Books, 1989), p. 13.

9 Hans Urs von Balthasar, *Prayer*, p. 89.

10 Gordon MacDonald, *Restoring Your Spiritual Passion* (Nashville: Oliver Nelson Books, 1986), p. 26.

Chapter 2 – Just Imagine

1 Reginald Bibby, *Fragmented Gods* (Toronto: Irwin Publishers, 1987), p. 168.

2 Eugene H. Peterson, *Reversed Thunder: The Revelation of John and the Praying Imagination* (San Francisco: Harper and Row, 1988), pp. 4, 2.

3 Ibid., pp. 8, 3.

4 Ibid., pp. 5, 2–3.

5 Eugene H. Peterson, *Under the Unpredictable Plant: An Exploration in Vocational Holiness* (Grand Rapids, MI: Eerdmans, 1992), p. 171.

6 Ibid., p. 6.

7 Eugene H. Peterson, *Answering God: The Psalms as Tools for Prayer* (San Francisco: HarperSanFrancisco, 1991), p. 28.

8 Ibid., p. 78.

9 Arthur Matthews, *Born for Battle* (Robesonia, PA: OMF Books, 1978), pp. 156–60.

10 Charles Colson, *The Body* (Nashville: W Publishing Group, 1994), p. 70. Reprinted by permission of W Publishing Group, Nashville, Tennessee. All rights reserved.

11 Lloyd C. Douglas, *The Robe* (New York: Houghton Mifflin, 1942), qtd. in D.G. Barnhouse, Commentary on Romans. From THE ROBE by Lloyd C. Douglas. Copyright, 1942 by Lloyd C. Douglas. Copyright © renewed 1969 by Virginia Douglas Dawson and Betty Douglas Wilson. Reprinted by permission of Houghton Mifflin Company. All rights reserved.

12 In his book *The Transforming Friendship*, James Houston points out how this temporary absence of God is a part of the maturing process. He writes: "This is … what happens in infant life. At first the mother gives her baby almost unlimited time and attention. … However, … [s]tep by step the mother withdraws her presence … .
This withdrawal is an important stage in the child's development. …
… [A] similar mixture of God's absence as well as his presence helps us to make prayer a personal, real experience. If we always experienced the presence of God whenever we prayed, we would never learn to distinguish between prayer and our own fantasies" (James Houston, *The Transforming Friendship* [Oxford: Lion, 1989], pp. 100, 102.)

13 Peterson, *Under the Unpredictable Plant*, pp. 171–72.

Chapter 3 – Psalm 84: The Highway to Zion

1 Ray Stedman, *Folk Psalms of Faith* (Glendale, CA: Regal Books, 1973), p. 219.

2 *Hymns of the Christian Life* (Camp Hill, PA: Christian Publications Inc., 1978), no. 64.

3 A.W. Tozer, *The Pursuit of God* (Camp Hill, PA: Christian Publications Inc., 1948), pp. 15–17.

Chapter 4 – Psalm 48: A Tale of Two Cities

1 Lloyd John Ogilvie, *Falling into Greatness* (Nashville: Thomas Nelson, 1984).

2 *Hymns of the Christian Life* (Camp Hill, PA: Christian Publications Inc., 1978), no. 397.

3 Charles Colson, *The Body* (Nashville: W Publishing Group, 1994), pp. 365–79.

4 Leonard Griffith, *Reactions to God: Man's Response to God's Activity in the Psalms* (London: Hodder and Stoughton, 1979), p. 77.

5 Ibid., pp. 77–78. Reproduced by permission of Hodder and Stoughton Limited.

6 Ibid., pp. 78–79. Reproduced by permission of Hodder and Stoughton Limited.

7 *Leadership* (Winter 1982).

8 Leonard Griffith, *Reactions to God: Man's Response to God's Activity in the Psalms* (London: Hodder and Stoughton, 1979), p. 81. Reproduced by permission of Hodder and Stoughton Limited.

Chapter 5 – Psalm 92: Getting Ready for Church

1 Eugene H. Peterson, "Should We Pay More Attention to the Lord's Day?" in *Tough Questions Christians Ask*, ed. David Neff (Wheaton, IL: Victor Books, 1989), p. 10.

2 Ibid., pp. 12–13.

3 Eugene H. Peterson, *Working the Angles: The Shape of Pastoral Integrity* (Grand Rapids, MI: Eerdmans, 1987).

4 Eugene H. Peterson, *Reversed Thunder:The Revelation of John and the Praying Imagination* (San Francisco: Harper and Row, 1988), pp. xii, 5, 6.

5 "Broken and Spilled Out" by Gloria Gaither and Bill George. © 1984 Yellow House Music (ASCAP) (Administered by Brentwood-Benson Music Publishing, Inc.) All Rights Reserved. Used By Permission. BROKEN AND SPILLED OUT Words by Gloria Gaither. Music by Bill George. Copyright © 1984 Gaither Music Company and Yellow House Music. All rights reserved. Used by permission.

6 *Hymns of the Christian Life* (Camp Hill, PA: Christian Publications Inc., 1978), no. 154.

7 Calvin Miller, *Spirit, Word and Story* (Dallas: Word Publishing, 1989), p. 9.

8 Bill Gothard, brochure about palm trees (personal communication)

9 Peterson, *Working the Angles*, 1987.

Chapter 6 – Psalm 127: Turning Houses into Homes

1 Friedrich Nietzsche, *Beyond Good and Evil*, trans. Helen Zimmern (London, 1907), Section 188, pp. 106–9, qtd. in Eugene H. Peterson, *A Long Obedience in the Same Direction* (Downers Grove, IL: InterVarsity Press, 1980).

2 See Germaine Greer, *Sex and Destiny: The Politics of Human Fertility* (London: Picador, 1985).

3 Jacques Ellul, qtd. in Eugene H. Peterson, *A Long Obedience in the Same Direction* (Downers Grove, IL: InterVarsity Press, 1980), p. 99.

4 Gordon MacDonald, *Ordering Your Private World* (Nashville: Thomas Nelson, 1984).

5 Leonard Griffith, *Reactions to God: Man's Response to God's Activity in the Psalms* (London: Hodder and Stoughton, 1979), p. 132.

Chapter 7 – Psalm 72: Mixing Politics and Religion

1 Bill Gothard, *The Unexpected Enemy of Justice and Mercy* (Oak Brook, IL: Institute in Basic Life Principles, 1982), pp. 6–8.

2 Tony Campolo, *A Reasonable Faith* (Waco, TX: Word Books, 1983).

3 World Relief newsletter.

4 World Relief newsletter.

Chapter 8 – Easter Music: A Medley
Based on Psalms 2, 110, and 118

1 Allan Bloom, *The Closing of the American Mind* (New York: Simon & Schuster, 1987), pp. 71–72.

2 Eugene H. Peterson, *Reversed Thunder: The Revelation of John and the Praying Imagination* (San Francisco: Harper and Row, 1988), p. 87.

3 Focus on the Family newsletter.

4 Focus on the Family newsletter.

5 *Hymns of the Christian Life* (Camp Hill, PA: Christian Publications Inc., 1978), no. 113.

6 Ibid., no. 359.

7 Leonard Griffith, *God in Man's Experience* (Nashville: W Publishing Group, 1969), p. 123. Reprinted by permission of W Publishing Group, Nashville, Tennessee. All rights reserved.

8 See James Montgomery Boice, *Philippians: An Expositional Commentary* (Grand Rapids: Zondervan, 1971).

Chapter 9 – Psalm 51: Recovering
from a King-Sized Failure

1 Versions of this story, attributed to Norman Vincent Peale, appear on a number of websites, where it is often cited as having been recounted by John Lavender in *Why Prayers Are Unanswered* (Wheaton: Tyndale House Publishers Inc., 1980).

2 Charles Colson, *Who Speaks for God?* (Westchester, IL: Crossway Books, 1985).

3 See Jonathan Edwards, *The Works of Jonathan Edwards*, vol. 1 (Edinburgh: Banner of Truth Trust, 1976).

4 Ibid., p. lxxxvi.

5 Qtd. in *Leadership* (Winter 1982), p. 50.

6 Andrew Murray, *The Holiest of All: An Exposition of the Epistle to the Hebrews* (New Kensington, PA: Whitaker House, 1996). Used by permission of the publisher.

Chapter 10 – A Tornado in Alabama: A Medley
Based on Psalms 22, 129, and 139

1 Eugene H. Peterson, *A Long Obedience in the Same Direction* (Downers Grove, IL: InterVarsity Press, 1980), p. 124.

2 Ibid., p. 125.

3 I am indebted to Ron Hembree, who, in a casual conversation, "clued me in" to this threefold description, in Psalm 139, of the God who knows us, is with us, and has made us.

4 *Hymns of the Christian Life* (Camp Hill, PA: Christian Publications Inc., 1978), no. 92.

Chapter 11 – Psalm 37: When You're Hot
under the Collar

1 *Leadership* (Winter 1985).

2 R.K. Johnston, *Psalms for God's People* (Ventura, CA: Regal Books, 1982), pp. 158–59. Copyright 1982 Gospel Light/Regal Books, Ventura, CA 93003. Used by Permission.

3 Qtd. in Ron Hembree, *Mark* (Plainfield, NJ: Logos International, 1979).

Chapter 12 – Psalm 90: If Only I Had More Time

1 Leonard Griffith, *Reactions to God: Man's Response to God's Activity in the Psalms* (London: Hodder and Stoughton, 1979), p. 100.

2 *Hymns of the Christian Life* (Camp Hill, PA: Christian Publications Inc., 1978), no. 13.

3 A.W. Tozer, *The Knowledge of the Holy* (New York: HarperCollins, 1961), p. 72.

4 J.I. Packer, *Knowing God* (London: Hodder and Stoughton, 1973), p. 97. Reproduced by permission of Hodder and Stoughton Limited. Also used by permission of InterVarsity Press, P.O. Box 1400, Downers Grove, IL 60515. www.ivpress.com

5 Ibid.

6 Ibid.

7 Ibid.

8 *Hymns of the Christian Life*, no. 25.

9 Lloyd John Ogilvie, *Falling into Greatness* (Nashville: Thomas Nelson, 1984).

10 Eugene H. Peterson, *Reversed Thunder: The Revelation of John and the Praying Imagination* (San Francisco: Harper and Row, 1988).

Bibliography

Augustine of Hippo, *The Confessions of St. Augustine*, trans. Henry Chadwick. Oxford: Oxford University Press, 1998.

Bibby, Reginald. *Fragmented Gods*. Toronto: Irwin Publishers, 1987.

Bloom, Allan. *The Closing of the American Mind*. New York: Simon & Schuster, 1987.

Boice, James Montgomery. *Philippians: An Expositional Commentary* (Grand Rapids: Zondervan, 1971).

Campolo, Tony. *A Reasonable Faith*. Waco, TX: Word Books, 1983.

Christensen, Larry. *The Christian Family*. Minneapolis: Bethany Fellowship Inc., 1970.

Colson, Charles. *The Body*. Nashville: W Publishing Group, 1994.

_____. *Who Speaks for God?* Westchester, IL: Crossway Books, 1985.

Edwards, Jonathan. *The Works of Jonathan Edwards*. Vol. 1. Edinburgh: Banner of Truth Trust, 1976.

Gothard, Bill. *The Unexpected Enemy of Justice and Mercy*. Oak Brook, IL: Institute in Basic Life Principles, 1982.

Griffith, Leonard. *God in Man's Experience*. Nashville: W Publishing Group, 1969.

_____. *Reactions to God: Man's Response to God's Activity in the Psalms*. London: Hodder and Stoughton, 1979.

Houston, James. *The Transforming Friendship*. Oxford: Lion, 1989.

Hymns of the Christian Life. Camp Hill, PA: Christian Publications Inc., 1978.

Johnston, R.K. *Psalms for God's People*. Ventura, CA: Regal Books, 1982.

MacDonald, Gordon. *Ordering Your Private World*. Nashville: Thomas Nelson, 1984.

_____. *Restoring Your Spiritual Passion*. Nashville: Oliver Nelson Books, 1986.

Matthews, Arthur. *Born for Battle*. Robesonia, PA: OMF Books, 1978.

Miller, Calvin. Spirit, *Word and Story*. Dallas: Word Publishing, 1989.

Murray, Andrew. *The Holiest of All: An Exposition of the Epistle to the Hebrews*. New Kensington, PA: Whitaker House, 1996.

Neff, David, ed. *Tough Questions Christians Ask*. Wheaton, IL: Victor Books, 1989.

Ogilvie, Lloyd John. *Falling into Greatness*. Nashville: Thomas Nelson, 1984.

Packer, J.I. *Knowing God*. London: Hodder and Stoughton, 1973.

Peterson, Eugene H. *Answering God: The Psalms as Tools for Prayer*. San Francisco: HarperSanFrancisco, 1991.

_____. *A Long Obedience in the Same Direction*. Downers Grove, IL: InterVarsity Press, 1980.

_____. *Reversed Thunder: The Revelation of John and the Praying Imagination*. San Francisco: Harper and Row, 1988.

_____. "Should We Pay More Attention to the Lord's Day?" in *Tough Questions Christians Ask*. Edited by David Neff. Wheaton, IL: Victor Books, 1989.

_____. *Under the Unpredictable Plant: An Exploration in Vocational Holiness*. Grand Rapids, MI: Eerdmans, 1992.

_____. *Working the Angles: The Shape of Pastoral Integrity*. Grand Rapids, MI: Eerdmans, 1987.

Piper, John. *Let the Nations Be Glad*. Grand Rapids, MI: Baker Books, 1993.

Stedman, Ray. *Folk Psalms of Faith*. Glendale, CA: Regal Books, 1973.

Tozer, A.W. *The Knowledge of the Holy*. New York: HarperCollins, 1961.

von Balthasar, Hans Urs. *Prayer*. San Francisco: Ignatius Press, 1986.